Philip Sidney

DEFENCE OF POESIE, ASTROPHIL AND STELLA AND OTHER WRITINGS

Edited by
ELIZABETH PORGES WATSON
University of Nottingham

EVERYMAN
J. M. DENT · LONDON
CHARLES E. TUTTLE
VERMONT</>

Introduction and other critical material copyright © J. M. Dent 1997

This edition first published by Everyman Paperbacks in 1997

Reprinted 1999

All rights reserved

J. M. Dent
Orion Publishing Group
Orion House, 5 Upper St Martin's Lane,
London WC2H 9EA
and
Charles E. Tuttle Co., Inc.
28 South Main Street
Rutland, Vermont 05701, USA

Typeset in Sabon by CentraCet Ltd, Cambridge
Printed in Great Britain by
The Guernsey Press Co. Ltd, Guernsey, C.I.

British Library Cataloguing-in-Publication Data
is available upon request.

ISBN 0 460 87659 7

CONTENTS

*For Pete Russell and Carina Campbell
who deserve a* **Third Pastorall.**

NOTE ON THE AUTHOR AND EDITOR

SIR PHILIP SIDNEY, 1554–86, was among the first great writers of the Elizabethan age. By vocation and training he was a courtier, soldier and diplomat, but his reputation in England and abroad was also that of a fine scholar of both classical and modern disciplines, as the enormous range of learned works dedicated to him indicates. His poetry, which includes the first and one of the greatest Elizabethan love-sonnet sequences, *Astrophil and Stella*, like his great heroic romance *Arcadia*, circulated widely and influentially in manuscript, though they remained unpublished in his lifetime. His writing, verse and prose, is innovative and sophisticated: wit, irony and delight play in various registers against a deeply serious and perceptive sensibility.

ELIZABETH PORGES WATSON took her degree in English Language and Literature at Oxford, and has been a lecturer in English at Nottingham University for several years. She works chiefly in the late medieval and Renaissance periods, and her publications include *Spenser* in the Routledge English Texts Series, as well as numerous articles on Spenserian and related topics.

CHRONOLOGY OF SIDNEY'S LIFE

Year   Age   Life

1554   **Born at Penshurst, 30 November**

CHRONOLOGY OF HIS TIMES

(Note: titles including love sonnets are marked †)

Year	Artistic Events	Historic Events
1550	Ronsard: *Odes* Langland's *Piers Plowman* printed (B Text) Hunnis: *Certain Psalms in English Metre* Vasari begins *Lives of the Artists*	Sir William Cecil, English Secretary of State
1551	More's *Utopia* translated into English Palestrina Director of Music, St Peter's Rome	Turks capture Tripoli Gesner's *Historia Animalium*: modern zoology
1552	Ronsard: *Amours* I† Titian, Michelangelo, working in Italy Jodelle: *Cléopatre*	
1553	Douglas's translation of *The Aeneid* printed More: *Dialogue of Comfort* printed	Edward VI of England dies (born 1537). His elder sister Mary Tudor becomes Queen
1554	Works by Lydgate and Lindsay printed Opening of Stationers' Registers (−1640)	Mary I marries Philip of Spain, Sidney's godfather. Mary attempts to restore Catholicism in England
1555	Ronsard: *Hymnes* Baldwin edits first (suppressed) edition of *Mirror for Magistrates*	Peace of Augsburg: Catholics and Lutherans to have equal rights John Knox returns to Scotland from exile in Geneva Latimer and Ridley burnt
1556	Genevan Psalter printed abroad	Emperor Charles V, father of Philip of Spain, abdicates

Year   Age   Life

1559   5   His father, Sir Henry Sidney, Lord President of Wales

1561   7   Birth of his sister, Mary, later Countess of Pembroke

Year	Artistic Events	Historic Events
1557	More: *English Works* (ed.) Rastell Tottel's *Miscellany*† (frequent editions –1587. Includes poems by Wyatt, Surrey, Vaux and others)	Influenza pandemic in Europe
1558	Margaret of Navarre begins *Heptameron* John Knox: . . . *Against the Monstrous Regiment of Women* First of Heywood's Senecan translations: *Troas* *Mirror for Magistrates* printed (frequent reprints/expansions –1610)	England loses Calais Mary I dies. Elizabeth I becomes Queen Mary Stuart, Queen of Scots, marries the future Francis II of France (1559–60) William Cecil Principal Secretary of State (see 1550) Margaret of Parma, sister of Philip of Spain, becomes his Regent in the Netherlands (–1567)
1559	Montemayor: *Diana* Elizabethan Prayer Book	Mary Stuart, Queen of Scots and of France, claims English crown
1560	Ronsard: *Les Discours* Uffizi in Florence founded Westminster School founded Geneva Bible	Church of Scotland founded Charles IX succeeds Francis II in France, with his mother, Catherine de Medici, as Regent
1561	Hoby translates Castiglione's *Il Cortegiano* Eden translates Cortés' *Art of Navigation* Merchant Taylors' School founded Palladio working in Italy Norton translates Calvin's *Institution of the Christian Religion* (1535) Stow's edition of Chaucer	Edict of Orleans suspends persecution of Huguenots Mary Queen of Scots leaves France to take up the rule of Scotland Scottish Church Ministers draw up Confessions of Faith First Calvinist refugees from Flanders in England
1562	Tasso: *Rinaldo* Tintoretto and Veronese working in Italy: Brueghel the Elder in Flanders Middle Temple Hall, London, built	Wars of Religion begins in France French attempt to colonise Florida Hawkins's first voyage to the New World

Year   Age   Life

1563   9   Birth of his brother, Robert

1564   10   Enters third form of the newly established Shrewsbury
              School, at the same time as his lifelong friend Fulke Greville

Year	Artistic Events	Historic Events
1563	William Byrd organist, Lincoln Flowering of mystical writing in Spain Foxe, *Book of Martyrs*: first English edition Googe: *Eclogs, Epitaphs and Sonnets*†	Council of Trent ends (begun 1543): Counter Reformation begins Plague throughout Europe: 20,000 dead in London Catholic Index of Prohibited Books
1564	Marlowe born (died 1593) Shakespeare born (died 1616) Galileo born (died 1642)	Robert Lord Dudley made Earl of Leicester English Merchant Adventurers granted new Royal Charter Spain occupies Philippines Hawkins's second voyage to the New World
1565	Golding's translation of Ovid's *Metamorphoses* I–IV Tasso Court Poet at Ferrara Ronsard: *Elegies* Norton and Sackville, *Gorboduc*	Malta besieged by Turkish fleet: relieved by Spain Royal Exchange, London, founded Royal College of Physicians, London, permits human dissection Hawkins introduces tobacco and sweet potatoes Mary Queen of Scots marries Lord Darnley
1566	Painter's *Palace of Pleasure*: Italian novellas in English Adlington translates Apuleius' *Golden Ass*	Mary Queen of Scots' son born: James I (1603–25) Calvinist riots in Netherlands Margaret of Parma dismisses Inquisition
1567	Turberville: *Epitaphs, Epigrams Songs, Sonnets*† Hake translates à Kempis's *Imitation of Christ*	Margaret of Parma resigns Regency of Netherlands Duke of Alva begins reign of terror Mary Queen of Scots forced to abdicate after Darnley's murder and her elopement with Bothwell

Year *Age* *Life*

1568   14   February, enters Christ Church, Oxford

1571   17   Plague in Oxford. Leaves without taking a degree

1572   18   May, licensed to travel abroad to learn languages. In Paris, stays with Sir Francis Walsingham, until just after the Massacre of St Bartholomew, 24 August. Leaves for Germany

Year	Artistic Events	Historic Events
1568	Bishop's Bible Building of Longleat House begun Skelton's collected Works printed	Mary Queen of Scots takes refuge in England English College at Douai founded to train Jesuits for missionary work in England Mercator's Projection for charts
1569	Arcilla's *Araucana* (epic on Spanish conquest of Chile) Hilliard, Eworth, working in England Underdowne's translation of Heliodorus's *Æthiopica*	Catholic insurrection in North of England suppressed Poland united with Lithuania
1570	Barber's *The Bruce* and Henryson's *Fables* printed Ortelius: first modern atlas Ascham: *Scholemaster* Polyphonic a cappella style at its height: Palestrina, di Lasso Castelvetro urges introduction of Aristotelean rules into drama	Elizabeth I excommunicated Turks sack Nicosia: declare war on Venice
1571	Act for Incorporation of Oxford and Cambridge Universities	Cecil created Lord Burghley Alliance between Spain and Venice against Turks Turkish fleet routed at Lepanto Clergy assent to Thirty-Nine Articles enforced by Act of Parliament
1572	Camoens: *Lusiadas* Ronsard: *Franciade* Byrd and Tallis organists at Chapel Royal Society of Antiquarians founded	Dutch War of Independence begins St Bartholomew's Day Massacre Walsingham Secretary of State Drake attacks Spanish harbours in America Burghley made Lord High Treasurer Poland becomes an elective monarchy Tycho Brahe observes a nova in the Milky Way

Year	Age	Life
1573	19	In Frankfurt until the spring. Meets Languet and other Protestant scholars. In summer travels to Vienna and Hungary. In November leaves for Italy
1574	20	Visits Venice, Padua, Florence, Genoa. Returns to Vienna in late summer: brief visit to Poland
1575	21	Leaves Vienna in spring: travels through Prague, Dresden, Heidelburg, Strasbourg to Antwerp. Sails for England in June. In August his father appointed Lord Deputy of Ireland
1576	22	In the spring succeeds his father as Royal Cupbearer. Late summer, visits his father in Ireland. Takes part in the suppression of the Earl of Clanricarde's rebellion. Returns to Court
1577	23	In February appointed Ambassador to the German Emperor Rudolph II, and to the Elector Palatine Louis VI and his brother Prince Casimir, to convey the Queen's condolences on the deaths of their fathers. Stands proxy for the Earl of Leicester at the Christening of the Prince of Orange's second daughter. His sister Mary marries the Earl of Pembroke. Returns to England in June. Begins *Old Arcadia*. In the autumn writes *Discourse on Irish Affairs*, defending his father's policy in Ireland

Year	Artistic Events	Historic Events
1573	Tasso: *Aminta* Bandello: *Novelle*	Duke of Alva returns to Spain War ends between Turks and Venice Walsingham made Chief Secretary of State
1574	Burbage licensed to open a theatre in London Languet: *Vindiciae contra Tyrannos* (pro-Huguenot) Lipsius edits Tacitus' *Annals*	Spain loses Tunis to Turks Portuguese colonise Angola and found Sao Paulo, Brazil Berlin University founded
1575	Rolland: *Court of Venus* Gascoigne: *Posies* Anon: *Gammer Gurton's Needle* Archbishop Parker leaves his collection of medieval mss to Corpus Christi, Cambridge Saxton's *County Atlas of England and Wales*	Charles IX of France succeeded by Henry III Stephen Báthory becomes King of Poland Edward Grindal becomes Archbishop of Canterbury State bankruptcy in Spain
1576	Burbage's 'Theatre' opens in December Gascoigne: *Steele Glas* Clusius' pioneer botanical work on Iberian flora	Frobisher discovers Frobisher Bay, Canada Don John of Austria, Regent of Netherlands Rudolph II succeeds Maximilian II as Emperor Spanish sack Antwerp
1577	'Curtain', London's second playhouse, opens Holinshed's *Chronicles* Harrison: *Description of England* Eden: *Travels in the East and West Indies* El Greco, Rubens, Caravaggio working in Spain, Netherlands and Italy	Henry of Navarre head of Huguenot party Don John's attempts to settle Netherlands rejected by William of Orange Surrender of Danzig ends opposition to Báthory's rule in Poland Drake begins circumnavigation of the globe

Year *Age* *Life*

1578 24 Writes playlet, *The Lady of May*, performed for the Queen during a visit to the Earl of Leicester at Wanstead. Continues writing poems connected with *Old Arcadia*, and other poems to be included later in *Certaine Sonets*

1579 25 With his father, acts as host to Prince Casimir. Writes to the Queen advising strongly against her proposed marriage with the Catholic French Duc d'Alençon. Spenser's *The Shephearde's Calendar* dedicated to him.

1580 26 Completes *Old Arcadia* in the summer, while staying with his sister, Mary. His father again Lord President of Wales

1581 27 Active in Court affairs. Member of Parliament for Kent. His aunt, Lady Huntingdon, brings her ward, Penelope Devereux ('Stella') to Court in January: affiances her to Lord Rich. They marry in November. Sidney leaves Court, December–March

1582 28 Spends summer with his father in Wales. *Astrophil and Stella* probably composed during this time. Also writing *Defence of Poesie*

Year	Artistic Events	Historic Events
1578	Du Bartas: *La Semaine* Ronsard: *Sonnets pour Hélène*† Lyly: *Euphues* Catacombs in Rome discovered	James VI (later I of England) assumes rule of Scotland Sebastian, King of Portugal killed in Morocco Death of Don John: Duke of Parma succeeds as Governor of Netherlands Negotiations for a proposed marriage between Elizabeth I and the Catholic Duc d'Alençon arouse strong feeling in England
1579	Spenser: *The Shephearde's Calendar* Pamphlet war initiated by Puritan attacks on the stage – Gosson, Lodge: later Stubbes, Nashe St John of the Cross: *The Dark Night of the Soul* North's translation of Plutarch's *Lives*	English–Dutch alliance Union of Utrecht: foundation of Dutch Republic Drake claims New Albion, California, for England
1580	Montaigne: first *Essais* Stow: *Chronicles of England*	Elizabeth I breaks off French marriage negotiations Drake returns to England Philip of Spain claims vacant Portuguese throne. Portugal invaded
1581	Heywood etc. translate Seneca's *Tragedies* Mulcaster: *Positions* Tasso: *Gerusalemme Liberata*	Portugal submits to Philip II Campion, Jesuit missionary, executed in England for treason Elizabeth I knights Drake
1582	Hakluyt begins *Voyages* Edinburgh University founded Watson: *Ecatompathia*† Rheims and Douai Bible (Catholic)	First English colony in Newfoundland

Year	Age	Life
1583	29	Knighted in January. Marries Frances, Walsingham's daughter and heir, 21 September. Writes *Two Pastoralls*, and translates *First Week* of Du Bartas (now lost). Begins translation of Mornay's *De la Vérité de la Religion Chréstienne* (never completed)
1584	30	Begins new and extensive expansion of *Arcadia – The New Arcadia* (not completed). Meets Giordano Bruno. With Francis Drake on the Parliamentary Committee for Raleigh's Virginia Bill
1585	31	Begins metaphrase of the *Psalms*: 1–43 completed. Prevented by the Queen's command from sailing with Drake to the West Indies; appointed Governor of Flushing. Sails for the Netherlands in November. There acquits himself notably under constant military and diplomatic pressures
1586	32	His father dies. He himself is wounded in a skirmish outside Zutphen, 22 September. Dies 17 October of subsequent infection
1587		Buried in St Paul's, magnificently, 16 February, at Walsingham's expense. Collections of elegies published by Oxford, Cambridge and Louvain Universities, as well as by many individual poets
1588		A few of Sidney's poems begin to appear in print

Year	Artistic Events	Historic Events
1583	Queen's Company of Players formed	Somerville and Throgmorton plots against Elizabeth I English trading expeditions to India and Middle East
1584	Lyly: *Alexander and Campaspe* Scot: *Discoverie of Witchcraft* Bruno: *Spaccio della Bestia Trionfante* Peele: *Arraignment of Paris*	William of Orange assassinated Raleigh discovers, names and annexes Virginia Banco di Rialto founded: Venice
1585	Shakespeare comes to London Guarini: *Il Pastor Fido* Cervantes: *Galatea* Alleyn head of Lord Chamberlain's Men and Lord Admiral's Company	Henry III and Elizabeth I refuse sovereignty of the Netherlands: Elizabeth I takes them under her protection Drake attacks Vigo and San Domingo
1586	Webbe: *Discourse of English Poesie* Camden: *Britannia*	Babington Plot: trial of Mary Queen of Scots, who names Philip of Spain as heir to her claim to the English throne
1587	Whetstone: *Life* (in verse) of Sir Philip Sidney Monteverdi: first book of madrigals Angell and Day: translation of Longus' *Daphnis and Chloe* from Amyot's French version	Execution of Mary, Queen of Scots
1588	Vatican Library opens in Rome Greene starts to popularise the pastoral romance in England: *Pandosto* Fraunce: *Arcadia–Rhetorick* Anti-Prelatical pamphlet war: Marprelate tracts/replies	The Spanish Armada sails against England, and is defeated
1589	Development of English critical writing: Puttenham, Nashe Galileo Professor of Mathematics at Pisa	Henry III of France assassinated. Henry of Navarre (Henry IV) first Bourbon King of France Unsuccessful attempt by Drake to capture Lisbon

Year	Age	Life
1590		Fulke Greville edits and publishes the incomplete *New Arcadia*
1591		Thomas Newman prints two editions of *Astrophil and Stella* in corrupt texts, the first of which has Nashe's *Preface*
1593		Mary, Countess of Pembroke, appends the last three Books of *Old Arcadia* to Greville's edition of the incomplete *New Arcadia*
1595		Editions of the *Defence of Poesie* by Ponsonby and Olney (*An Apologie for Poetrie*)

Year	Artistic Events	Historic Events
1590	Spenser: *Faerie Queene* I–III Shakespeare's earliest plays performed Marlowe: *Tamburlaine* Start of great period of English drama Fowler: *Tarantula of Love*† Galileo: *De Motu*	Walsingham dies Catholic League in France opposes Henry IV
1591	Spenser: *Complaints* Trinity College, Dublin, founded by Elizabeth I	Henry IV excommunicated. Elizabeth I sends money and an expedition under Essex to his help
1592	Henslowe begins his Diary Kyd: *Spanish Tragedy* Daniel: *Delia*† Ruins of Pompeii discovered	Essex is recalled Outbreak of plague in London
1593	Shakespeare: *Venus and Adonis* Barnes: *Parthenophil and Parthenope*† Fletcher: *Licia*† Lodge: *Phillis*† (Shakespeare likely to have begun writing Sonnets: printed 1609)	Henry IV converts to Rome
1594	Hooker: *Ecclesiastical Polity* 1–4 Nashe: *Unfortunate Traveller* Shakespeare: *Lucrece* Anon: *Zepheria*† Constable: *Diana*† Drayton: *Ideas Mirrour*† Percy: *Coelia*† Morley: *Madrigals to Four Voices*	Edict of St Germain-en-Laye grants Huguenots freedom of worship
1595	Continued growth of English drama Maunsell: *Catalogue of English Printed Books* Spenser: *Amoretti*†, *Epithalamion, Colin Clouts Come Home Againe* (with elegies on Sidney)	Henry IV declares war on Spain Spanish raid on Cornwall Last voyage of Drake and Hawkins to Spanish Main Raleigh explores the Orinoco

Year   Age   Life

1598   Mary, Countess of Pembroke's collected edition of her
              brother's work: the standard edition until this century. She
              dedicates her revised and completed version of Sidney's
              metaphrase of the *Psalms of David* to the Queen. No early
              edition exists

1602   Sidney's *Two Pastoralls* appear for the first time in an
              anthology compiled by Frances Davison: *A Poetical
              Rhapsody*

Year	Artistic Events	Historic Events
1596	Spenser: *Faerie Queene* IV–VI, with revised edition of I–III, *Fowre Hymnes, Prothalamion* Griffin: *Fidessa*[†] Lynche: *Diella*[†] Smith: *Chloris*[†]	English sack Cadiz Barents discovers Spitzbergen Spanish take Calais
1597	Shakespeare now well established: buys New Place in Stratford James VI of Scotland: *Demonologie* Bacon: first *Essays* Dowland: *First Book of Songs*	Second Spanish Armada: scattered by storms Spain and France open peace negotiations
1598	Speght's edition of Chaucer Meres: *Palladis Tamia* First parts of Chapman's translation of Homer printed Marlowe (completed by Chapman): *Hero and Leander* Hakluyt: *Voyages* (enlarged) Young: translation of Montemayor's *Diana*	Edict of Nantes Death of Burghley Death of Philip II of Spain

INTRODUCTION

Sidney's Life

Early years and formal education

> Drawn was thy race aright from princely line,
> Nor less than such, by gifts that nature gave,
> The common mother that all creatures have,
> Doth virtue show, and princely lineage shine.
>
> A king gave thee thy name; a kingly mind
> That God thee gave . . .
> Sir Walter Raleigh, *An Epitaph upon . . . Sir Philip Sidney*

Philip Sidney's family circumstances at and around the time of his birth in 1554 are relevant to any consideration of his own adult opinions, ambitions and career. Both his parents' families had Protestant sympathies, and had prospered under Edward VI and his Council of Regency. Neither looked forward happily to the accession of Mary, a devout Catholic. His mother's family was deeply embroiled in the bloodshed and disorder that followed Edward's death in 1553: his uncle, Lord Guildford Dudley, had married Lady Jane Grey, and both were executed after the attempt to make her Queen had failed. So was Philip's grandfather, John Dudley, Duke of Northumberland, whose ambition to replace the Tudor with a Dudley dynasty had motivated both the marriage and the unsuccessful uprising. Philip's four other uncles, Guildford Dudley's brothers, narrowly escaped the same fate. His father, Sir Henry Sidney, possessed perhaps of more foresight, changed his ground to support Mary in time to escape real involvement. In the year following Mary's Coronation in October 1553 he was sent on embassy, with the Earl of Bedford who had acted with similar speed and discretion, to conclude the very unpopular marriage treaty between Mary and Philip of Spain. His son was born on

30 November, four months after the royal wedding. Philip stood as godfather to the child, who was called after him.

Mary died in 1558, when Philip was four years old. The accession of Elizabeth I, and her subtly temperate settlement of a Protestant Church in England, brought with it new shifts, stresses and possibilities for her Catholic and, more particularly here, her non-Catholic subjects. But Elizabeth had a long and exact memory. Her sister's reign and its tragic prelude had been a time of great difficulty and danger for herself. The fortunes of the Sidney and Dudley families at that time may well have weighted other considerations, inclining her to certain ambivalences in her later dealings with both. Philip Sidney's failure to gain early advancement is the present, and outstanding, case in point.

In 1559 Sir Henry Sidney, was made Lord President of Wales, a post he held until his death in 1586, three times in conjunction with the far more arduous office of Lord Deputy in Ireland. These duties, and some missions abroad, kept him from Court for much of his lifetime. From the age of about seven Philip was in the charge of a tutor, by whom he was grounded in Latin and French. In 1564 he was sent to Shrewsbury School, not far from his father's presidential seat in Ludlow. The founding Headmaster, Thomas Ashton, was a fine scholar, and as his later career shows, a sensitive diplomat. The religious bias of the school was towards Calvinist Protestantism. The subject teaching reflected Ashton's up-to-date views. We know from account books and other sources that Philip studied the major Latin authors in depth, and some Greek, as well as French: the inclusion in the syllabus of a modern language was unusual at this time. He also learnt Latin composition; a necessity in any public career when Latin was still the international language of learning and diplomacy. A fellow pupil and exact contemporary was Fulke Greville, his lifetime friend and posthumous editor and biographer.

Only two of Philip's uncles had survived into Elizabeth's reign: Ambrose Dudley, later Earl of Warwick, and Robert Dudley, later Earl of Leicester foremost among Elizabeth's nobility and high in her favour. Until the birth of a son in 1579 by Leicester's marriage to Lettice Knollys, Philip was the presumptive heir of both. Leicester took the earliest possible opportunity of introducing his young nephew to the royal notice, taking him to Oxford in 1566, when he was Chancellor of the University, for the celebrations taking place there in honour of the Queen's visit.

In February 1568 Philip went to Oxford again, to Christ Church as a student. At that period he was not unusually young for university studies, and while as the Chancellor's nephew he would have received many privileges, he was far from wasting his time academically. Studies were categorised as grammar, rhetoric and dialect, and all teaching was in Latin, including *ex tempore* dispute. In addition to gaining close familiarity with the authors prescribed, especially Cicero and Aristotle in Latin translation, he studied ancient history and philosophy. He would also have been kept well aware of current Protestant theological debate: the greater number of his student contemporaries were intending to follow a career in the Church. At or around this time he made an English version of the first two Books of Aristotle's *Rhetoric*, and this branch of his studies certainly contributed much to the development of his own style, his feeling for language and the possibilities of its controlled manipulation. Mere imitation of style he found invidious. Writing to his younger brother Robert in October 1580 (III. p. 132[1]), he warns him of: 'Ciceronianisme the chiefe abuse of Oxford', whereby those who attend only to the words come to neglect the sense. His own Latin style is sound but not pedantic.

In the spring of 1571 the University was closed because of an outbreak of plague. Philip did not return to take a degree. Just then his family were in London, and he probably spent some part of that year with them. For someone in his position foreign travel required official permission, and in May 1572 he was licensed to travel abroad with three servants and four horses 'for attaining the knowledge of foreign languages'.

Travels in Europe

> To learne the enterdeale of Princes strange,
> To marke th'intent of Counsells, and the change
> Of states, and eke of priuate men somewhile,
> Supplanted by fine falshood and faire guile;
> Of all the which he gathereth, what is fit
> T'enrich the storehouse of his powerful wit,
> Which through wise speaches, and graue conference
> He daylie eekes, and brings to excellence.

> Such is the rightful Courtier in his kind.
> Edmund Spenser, *Mother Hubberd's Tale* ll. 758–93

These lines are taken from Spenser's summary of the qualities and skills proper to 'the rightful Courtier'; part of a word portrait generally assumed to be based on Sidney. The figure of the courtier was much discussed at this time. He might be a fool and corrupt; Spenser has much to say on the negative side also in the same poem. But the highest expectations of him were high indeed. Books were written on the subject, of which Castiglione's *Il Cortegiano*, 1528, translated into English by Sir Thomas Hoby as *The Courtier* in 1561, is the most famous and influential. Sidney set out on his travels with such tenets as those of Castiglione very much in mind. Certainly he was to miss no opportunity of expanding his own interests in learning and the arts. But he was first and foremost his Queen's servant. Some years later in another letter to his brother Robert he advises him on his responsibilities while travelling abroad. Much may be learned, he says, from the example of laws and customs good or evil in themselves. More particularly:

> ... soe as you cannott tell what the Queen of England is able to doe, defensivelie, or offencivelie, but bye through compare what they are able to doe, with whome shee is to bee matched. (III. p. 125)

To this end he should note all possibly observable details of naval and military strength and its financing, readiness for war, terrain, social content or unrest, as well as indications of change in foreign policy. To assimilate and retain with any accuracy such a mass of shifting information over a period of time would be impossible for most people today. Sidney's education however, his brother's and that of their contemporaries, included rigorous training of the memory, and its exercise as an art.[2]

Sidney went first to Paris, and lodged with Sir Francis Walsingham, then ambassador. He rapidly made his mark in courtly and intellectual society: his extraordinary international reputation for grace, wit and learning dates from the three months he spent there. This must have been an intensely exciting time for him, with new possibilities of every kind of fresh adult experience crowding in. It was cut very brutally short. The massacre of Protestants that took place on St Bartholomew's

Day, 24 August, shocked the whole of Europe. Sidney may well have been still in Paris, to see from the safety of the embassy some part of the horror in which many of his new friends were among the killers and their victims. In any case he would have heard the dreadful details immediately, and at first hand. He left France for Germany immediately afterwards, and never returned there.

After a stay in Heidelburg he went to Frankfurt, where he spent the winter as a guest of the learned printer Andrew Wechel, a French Huguenot refugee. At this time, and in the course of his travels through Germany and beyond in the spring and summer following, he was introduced to many scholars and men eminent in various fields. For all of them, as for Sidney himself, Latin was a familiar spoken language: this was as well, since Sidney disliked the harshness of the German language intensely, and refused even to attempt to learn it. Outstanding among his new acquaintances was Hubert Languet, at this time in the service of the Elector of Saxony. Languet was much the elder, an ardent Protestant, a philosopher, and diplomat of wide experience. His influence on Sidney's political and religious perspectives was formative and lasting: their affection deep and mutual. If Languet's fatherly concern for his young friend may at times have been irksome, as his complaints of Sidney's laggard responses to his letters seem to indicate, the real value Sidney set on his friendship was high. In a Song given to his own *persona*, Philisides, in the *Old Arcadia* Sidney gives this value definition:

> The songe I sange old Languet had me taught,
> Languet, the shepheard best sweet *Ister* knewe,
> For clerkly reed, and hating what is naught,
> For faithfull hart, cleane hands, and mouth as true:
> With his sweet skill my skillesse youth he drewe,
>   To have a feeling tast of him that sitts
>   Beyond the heaven, far more beyond your witts . . .
>
> He liked me, but pitied lustfull youth:
> His good strong staff my slippry yeares upbore:
> He still hop'd well, because I loved truth . . . (ll. 66. p. 99)[3]

Although 'shepherd' is commonly used at this time to mean 'poet', as for example in Sidney's own *Two Pastoralls* (see below, pp. 131–4) the meaning here is rather that of 'mentor'.

Sidney's correspondence with Languet shows no interest in contemporary literature, and his new European acquaintance-ships, greatly enlarged in Germany, Austria and later in Italy by Languet's letters of introduction, were among scholars and statesmen rather than poets. Of his own literary ambitions, if indeed they yet existed, we know nothing. He received many dedications at this time and throughout his life, but though the most famous of these is Spenser's, *The Shepheard's Calendar* in 1579, the vast majority were of works of learning, many of them theological.

In the summer of 1573 he left Frankfurt for Vienna. From this time on his activities can be traced to a large extent through references in his letters to Languet: he continued with his classical studies, and read Machiavelli as well as modern history, especially where this was relevant to his travels. In Vienna he also pursued studies in music and astronomy, besides taking advantage of the teaching of the master equestrian, Pugliano (see below p. 83). His own reputation for horsemanship was high, and his love of this aspect of chivalric skill appears in his frequent use of imagery connected with it. (See below p. 24, n.) He made a brief visit to Hungary, with an introduction from Languet, before travelling to Venice in November.

Even in Italy, Sidney's immediate contacts were chiefly, though by no means exclusively, among leading Protestants. This was not out of prejudice: his very real hatred of Catholi-cism, explicit in his letters and elsewhere, did not exclude Catholics from his personal friendship in England and abroad. But the public arena to which he aspired was military and political, and his future place in it would be with the Protestant powers.

He found time for study in Venice and Padua, as well as for having his portrait painted by Veronese. This was sent as a promised gift to Languet, who received it with admiration and delight, only complaining that the expression was perhaps too grave. This portrait is now lost; if it still exists it has not yet been identified. He also visited Genoa and Florence, but he did not go to Rome, or to any of the southern parts of Italy. During this time he certainly became fluent in Italian: he would have received help here from his attendant travelling companion, Ludovick Bryskett, who was an Italian by birth, his name being an anglicisation of Bruschetti. Bryskett later left his position in the Sidney household for a post in Ireland, where he was a close friend of Spenser. In his *Pastorall Aeglogue*, published with other elegies on Sidney in 1595, he says that Sidney and he travelled into Italy 'still with the Muses sporting'. This may mean nothing beyond their enjoyment of conversation about learning and the arts in general, but is possibly more specific. It seems likely that it was at this time that Sidney began to acquire that familiarity with Italian poetry, epic and romance which is evident in his own writing, but he makes no mention of this, for example, in his letters. Not that there is reason why he should: works of this kind he would have regarded for the most part as leisure reading, as he was to commend his own *Arcadia* to his sister Mary, that she should, 'Read it, then, at your idle tymes.' (I. 4)

Sidney's reputation for learning and courtly excellence had preceded him to Italy, and the dedications of learned and theological works he received at this time and later shows that he upheld it. He appeared as a living refutation of the common Italian assumption that all Northern Europeans, and the English in particular, were uncultured barbarians. He made new friends and contacts not only among the great Italian families but also among English expatriates, including some recusant Catholics. Of the profound impressions made on him by Italian art – sculpture, painting, architecture and literature – he says almost nothing in his correspondence at the time. Sidney's own likely sense of priorities apart, it is probable that the necessary assimilation of rich and crowded aesthetic experience into his own imagination needed time to be recognised, much less drawn upon.

In the later summer of 1574 he returned to Vienna. He made a brief visit to Poland, and then left Vienna in the following spring. He travelled leisurely by way of the major cities to Antwerp, taking ship there for England in June.

Courtier in waiting

Now though his short life and private fortune were, as I said, no proper stages to act any greatness of good or evil upon, yet are there (even from these little centres of his) lines to be drawn not astronomical or imaginary, but real lineaments – such as infancy is of man's estate – out of which nature often sparkleth brighter rays in some than ordinarilly appear in the ripeness of many others.[4]

On his return to England Sidney renewed his friendship with Fulke Greville, who was later to be his biographer, and later still to sum up his own career in his chosen epitaph: Servant to Queen Elizabeth, Counsellor to King James, Friend to Sir Philip Sidney. In the passage quoted above he is discussing Sidney's public life, the career towards which his education, inclinations and experience had directed him from childhood. In 1575 the promise upon which Greville so finely dwells must have seemed to Sidney himself and to many others on the verge of great fulfilment. This never took place.

Reasons for this have been put forward by every one of Sidney's biographers. My own opinion is that there were three main factors standing in the way of his public career, each exacerbated by the timing of events equally outside his immediate control. The first and second have been pinpointed by Katherine Duncan-Jones: '. . . the Queen's caution. Sidney may have been rather *too* successful on the Continent for her liking, as he could not be trusted not to take independent initiative'.[5] The second was Leicester's attitude towards him expressed in conversation again with Greville: '. . . who told me (after Sir Philip's and not long before his own death) that when he undertook the government of the Low Countries he carried his nephew over with him as one among the rest, not only dispising his youth for a counsellor, but withal bearing his hand upon him for a forward young man'.[6] Leicester's feelings for Sidney may well have included some jealousy and resentment: until the birth in 1579 of his only legitimate son, the short-lived Lord Denbigh, Sidney was Leicester's presumptive heir, and may also have appeared to be a potential usurper of his present greatness and influence.

What seems to me to have been a third and crucial impediment to Sidney's early advancement was simply his family history. The Queen's most uncomfortable memories of this are likely to have been sharply revived during the month following Sidney's return to England, when Leicester entertained her at Kenilworth. The enormously elaborate celebrations had a specific end in view: in the event they amounted to perhaps the most expensively unsuccessful proposal of marriage in recorded history. The Queen's reactions made the outcome clear fairly early on, and tactful modifications were hastily made.[7] If, as seems probable, Sidney was present, and even if he were not, his position is likely to have been doubly affected. Leicester's disappointed ambition may well have irritated any kind of latent resentment against his nephew. And the Queen herself, whose personal feelings for Leicester never blinded her political perceptions, can hardly have helped seeing in the whole occasion a resurgence of his father's dynastic pretensions which had given so tragic an opening to her sister Mary's reign. As Leicester's heir, Sidney had been quite innocently wrong-footed.

He succeeded his father as Royal Cupbearer in the spring of 1576: a gratifying title, but one carrying no political responsibility. In the August following, Sir Henry Sidney was appointed Lord Deputy of Ireland for the third time.[8] Sidney visited him in the summer, when he took part in the suppression of the Earl of Clanricarde's rebellion. He was deeply interested in his father's administration and its problems; indeed there is some evidence that he would have been happy to succeed his father as Lord Deputy.[9] It was on this first-hand experience that he was to base his earliest surviving work, the *Discourse on Irish Affairs*, written late in 1577 (III. 46–50), defending his father's policies.

That spring saw what must have seemed to be the real start of his public career. The Queen sent him as her ambassador to convey her condolences to the courts of the Emperor Rudolph II, the Elector Palatine and his brother Prince Casimir on the recent deaths of their fathers. His letter to Walsingham, dated 3 May (III, pp. 109–114), makes it clear that he discharged this ostensible part of his duties with tact and grace. It is equally clear that his commission went further:

> . . . I enformed my self as well as I coold of suche particularities as I receaved in my enstructions, as of the 1. Emperours disposicion and his brethren. 2. By whose Advise he is directed. 3. When it is lykely he shall marry. 4. What princes in Jermany are moste affected to him. 5. In what state he is lefte for revenews. 6. What good agreement there is betwixte him and his brethren. 7. And what partage[10] they have. In these thinges I shall at my returne more largely be hable and with more leysure to declare it . . .

In the course of his travels he met many old friends. The most important of his new contacts took place in May, in the

Lowlands, when by the Queen's command he attended the Christening of William of Orange's second daughter, Elizabeth. The impression he made on the great Protestant leader is evident from a passage in Fulke Greville, relating to a conversation he had with the Prince in 1579. Also clear is the fact that Sidney's enforcedly low public profile over the intervening two years had become anomalous abroad, and bitterly painful to himself:

> ... that I would first commend his [William of Orange's] own humble service ... to the Queen, and after crave leave freely to open his knowledge and opinions of a fellow-servant of his that (as he heard) lived employed under her ... he protested unto me (and for her service) that, if he could judge, her Majesty had one of the ripest and greatest counsellors of state, in Sir Philip Sidney, that at day lived in Europe; to the trial of which he was pleased to leave his own credit engaged till her Majesty might please to employ this gentleman, either among her friends or enemies.
>
> At my return into England ... this ... I acquainted Sir Philip with ... Unto which he, at the first sight opposing ... yet, for my satisfaction, freely added these words: first, that the Queen had the life itself daily attending her, and if she either did not or would not value it so high, the commendation of that worthy prince could be no more (at the best) than a lively picture of that life, and so of far less credit and estimation with her. His next reason was because princes love not that foreign powers should have extraordinary interest in their subjects, much less to be taught by them how they should place their own, as arguments either upbraiding ignorance or lack of large rewarding goodness in them.[11]

There was no sequel to Sidney's embassy of 1577. Whether or not he then failed some hidden test of discretion or restraint, no comparable opportunity was to be offered him until the year before his death. It is likely that his loss, and possibly the Queen's, is our gain. He had leisure, and though it was unwelcome, he put it to use.

Courtier and Poet: necessity and choice

> Neere *Wilton* sweete, huge heapes of stones are found,
> But so confusde, that neither any eye
> Can count them just, nor reason reason trye
> What force brought them to so unlikely ground.

> To stranger weights my minde's waste soile is bound,
> Of passyon's hills reaching to reason's skie,
> From fancie's earth passing all numbers' bound,
> Passing all ghesse, whence into me should fly
> So mazde a masse, or if in me it growes,
> A simple soule should breed so mixed woes.
>
> Sidney, *The 7 Wonders of England*, 1–10.[12] *Certaine Sonets*, 22

Shortly before Sidney's return to England in June 1577 his sister Mary married Henry Herbert, Earl of Pembroke. In the summer of that year Sidney paid the first of many visits to their seat in Wiltshire: '*Wilton* sweete'. The lines quoted above form the first section of a poem whose structure is probably based on one by Petrarch[13], comparing his state of mind to seven natural wonders; here Stonehenge, the nature and origin of which was much debated at this time. The number seven refers to the Wonders of the ancient world, but Sidney's are English, and prodigies of nature rather than of art. It is not one of his more successful poems, but the ingenious alignment of his state of mind with these selected curiosities of his native land is doubly indicative of his own deep sense of national identity, and of his frustrated alienation from its central expression through public responsibility.

It was most probably during his first visit to Wilton that he began work on the first version of his romance *Arcadia* (*Old Arcadia*). This was not printed until 1912, when Feuillerat's edition appeared, based on then recently discovered manuscripts. The dedication to his sister[14] was prefaced to the revised version (the *New Arcadia*) when this was printed after Sidney's death, but it refers to the work as completed: 'But you desired me to do it ... Now, it is done onelie for you, onely to you.' This indicates that it was written for the *Old Arcadia* when Sidney finished it in 1580. The deprecatory tone of the dedication must be taken in context: Sidney would have regarded his *Discourse*, written late in 1577 in defence of his father's Irish policies, or his widely circulated open *Letter* to the Queen written in 1579 advising her against her proposed marriage with the French Catholic Duc d'Alençon, as of central relevance to his public vocation as a courtier, important in a way that no work simply of his own invention could be. Sidney refers to his romance as 'a trifle, and that triflinglie handled', but the

surviving manuscripts show that he was making careful changes
and revisions before deciding to undertake a complete rewriting.
What may well have started as an experimental game continued
in delighted earnest. The plan of the work is startlingly original:
the tragi-comic prose narrative, interspersed with poems keyed
into character and situation, is shaped dramatically into five
'Actes'. The first four of these conclude with pastoral songs or
games, the elegantly varied lyrics for which are unfortunately
too closely involved with character and action and with each
other to make selection fair. Sidney's choice and development of
a dramatic structure sustained by the subtle use of lyric registers
is elegantly handled, and looks forward to other of his major
works, *Astrophil and Stella* in particular.

His playlet, *The Lady of May* (see below, pp. 3–14), is his only
simply dramatic work, written for the entertainment of the
Queen on her visit to Leicester's seat at Wanstead in May 1578.
Like *The Arraignment of Paris*, by the professional poet and
playwright George Peele, published in 1594, and like the court
masques of Ben Jonson and others performed in the next reign, it
depends for its effective denouement on the presence of royalty.
Unlike these, but like a number of other entertainments offered
to Elizabeth[15] it gives her an active role to play. The ending
depends on her decision as to which of the two suitors of the
May Lady is worthiest of her love. Sidney has provided for either
choice, but it is clear that the Queen's verdict, in favour of the
gentle shepherd Espilus and against his rival, the bold forester
Therion, was not the one expected. See below pp. 13 and n. It
makes graceful play with the pastoral registers of lyric and
comedy, has a compact structure, and shows a sharp ear for
dialogue. It is possible that had he lived longer Sidney might have
written tragedies, for study rather than performance, as did Fulke
Greville, for example.[16] Certainly he would not have contem-
plated writing for the public stage, a professional field, and one
not yet highly regarded in terms of learning or influence.[17]

It is likely that Sidney spent a good part of this year in court
attendance. At the same time he was working on the *Old
Arcadia*, and poems related to it, as he says in the dedication,
'By sheets', sent to his sister, 'as soon as they were done'.
Probably he was also working on some at least of the poems to
be included in *Certaine Sonets* (see below, pp. 15–22).

In February 1579 the Protestant Prince Casimir visited England, at the same time as Sidney's valued friend Languet. Sidney had met the Prince while on embassy two years before, and this acquaintanceship may have been the reason that Sidney and his father were assigned as his official hosts. The Queen distinguished Casimir by making him a Knight of the Garter: a rare honour for a foreigner, one probably calculated to gain approval from her Protestant subjects and allies abroad at a time when negotiations were being reopened for a proposed marriage between herself and the Catholic French Duc d'Alençon.

There was strong popular opposition to this match. At Court Burghley headed the party favouring it, and Leicester the opposing faction. Sidney supported his uncle: his famous quarrel on the tennis court with the Earl of Oxford may well have been sparked off by their disagreement on this wider issue. Sidney's widely circulated open *Letter* to the Queen is clearly argued, and, taken in its context, not immoderately. It was probably composed in the autumn of 1579. Languet, who wrote to Sidney in January 1580, advising him to be discreet in expressing his opinions, and to be careful of avoiding offence to the French party, wrote again in October of the same year with the telling comment:

Since ... you were ordered to write as you did by those whom you were bound to obey, no fair-judging man can blame you for putting forward freely what you thought good for your country ...[18]

It is likely that the *Letter* was written at Leicester's instigation, and perhaps also Walsingham's. In either case, the Queen seems not to have taken any great offence. Sidney spent much of his time during this period away from court: his quarrel with the Earl of Oxford, his shortage of money, his sense of political powerlessness may have been contributory reasons for this, but he suffered no actual banishment. The Queen's real anger was reserved for Leicester, when the news of his secret marriage to Lettice Knollys in the previous year was broken to her by the French ambassador and Simier, d'Alençon's representative, with the object of discrediting their most formidable opponent. Elizabeth's furious reaction to this slight to herself as Queen as well as woman is understandable, but was shortlived. Sidney, who could hardly not have known of his uncle's clandestine match, may well have felt absence for a time to be the better part of discretion. The *Letter* offered counsel to his ruler, as a

dutiful courtier was bound to do, and in that spirit it seems to
have been received. It is likely that Spenser's dedication of *The
Shephearde's Calendar* to Sidney in November 1579 was
prompted not only by his reputation for 'learning and chevalrie',
but by the poet's whole-hearted support for the opinions held
by Leicester's party and expressed in Sidney's *Letter*.[19]

Spenser may possibly have intended originally to dedicate his
poem to Leicester himself, who had shown him some favour
and patronage. Spenser and Sidney certainly met, but it can only
have been occasionally, and over a period of a few months,
before Spenser took up the post of Secretary to Lord Grey in
Ireland in August 1580. Their common interest in English letters
may well have sparked off both their energies in directions that
differ very widely: there is virtually no trace of direct influence
perceptible on either side.[20] At this time Spenser shared Sidney's
interest in metrical experiment and reform, as his letters to his
Cambridge tutor, Gabriel Hervey, indicate. Even there, where
Spenser is making much of his fresh acquaintance with 'the
twoo worthy Gentlemen, Master *Sidney* and Master *Dyer*', his
enthusiasm for the formulation of 'certaine Lawes and rules of
Quantities of English sillables, for English verse' has a transient
ring. Hindsight may be responsible for this; we know what
became of 'my *Faery Queene*' here mentioned so much more
casually[21]. It is however possible that discussion of Spenser's
plans for his epic, and perhaps the sight of some completed
passages, did have some later influence on Sidney's approach to
the revision of *Arcadia*, in ways to be considered presently.

Sidney's technical interest in work being done on classical
versification by continental as well as English scholars, and in
its potential for poets writing in English, is evident in the songs
written for the *Old Arcadia*, and in many of the poems included
in *Certaine Sonets*[22]. It is a part of his inclusive interest in
poetics, and in what he saw as the unrealised potential of
English poetry. Many of the points he approached in his own
writing are drawn out for consideration in the *Defence of Poesie*
which he may have begun to plan during the later part of 1580,
when he also completed the *Old Arcadia*.

Courtier and Poet: voices and action

Read the Countesse of Pembrookes Arcadia, a gallant Legendary,
full of pleasurable acidents and proffitable discourses; for three

thinges especially very notable – for amorous Courting (he was
young in yeeres), for sage counselling (he was ripe in iudgement),
and for valourous fighting (his soueraine profession was Armes).
Gabriel Hervey, *Peirce's Supererogation*, 1593[23]

Hervey is here extolling the *New Arcadia*, which first appeared
in print in Fulke Greville's edition of 1590. His alignment of its
qualities with those of its author is perhaps no more than an
elegant trope, but it points to an important development in
Sidney's writing. In whatever light-hearted spirit he may have
begun to write the *Old Arcadia*, he lavished a great deal of care
and experimental artistry on its completion. Its imagined world
is in itself coherent and virtually self-contained in a way that
none of his later original works are. His own pastoral *persona*,
Philisides, has a supporting role in the action, which has been
compared by Katherine Duncan-Jones[24] to that of Chaucer in
The Canterbury Tales, but both his feet are on Arcadian soil.
He may glance outside, notably to pay tribute to Languet in the
passage quoted earlier (p. xxxi), but that is all. The manipulation of Astrophil's concerns in relation to Sidney's own, and the
uses made throughout the expanded narrative analysis of the
New Arcadia's history and its makers to express and define his
own political thinking and preoccupations is very much more
complex. In both he is exploiting the techniques of dramatic
projection formulated in the *Old Arcadia* to new and sometimes
bewildering subtlety of effect. From the end of 1580, when the
Old Arcadia was finished, an emerging sense of balance becomes
perceptible between Sidney's public career and interests and his
literary activities, in the relevance of which he seems to have felt
new and justified confidence.

In April 1581 Sidney became Member of Parliament for Kent,
and for most of this year he divided his time between London
and Wilton. In May he certainly had a major part in devising an
entertainment for the visit of the French legation to discuss the
still on-going marriage proposal of the Duc d'Alençon: *The
Triumph of the Four Foster Children of Desire*. His *Letter* had
made Sidney's views on the marriage well known, and, apart from
impressing the French visitors with its splendour and elegance,
the central point of the *Triumph*, though most gracefully
handled, was that the Queen was unattainable.[25] In the event,
although d'Alençon himself came to England in November, it

was clear by then that the negotiations would come to nothing, for a number of reasons, one of which was the pressure of public feeling.

In January Sidney's aunt, Lady Huntingdon, had brought her young ward, Penelope Devereux, to court. Much earlier there had been some thought of a future marriage between her and Sidney, but nothing had come of it. They would now have renewed acquaintance, and taken part together in various court festivities: it is likely for example that Penelope was present at the *Triumph*, and that she saw Sidney take part in the mounted tilt and foot tourney that formed part of the entertainment. A marriage was arranged between her and Lord Rich, and this took place in November. Sidney was away from court from December until March 1582: he was one of the escort of nobility and gentry who accompanied d'Alençon to Antwerp in February at the conclusion of his abortive visit.

Penelope Rich was the matrix for Stella, in *Astrophil and Stella* (see below, pp. 23–81), which Sidney may have begun as early as the winter of 1581, and which was probably completed during the summer of the following year, while he was staying with his father in Wales. In the course of the sequence he makes three overt references to Penelope's married name, Rich: in Sonnets 24, 35 and 37. The sequence ostensibly expresses the painful course of a hopeless love exacerbated by the struggle between Virtue and Desire, but given the dates and circumstances of composition, it can hardly be intended as any kind of factual transcription, even if it were not completed until some time in 1583. Sidney may well have taken account of such a reading as a possibility, however. The sequence was not printed until after his death, and though none of the surviving manuscripts can be dated earlier than this the custom of circulating poems among friends, and so to friends of friends, was widespread. *Astrophil and Stella* is the first of the great Elizabethan love-sonnet sequences, and like others written later, it may have anticipated readings of different kinds, on different levels of awareness and intimacy, of which the convention of autobiographical record is only the most obvious.[26]

In his preface to Thomas Newman's pirated first edition of *Astophil and Stella* that appeared 1591, Thomas Nashe aptly couches his summary of the poem in dramatic terms:

... this Theater of pleasure ... here you shal find a paper stage streud with pearle, an artificial heau'n to overshadow the fair frame, and christal wals to encounter your curious eyes, while the tragicomody of loue is performed by starlight ... The argument cruell chastitie, the Prologue hope, the Epilogue dispaire.[27]

Astrophil himself is a *persona* of great complexity: the courtier as poet, the poet as lover, the lover as courtier: three interlocking circles, projecting and analysing these preoccupations of Sidney himself from their overlapping centre. Stella is in no literal sense Penelope Rich: by the end of the sequence the discrepancy between Astrophil's imagined extrapolation of her as 'the onely Planet of my light' (*AS* 68) and any kind of likely reality has become painfully clear.

Nashe's outline of the structure is over simple, in that the 'argument' is not so much Stella's 'cruell chastitie' as the morally debilitating and claustrophobic effects of Astrophil's frustration in a situation of his own subjective making. Among the many ironies of allusion and cross-reference that play across the sequence are those where expectations of Petrarch's resolution, where the Lady acts as monitor of the transition from human love to divine grace, are undercut by Astrophil's growing self-absorption counterpointed by Stella's unwitting inadequacy. The stages of this progression are, as Nashe suggests, clearly marked: an unbroken run of sonnets, 1–63, presents the exquisite struggle towards an ideal admitted while still being bitterly resented:

> And therefore by her *Love's* authority,
> Willd me these tempests of vaine love to flie,
> And anchor fast my selfe on *Vertue's* shore. (62)

Then control slips into a reiterative downward spiral of false elation, depressive nightmare and self-mockery, the shifts pointed by intervening lyrics, both dramatic and monologue. In the final sonnet, 108, Astrophil's identity as a lover has become indistinguishable from the figure of Cupid, symbiotic with his egocentric concept of love itself:

> Most rude *Dispaire* my daily unbidden guest
> Clips streight my wings, streight wraps me in his night.

The *Defence of Poesie* (see below, pp. 83–129), was probably being written over the same period as *Astrophil and Stella*. It was not printed until after Sidney's death; two editions appeared in 1595, the first by William Ponsonby, under the title used here, *The Defence of Poesie*, and the second by Henry Olney, as *An Apologie for Poetrie*. Early editions were for the most part based on Ponsonby, and his is the title in most general use. There is warrant for both titles, however. Like other of Sidney's works the *Defence* was circulated in manuscript before appearing in print, and while Sidney speaks of his work as a 'defence', Sir John Harington, for example, in his own *Briefe Apologie of Poetrie*, 1591, refers to 'Sir *Philip Sidneys* Apologie'.[28]

Either title needs some explanation for a modern readership. Literary criticism at this period is grounded in moral controversy, even where a writer may be chiefly interested in techniques of versification and form; an example is Puttenham's *Arte of English Poesie*, published in 1589, but probably written earlier. Puritan attacks on stage-plays in particular extended to other genres; love poetry and any fictitious writing were especially condemned as being respectively corrupting and literally untrue. The primary derivation of 'poetry' from the Greek verb ποιεῖν 'to make' allowed the general extension of its meaning to include imaginative prose. Professional writers engaged in pamphlet debate on both sides: Stephen Gosson's *The School of Abuse. Conteining a plesaunt invective against Poets, Pipers, Plaiers, Jesters and such like Catterpillars of a Commonwealth*, 1579, was answered almost at once by Thomas Lodge in his *Defence of Poetry*.[29] As Smith points out, however, in his general discussion of this situation,[30] 'The controversy was carried on from different standpoints.' The defenders of poetry, Sidney preeminently among them, were in full agreement with the Puritan condemnation of lewdness and social abuse in literature, dramatic and otherwise, but their real concerns were with its opposite potential for good, and with authoritative precedent and proof of this, ancient and modern. Their opponents dictated certain starting points, even determined certain approaches, but beyond these there was little real engagement.

That Gosson dedicated his *School of Abuse* to Sidney indicates as much. Sidney's Puritan sympathies were well known, as was his learning. The dedication implies that Gosson assumed his views to be inclusively applicable, in a way that now appears almost pathetically inappropriate. It may well have startled Sidney himself, given Spenser's comment in his Letter to Gabriel Harvey dated early in October 1579:

> Newe Bookes I heare of none, but only of one, that writing a certaine Booke, called *The School of Abuse*, and dedicating it to Maister *Sidney*, was for hys labor scorned: if at leaste it be in the goodnesse of that nature to scorne.[31]

Spenser saw himself first of all as a poet. His direct involvement with these and related critical issues makes an interesting contrast with the argumentative perspectives taken by Sidney or Harington, courtiers by career and vocation. Spenser's early work contains some parodic attacks on incompetence in poetry combined with contempt for its moral abuse and the perversity of fashionable taste:

> Or it mens follies mote be forst to fayne,
> And rolle with rest in rymes of rybaudrye[32]
> Or as it sprong, it wither must agayne.
>
> (*October*, ll. 76–8)

His mature poetic practice was epic, and the stated purpose of his *Faerie Queene*, '. . . to fashion a gentleman or noble person in vertuous and gentle discipline'.[33] Like Sidney, he writes within assured parameters: unlike Sidney he found no need to give these abstract definition.

It is possible that Gosson's *Abuse* was at least a partial catalyst for Sidney's *Defence*, written about three years later. Sidney's work is in no sense a direct reply to Gosson; rather it affirms what Gosson and others were choosing to ignore or simply not to recognise; the power of poetry, and the corresponding responsibility of the poet:

> Nay truely, though I yeeld that Poesie may not onely be abused, but that beeing abused, by the reason of his sweete charming force, it can doe more hurt than any other Armie of words, yet . . . it is a good reason, that whatsoever, being abused, doth most harme, beeing rightly used (and upon the right use of each thing conceiveth his title), doth most good (p.113).

Sidney establishes his own position at the very outset, recalling his visit to the Imperial Court in Vienna in 1573, when he had studied horsemanship under the famous master Pugliano. His

teacher's enthusiasm for his art carries the noblest associations
of Sidney's world: skilled horsemen are 'the Masters of warre,
and ornaments of peace ... triumphers both in Camps and
Courts'. Sidney then draws a witty and self-deprecating parallel
with his own feeling for poetry as apparently tangential to his
courtly and chivalric concerns:

> ... in these my not old yeres and idelest times, having slipt into
> the title of a Poet, am provoked to say something unto you in the
> defence of that my unelected vocation (p. 83).

Sidney's modesty here carries an underlying irony: later he will
refute the specific charge that poetry encourages idleness with
the examples of Homer and Ariosto among others: 'For Poetrie
is the companion of Campes' (p. 114).

The wry, detached ease of his opening, and of his style
throughout, is in fact deceptive. Like accomplished sword-play,
it has strength and control behind it. It is only after he has
examined the nature of poetry, its functions and kinds throughout history and its relation to other disciplines of the mind that
he specifically refutes its critics and the charges they bring, from
a position of achieved advantage. Then he suspends his general
conclusion, that '... the ever-praise-worthy Poesie is full of
vertue-breeding delightfulnes, and voyde of no gyfte that ought
to be in the noble name of learning' (p. 128), to discuss the
particular continuum and potential of English poetry and the
English language.

Two things need to be borne in mind in reading this section.
The first is the changes in language that had taken place since
the time of Chaucer, in particular the loss of the final 'e'.
Chaucer's meaning was often obscured for sixteenth-century
readers, and his scansion blurred. These are major reasons for
the 'great wants' Sidney finds in his work, 'fitte to be forgiven in
so reverent antiquity' (p. 120). The second is the time of writing.
In 1582 Shakespeare and Marlowe were both eighteen, and
neither would come to London for about four years. Spenser's
The Shepheard's Calendar had appeared in 1579, and carried
an overt statement of epic intent, but Books I–III of *The Faerie
Queene* would not appear in print until 1590. Sidney himself
had written or was writing the first of the great love-sonnet
sequences: he could hardly foresee its successors. His statement
that, 'our tongue is most fit to honor Poesie, and to bee honored

by Poesie' (p. 128), is made in faith and hope. Both were to be gloriously fulfilled; very soon, but still not in his lifetime.

In January 1583 Sidney stood proxy for the absent Prince Casimir at his official installation as Knight of the Garter. His own knighthood resulted from his performance of this duty, rather than being bestowed on him as a personal honour. In the following months he may have finished the *Defence*, and perhaps *Astrophil and Stella*. He also undertook two works of serious translation from contemporary French writers. The first of these, the *First Week* of the Huguenot poet Du Bartas's encyclopedic epic dealing with the Creation,[34] is now known only from a number of contemporary references.[35] Du Bartas was acquainted with Sidney personally, and may well have known of this project. Sidney also began but left unfinished a translation of *De la Verité de la Religion Chréstienne* which had been published in 1581 by their mutual friend Du Plessis Mornay. Arthur Golding claimed that his own translation, published in 1587, was a completion of Sidney's, but this claim, made as a reliable selling point, is very dubious in itself. These works would have attracted Sidney by their subject matter, and the scope and complexity of Du Bartas's poem would also have provided a technical challenge. We cannot know how Sidney tried to meet this, but his translations, or rather metaphrases of the Psalms, probably begun somewhat later, show a subtle versatility which would certainly here have been evident in very different ways.

These works of translation, which in the case of the Psalms are also in a tradition of personal devotion,[36] seem to me to indicate not so much a change of direction in Sidney's writing, as a greater inclusiveness. Far from his abandoning earlier interests, his revision of *Arcadia*, the *New Arcadia*, which he began in this year or the year following, shows how these were expanding in richness and maturity. At or about this time he also wrote the *Two Pastoralls* (see below, pp. 131–41), in which his long-established friendship with Edward Dyer and Fulke Greville is celebrated in terms of poetic fellowship.

On 21 September 1583 he married Frances Walsingham, daughter and heir of Elizabeth's Secretary of State. This is not likely to have been a sudden undertaking; as early as 17 December 1581, Sidney wrote to Walsingham from Wilton that, 'The

countrei afoordes no other stuff for lettres but humble saluta-
cions, which in deed humbli and hartily I sent to yowr self my
good Ladi and my ecceeding like to be good frend',[37] where 'my
good Ladi' might be either Lady Walsingham, his future mother-
in-law, or Frances herself. Either would at least hint at a
proposed courtship, and the match was in every way suitable.
Walsingham was, like Sidney, very strongly of the militantly
Protestant party, and the acquaintance with Frances is likely to
have been long-standing. There is very little indication as to how
and to what extent their personal feelings were involved. None
of their letters has survived, and, apart from his Will where she
is named as executrix, we have only three references to her in
Sidney's other correspondence, all in letters to Walsingham. In
one, written from Utrecht on 24 March 1586, he asks whether
a letter sent to him enclosed in one to his wife ever arrived, and
then in a postscript he expresses concern as to the conditions
Frances may have to face if she joins him in the Lowlands as
planned.[38] On 28 June he writes again, saying that he is about
to leave Utrecht for Flushing, 'whence I heer that your daughter
is very well and merry'.[39] Frances remains a shadowy figure: as
Sidney's wife and widow, in her second marriage in 1590 to the
glamorous and eventually self-destructive Earl of Essex, and in
her third to Lord Clanricarde. This is merely accident, and no
indication of her character. Had we even some of the letters
exchanged between her and Sidney, for example, they might
have told us a great deal about both correspondents.

During 1584, the year following his marriage, Sidney worked
on his revision and expansion of *Arcadia*, which he was never
to complete. Fulke Greville has supplied a number of hints as to
the intended working out of the plot, and he takes Sidney's
purpose in the revision to have been deeply and seriously
considered:

> . . . his intent and scope was to turn the barren philosophy precepts
> into pregnant images of life . . . In which traverses I know his
> purpose was to limn out such exact pictures of every posture in
> the mind that any man . . . might (as in a glass) see how to set a
> good countenance upon all the discountenances of adversity, and
> a stay upon the exorbitant smilings of chance.[40]

Sidney enriches his central plot, using a subtle complex of
digressions to draw variety into its newly opened registers of

epic and heroic responsibility. Greville's analysis is likely to be based on the memory of discussions with Sidney himself, and what he says accords with Sidney's own opinions given in the *Defence* as to the inferiority of philosophy to poetry (here including prose fiction) as a morally educative force: 'the peerelesse Poet ... yeeldeth to the powers of the mind that whereof the philosopher bestoweth but wordish description: which doth neyther strike, pierce nor possesse the sight of the soule so much as that other doth' (p. 95). What Greville omits is the element of sheer delight; in character, in the emblematic pointing of description and setting, in beauty, wit, and virtuoso play with language for effects running through farce to tragedy. Greville's own cast of mind was sober to the point of pessimism, and his profound and illuminating admiration of his friend's work misses something of its more generous balance.

In February 1584 Sidney met the former Dominican Giordano Bruno,[41] a militantly controversial philosopher who was now including England in the course of his wide European travels. His extraordinary, eccentric and far-reaching cast of mind was to bring him to the stake fifteen years later, when he was unwise enough to return to Italy. Whether or not Sidney was familiar with any of his works before their meeting, he would certainly have known of Bruno's reputation; of his passionate and quasimystical fascination with number, with memory, with the divine capacity of the human intelligence. He was among a distinguished company who heard Bruno's exposition of his philosophy at Oxford, in debates which triggered off a lengthy and vituperative controversy: summarised simplistically, Bruno argued for a magical universe, capable of perception and control through intellect and imagination properly trained. His opponents saw his thesis as invalid and its effects as unlawful. It is unlikely that Sidney was in any full sense a convert to Bruno's views, and the nature and extent of their influence on him remains conjectural. They certainly interested him however. Fulke Greville held a supper party in February, to entertain Bruno, where Sidney was among those who met to discuss the philosopher's views with him informally. Bruno subsequently dedicated two works to Sidney: his philosophic manifesto *Spaccio della Bestia Trionfante*, 1584, and a volume of mystical poetry, *De gli Eroici Furori*, 1585. We do not know Sidney's opinion of either of these, but there is evidence that Alexander

Dicson, Bruno's most convinced and outspoken English sup-
porter, was at least for a time in attendance on him.[42]

There are two areas in particular where Bruno's thinking may
well have engaged Sidney's imagination, besides his general
interest in the use and training of memory as an art (see above,
p. xxx). Sidney's view of the poet as manipulating his reader's
response to image and allusion is sufficiently close to Bruno's
deployment of revelatory symbol to allow interplay between the
two. Similarly Bruno's perception of the universe as a spiritual
mystery capable of mathematical comprehension is variously
expressed in terms that would have been less familiar to Sidney
than the fundamental thesis itself. Mathematics, chemistry and
number at this period easily became mysterious. Sidney's interest
in aspects of mathematical learning that we have come to
subdivide into the 'occult sciences', was not at all unusual nor
incompatible with opinions that have often tended to associate
him with Bruno's Puritan opponents. At least from the time of
his leaving Oxford he was closely acquainted with John Dee, a
brilliant mathematician, astrologer to the Queen and lifelong
student of the occult: Shakespeare's Prospero approximates
closely to the way Dee saw himself, or would have wished to be
seen.

Sidney's own concerns were not centrally in this area, and the
extent to which he drew on it is still being explored.[43] It remains
true, however, as Yates has pointed out, that 'The only English,
or rather Welsh, character who might have acted as some
preparation for the arrival of Bruno is John Dee.'[44] Sidney, who
had studied with Dee in company with Fulke Greville and
Edward Dyer, was in a good position to take such advantage of
Bruno's teaching as suited him. Interestingly, the same sonnet,
Astrophil and Stella 26: 'Though dustie wits dare scorne Astrologie', has been cited by both French and Yates as showing the
influence on Sidney's writing of Dee and Bruno respectively.[45]

A very different range of Sidney's interest is also likely to have
been coloured by Dee. The New World, and its potential for
wealth, colonisation and trade had not merely enlarged the map,
it had shifted its balance. The Atlantic, not the Mediterranean,
was the new route to fortune, fame and empire: the English
ports, London, Dover, Bristol, Plymouth were new gateways.
The Catholic Spanish hold on the Americas and their huge
wealth gave rise to national rivalry and political concern, with a

sharp cutting edge of Protestant zeal. Probably no one of Sidney's generation was immune to this heady complex of fascination and excitement. Sidney himself was involved in its practicalities as well: he had taken an active interest in plans for American colonisation from 1582 and probably earlier. In 1584 his work in the Ordnance Office carried special responsibility for the fortifications at Dover, and he served with Drake on the Parliamentary Committee for Raleigh's Virginia Bill. His own hopes and plans were far more wide-reaching: nothing less, as Fulke Greville reports, than 'that heroicall design of invading and possessing America'.[46] That design had already been formulated by Dee in his *General and rare memorials pertaining to the Perfect art of Navigation*, 1577. His arguments for what amounts to Elizabeth's divine right to world empire draw on a literal belief in the descent of the Welsh Tudors from ancient British royalty, and above all on the concept of Arthur having returned in Elizabeth's rule to fulfil her country's supreme destiny, religious and imperial. The idea itself is not unusual at this time. The ill-fated Entertainment at Kenilworth in 1575 made play with it, and it is the foundation of Spenser's *Faerie Queene*. Dee's arguments however are in no way figurative. Whether Sidney was convinced by them in their own literal terms we do not know. That their conclusions excited him and influenced the scope of his own parallel thinking is entirely probable.

It is likely that during 1584 and the year following Sidney continued to work on the *New Arcadia* and his translations from the French. He also began a metaphrase of the Psalms, using and developing a wide range of verse forms. He completed Psalms 1–43: his sister Mary continued and finished the work after his death. See below, pp. 135–41 and nn. He also wrote a *Defence* of his uncle, the Earl of Leicester, in answer to a libel on him, *Leicester's Commonwealth*, disseminated in England in the summer of 1584. It seems likely that while Walsingham and Leicester himself had clear assumptions as to its authorship, Sidney had not, and may well have thought it to be Jesuitical in origin. Certainly he was at this time strongly supporting legislation against members of the Jesuit Order, who were infiltrating Catholic supporters in England as missionaries and spies. The *Defence* is a curious work, which concentrates almost entirely on the refutation of the charge, very much subsidiary to the main attack being made on Leicester's character and political motives, that he 'hath no ancient nobility'. Katherine Duncan-Jones has suggested that Leicester, and perhaps Sidney himself, may already have been thinking of the possibility of appointment and service in the Netherlands, a contingency where 'the question of Leicester's exact rank may have been of crucial importance'.[47] It is probable that in any case the relevance of the *Defence* was short-lived; unlike Sidney's *Letter to the Queen*, it seems not to have circulated widely.

Late in the summer of 1585 Leicester was appointed Lieutenant-General of the English troops sent to the Netherlands in support of the Dutch provinces then in revolt against Spanish domination. Whether or not Sidney had hopes of accompanying him, he had alternative plans, made in careful secrecy. Fulke Greville, who was to go with him 'as his loving and beloved Achates on this journey', gives a detailed account of the planning of what was to have been the first step in Sidney's 'heroicall design': an expedition setting out in September for the West Indies, to be commanded jointly by Drake and by himself. Sidney could never have broached such a plan to the Queen with any hope of its acceptance. Drake's exploits she might allow and even encourage in the face of Spanish affront: Sidney's involvement could not have been so contained.

Greville's[48] account reflects Sidney's excitement in the project itself, and in the immediate practicalities of its concealment. Walsingham may just possibly have been taken in by Sidney's cover-story, that he intended to meet Don Antonio, Pretender to the throne of Portugal, on his expected arrival at Plymouth in order to escort him to the Court, but Walsingham was perhaps the least gullible man in Europe. Greville may well have had his own reservations: certainly once they had arrived in Plymouth he was aware, as it seems Sidney was not, of Drake's very understandable unease. There were delays, unexpected difficulties; time for discovery and recall. Sidney seems to have ignored the first summons sent him, but 'The next was a more imperial mandate'. The Queen recalled him to take up the appointment of Governor of Flushing. Drake sailed unaccompanied, so that the 'heroicall design', as Greville saw the event, ' – how exactly soever projected and digested in every minute[49] by Sir Philip – did yet prove impossible to be well acted by any other man's spirit than his own, how sufficient soever his associate were in all parts of navigation: whereby the success of this journey fell out to be rather fortunate in wealth than honour.'

Whatever private reproaches may have met Sidney on his return to Court, there seem to have been no public repercussions. He left England for the Netherlands in November, shortly after the birth of his daughter, Elizabeth.

Greville's self-presentation as Sidney's only and privileged confidant in his abortive enterprise with Drake may not be entirely accurate, but it is certainly very unlikely that he would have told his wife anything about his plans. All other considerations apart, she was Walsingham's daughter. Our sensibilities may be shaken at the thought of an imminently prospective father simply disappearing for an unforeseeable time on a hazardous voyage, but Sidney's priorities were those of his own age and upbringing. This was not a quixotic escapade, but perhaps his only chance to initiate a plan which he hoped and believed might lead to near limitless national expansion and glory; a motive far outweighing any coincident domestic responsibility.

Once in the Netherlands, Sidney redirected his hopes towards the Protestant cause in Europe: 'The placing of his thoughts upon which high pinnacle laid the present map of the Christian world beneath him.'[59] As early as his embassy of 1577, and then perhaps too enthusiastically for his Queen's liking, he had thought of that cause and England's potential contribution to it as carrying a religious mandate parallel in grandeur to that which might in the New World be combined with colonial achievement. On 24 March 1586 he wrote to Walsingham in terms that make his views clear, as well as indicating a growing perception of his sovereign's lack of sympathy with them:

> If her Majesty wear the fowntain I woold fear considring what I daily fynd that we shold wax dry, but she is but a means whom God useth and I know not whether I am deceaved but I am faithfully persuaded that if she shold withdraw herself other springes woold ryse to help this action. For me thinkes I see the great work indeed in hand, against the abusers of the world, wherein it is no greater fault to have confidence in mans power, than it is to hastily to despair of Gods work.[51]

The Queen's view of the usefulness and function of an English presence in the Netherlands was cautious and pragmatic: she did not want, and could not afford, the expense and long-term military commitment of an offensive war on the Continent. Leicester had infuriated her by accepting the title of Governor-General of the Netherlands in January, thereby giving a strong hint of such commitment, and the resulting tensions added to the constantly shifting complexities of military and diplomatic pressure with which Sidney was anyway contending.

In May his father died, and in June his mother, but he can have had little time for private grief. It is clear that whatever his ideological frustrations he was now finding real and responsible scope for energies and hard-won skills of mind and body. Over the eleven months he spent in the Netherlands he won admiration on all counts, even, in reluctant retrospect, from Leicester, whose feelings for his nephew had been anything but uncritical (see above, p. xxxiv): 'Notwithstanding, in short time he saw this sun so risen above the horizon that both he and all his stars were glad to fetch light from him.'[52]

On the morning of 22 September Sidney rode with Leicester in a company intending to intercept a baggage train approaching the town of Zutphen, then under siege. He was wounded in the thigh by a musket-shot, which broke the bone. Somehow he kept his seat, and rode his horse out of the fighting; an extraordinary feat of horsemanship and determination. He was taken to Arnhem, where despite the efforts of his surgeons, or, sadly, very likely as a result of them, the wound became infected. After many days of pain he died on 17 October. His wife and his younger brother Robert were with him when he died.

Sidney had incurred large personal expenses in equipping the troops under his command and in the course of his duties generally. He died in debt to an extent of which he was certainly unaware. He had left Walsingham with a power of attorney to sell part of his lands should it prove necessary, but this was nothing like adequate. Walsingham had eventually to find about £6,000 of his own to satisfy Sidney's creditors, and to meet the terms of his Will. By modern reckoning that is more than £60,000. As Walsingham told Leicester, he was left in 'a most hard and desperate state, which I weigh nothing in respect of the gentleman who was my chief worldly comfort'. The funeral was postponed until after Leicester's return from the Netherlands. Sidney was buried in St Paul's on 16 February 1587, with great magnificence. Besides representatives from the State of

Holland, the Lord Mayor of London and other City dignitaries and members of Sidney's immediate family, Francis Drake, Edward Dyer, Fulke Greville, and the Earls of Pembroke, Essex and Leicester were among the principal mourners.

Aftermath: Fame and achievement

> Whilest thus I looked, loe adowne the *Lee*,
> I saw an Harpe stroong all with siluer twyne,
> And made of golde and costlie yuorie,
> Swimming, that whilome[53] seemed to haue been
> The harpe, on which *Dan Orpheus* was seene
> Wylde beasts and forrests after him to lead,
> But was th'Harpe of *Philisides* now dead.
>
> At length out of the Riuer it was reard
> And borne aboue the cloudes to be diuin'd,[54]
> Whilst all the way most heuenly noyse was heard
> Of the strings, stirred with the warbling wind,
> That wrought both ioy and sorrow in my mind
> So now in heauen a signe it doth appeare,
> The Harpe well known beside the Northern Beare.
>
> Edmund Spenser, *The Ruines of Time* ll. 603–16.
> Dedicated to Sidney's sister, Mary, Countess of Pembroke, 1591.

Spenser's poem presents an historical retrospect of the city of St Albans, from her time as 'Princesse' of the northern reaches of the Roman Empire to his own day, mourning the deaths of Leicester in 1588 and of his brother the Earl of Warwick in 1590. It concludes with two groups each of six 'tragicke Pageants', the second of which is a series of emblematic apotheoses of Sidney as poet, warrior and 'Immortall spirite'.

Sidney's death was mourned in countless elegies; the Universities of Oxford and Cambridge published collections, for the most part in Latin, and Spenser is only one of the many individual poets who collected such elegies in English, including that by Ludovick Bryskett (see above, pp. xxxii–xxxiii) and also published their own over the next few years. In the passage quoted above, Spenser takes a classical myth which relates how Orpheus's lyre became the constellation Lyra, and by an elegant elision transfers it figuratively to Sidney's poetic immortality. This is more than a graceful compliment; Orpheus was seen both as an archetype of the Poet and as a founder of civilisation.

By transferring his key attribute in this way, Spenser is presenting Sidney as having initiated in England a new cycle of poetic and educative progress.

Spenser's myth-making here is metaphorical, and not invalid. Sidney had written the first of the great Elizabethan love-sonnet sequences and the finest critical essay of the period besides opening up whole new ranges of experimental techniques in verse and prose. The *Old* and *New Arcadias* are only now perhaps receiving due appreciation. But Sidney has also been subject to another kind of myth-making, which since the late seventeenth century has tended, partly through a misunderstanding of the conventions of Elizabethan biography, to distance his readers from his real aims and achievements.

Fulke Greville is chiefly responsible for this, through no fault of his own: biography at this time was not only an historical form but a poetic one, to be read and appreciated as such. A number of accounts of Sidney's life, and above all of his death, exist besides Greville's, and it is not surprising to find his dying represented consistently as exemplary of Christian fortitude and resignation. So it may well have been, but the letter written on the night before he died to Wyer, physician to the Duke of Cleves, shows that it was not easy: 'My Wyer, Come. Come. My life is endangered and I long for you. Alive or dead, I will not be ungrateful. I cannot write more, but with all my strength I beg you to hasten. Farewell. At Arnhem. Your Philip Sidney.'[55] For us this glimpse of desperation is valuable and touching. To his contemporaries it would have seemed in itself merely irrelevant.

Greville went further however. Throughout the *Dedication* he may well have had in mind Sidney's summary of the poet's power to transcend historical ambivalence:

> ... know whether [*Nature*] have brought forth ... so right a Prince as *Xenophon's Cyrus* ... not onely to make a *Cyrus* which had been but a particular excellencie, as *Nature* might have done, but to bestow a *Cyrus* upon the worlde, to make many *Cyrus's*, if they wil learne aright why and how that Maker made him. (See below, p. 89.)

In particular, of the three best-known traditions relating to Sidney's death two have taken their accepted colour from him: the third may even be his invention.

The first two raise questions of motive, and so of character. Accounts of the fatal skirmish outside Zutphen vary in detail, but there is general agreement that Sidney's wound, or at least its severity, was the result of his wearing no thigh armour. This seems to have been a fashion, presumably because it allowed greater manoeuvrability on horseback. Sir John Smythe, in 1590, attacks the practice as foolish and dangerous, and says specifically: 'The imitating of which unsoldierlike and fond arming cost that noble and worthy gentleman Sir Philip Sidney his life.'[56] Greville glosses Sidney's imprudence with care:

> ... with what alacrity soever he went to actions of honour, yet, remembering that upon just grounds the ancient sages describe the worthiest persons to be ever best armed, he had completely put on his; but meeting the marshall of the camp lightly armed ... the unspotted emulation of his heart to venture without any inequality made him cast off his cuisses, and so, by the secret influence of destiny, to disarm that part where God, it seems, resolved to strike him.[57]

That Sidney was in fact motivated by such quixotic chivalry is quite likely, and Greville may well have been told of it, but Sidney's reflections upon the precepts of 'the ancient sages' are as much Greville's own presumption as are his comments on the part played by providence.

Similarly, a number of sources agree that on his death-bed Sidney expressed a wish that his unfinished *New Arcadia* should be destroyed.[58] Greville, to whom the manuscript had been entrusted which he was in fact to publish in 1590, gives as Sidney's sole motive: '... that when his body declined and his piercing inward powers were lifted up to a purer horizon he then discovered not only the imperfection, but vanity of these shadows.'[59]

There may again be some truth in this. Equally, Sidney may not have wished to be judged by an unfinished work: an 'unpolished embryo' as Greville says. There is no suggestion that Sidney intended other of his secular works, not even *Astrophil and Stella*, to be included in the holocaust. In any case Sidney can hardly have been unmindful of Virgil's similar dying wish concerning the *Aeneid*: an analogue that may indeed have been intended to draw attention to his own evaluation of *Arcadia* as epic in intention and scale.

The third example is the most famous, and the most puzzling. Greville describes how Sidney was wounded and then rode back from the fighting:

> In which sad progress, passing along by the rest of the army where his uncle – the general – was, and being thirsty with excess of bleeding, he called for drink, which was presently brought him; but as he was putting the bottle to his mouth he saw a poor soldier carried along, who had eaten his last at the same feast, ghastly casting up his eyes at the bottle; which Sir Philip perceiving, took it from his head before he drank, and delivered it to the poor man with these words: 'Thy necessity is yet greater than mine.'[60]

Three main reasons have been adduced for thinking this story to be Greville's own fiction: that it appears nowhere else, that Greville was not himself in the Netherlands at the time of Sidney's death and that a very similar story is told by Plutarch of Alexander the Great.[61] If Greville did invent this episode, it would still have the same importance that I once heard the late Professor Dorothy Whitelock ascribe to the story of King Alfred's burning of the cakes: that it indicated very accurately the kind of person people thought Alfred was. Greville's account is in perfect keeping with the kind of man he took Sidney to be.

It seems to me however unlikely that the story has no basis at all. It would be out of keeping with Greville's treatment of other incidents where his information can only have been second-hand, but where we have other witnesses, as with the examples just discussed. He may well have heard the story, or its nucleus at least, and let his imagination work on the descriptive details, and perhaps on the painfully memorable words he gives to Sidney himself. The analogue with Alexander the Great can be taken as actually strengthening the likelihood of the story: Sidney might well have remembered it also, and acted on its example, just as some days later he was to echo Virgil's dying wish for the burning of the *Aeneid*.

Greville's love and admiration for Sidney and his own rather bleak values made his memory of him in some ways selective. He gives little hint of the humour, quick temper, irony and wide capacity for enjoyment that appear in Sidney's writings and letters. Such imperfections as rashness and pride are given noble colour, but are still apparent, as for example in the accounts of Sidney's time in Plymouth and of his arming before Zutphen.

Greville knew exactly what he was doing, and to his contemporaries it was transparent, but since then it has been open both to romantic idealisation and denigratory social realism. The *Dedication* is a work of piety, founded on a deeply felt sense of his subject's heroic status: 'this master-spirit'.[62] Greville's summary of his own career already quoted, carved on his tomb in St Mary's Church, Warwick, sets this in context and just proportion: 'Servant to Queen Elizabeth: Counsellor to King James: Friend to Sir Philip Sidney.'

Greville's *Dedication* was written probably between 1604 and 1614, but as early as 1590 he contributed directly to his friend's still widening fame by editing and publishing the unfinished *New Arcadia*. Greville would certainly have seen any wish of Sidney's for its destruction in the light of Virgil's example, and while exalting his friend's motives saw to it that, like Virgil, he was not obeyed. Even before Sidney's death his works, especially his poems, had a wide circulation in manuscript: in the years immediately following this seems to have increased. A few poems began to appear in print, and in 1591 there were two editions of *Astrophil and Stella*, both with corrupt texts. There were two editions of the *Defence* in 1595 (one with the title *An Apologie for Poetrie*, see below, p. 83 and n.). In 1593 Sidney's sister Mary Countess of Pembroke had also published another edition of the *Old Arcadia*. She reprinted this in 1598, together with the *Defence*, *Astrophil and Stella*, *Certaine Sonets* and *The Lady of May*, using manuscripts in her own possession. This collection was reprinted thirteen times before 1739, and remained the standard edition of Sidney's work until this century.

References

1. References to Sidney's correspondence and to other prose works not included here are taken from Feuillerat's edition, revised 1963: volume and page numbers. See Suggestions for Further Reading.

2. In another letter written to his brother, 18 October 1580, Sidney gives some details of this: III. pp. 130–3. The whole subject is discussed fully by Frances A. Yates, *The Art of Memory*, 1966. See Suggestions for Further Reading.

3. References to poems by Sidney not included here are taken from Ringler's edition: number and page number. See Suggestions for Further Reading.

4. Fulke Greville, Dedication, *Prose Works*, ed. Gouws 1986, p. 25. See Suggestions for Further Reading.

5. Katherine Duncan-Jones, *Sir Philip Sidney*, 1989. Introduction, p. xv. See Suggestions for Further Reading.

6. Gouws, p. 18.

7. George Gascoigne, *The Princely Pleasures at Kenilworth Castle*, 1576, gives what was planned as well as what actually took place. See Suggestions for Further Reading.

8. He had held this office previously, with brief intermissions and under unceasing pressure and criticism, from 1565.

9. Katherine Duncan-Jones (ed.), *Miscellaneous Prose of Sir Philip Sidney*, Oxford, 1973, pp. 3–7, gives an account of Sir Henry's administration, the bitter controversy surrounding it, and Sidney's own involvement with this. See Suggestions for Further Reading.

10. partage: sharing out.

11. Gouws, pp. 16–17.

12. Ringler, p. 149.

13. *Canzone*, 135: '*Qual piú diversa e nova*'.

14. III. 3–4.

15. For example in the course of the Kenilworth entertainment mentioned above (p. xxxiv), and centrally in that offered at Ditchley in 1592 (included in *Entertainments for Elizabeth I*, by Joan Wilson, 1980. See Suggestions for Further Reading.)

16. *Mustapha*, published in 1609, and *Alaham*, 1633, but both almost certainly written before 1600.

17. Ben Jonson's publication of his own works in the folio edition of 1616, and the posthumous First Folio of Shakespeare in 1623 indicate a change of attitude: they expect a serious readership. But the Puritan opposition to the theatre with which Sidney contended in the *Defence* (see below pp. 121 ff.) continued to grow until the theatres were reopened at the Restoration after their closure during the Commonwealth. Milton's *Arcades*, c. 1633, and *Comus*, 1634, were private entertainments. In his preface to *Samson Agonistes*, written towards the end of his life and published in 1634, Milton specifically rejects any idea that it should be actually performed.

18. *The Correspondence of Sir Philip Sidney and Hubert Languet*, ed. S. A. Pears, 1845, p. 187.

19. While it is generally agreed that the d'Alençon suit is glanced at in Spenser's *The Shephearde's Calendar*, especially in the *Februarie* Eclogue, there is much critical dispute as to the details. In *Mother Hubberd's Tale*, which he was also writing at about this time, the

issues were clear enough to mean that the poem was then refused publication. It appeared in 1591, possibly with some revisions, when the general moral could be taken without particular reference to an occasion by then no longer relevant.

20. See Ringler, Introduction, pp. xxxi–xxxiv.

21. *Poetical Works*, pp. 611–12, 635–6.

22. For detailed discussion of these and other formal innovations in Sidney's work, see Ringler, Introduction, pp. xxxi–xxxvi.

23. In G. Smith, *Elizabethan Critical Essays*, II. p. 263. See Suggestions for Further Reading.

24. *Sir Philip Sidney*, Introduction, p. x.

25. Henry Goldwell's detailed account of the *Triumph* is given by Katherine Duncan-Jones, *Sir Philip Sidney*, Appendix A, pp. 299–311. See Suggestions for Further Reading.

26. Michael Drayton's sequence *Idea* is a particularly telling example. It first appeared in 1593, and was revised and expanded in later editions. Its argument of hopeless and intransigent love would have had a rather different, wittily dramatised, reading by the lady herself. She was the daughter of Drayton's boyhood patron, Sir Henry Goodere, and at the time Drayton was working on the sequence both were middle aged; she was happily married, and Drayton was a close family friend.

27. Smith, *Elizabethan Critical Essays*, II p. 223.

28. Harington's essay, prefixed to his translation of Ariosto's *Orlando Furioso*, is reprinted in Smith, *Elizabethan Critical Essays*, II p. 194. See Suggestions for Further Reading.

29. The text of Lodge's *Defence*, prefixed by a list of contributions to the anti-stage controversy printed between 1577–87, appears in Smith, I p. 6.

30. Introduction, I pp. xiv–xxxi.

31. Spenser, *Poetical Works*, p. 635.

32. rybaudrye: indecency.

33. *Letter . . . to . . . Sir Walter Raleigh*, 1589, *Poetical Works*, p. 405.

34. Du Bartas's complete work, *La Semaine ou Creation du Monde*, which had an extremely high reputation, especially in England, was later translated into English by Joshua Sylvester, 1592–9.

35. See Ringler, p. 339.

36. A medieval tradition of Psalmic translation and metaphrase as devotional exercise continues into post-Reformation England. Sir Thomas Wyatt's *Penitential Psalms* are a well-known example.

37. III p. 139.

38. III pp. 167–8.
39. III. p. 177.
40. Gouws, pp. 10–11.
41. For a detailed account of Bruno's life and work see Frances A. Yates, *Giordano Bruno and the Hermetic Tradition*, Routledge and Kegan Paul, London, 1964. Yates also discusses Bruno's visit to England, and his acquaintance with Sidney in particular in *The Art of Memory*, Routledge and Kegan Paul, London, 1979, pp. 243–86 in the Ark paperback edition cited here: Routledge and Kegan Paul, London, 1984.
42. See Yates, *The Art of Memory*, p. 283.
43. Peter J. French gives perhaps an over-generous assessment of Dee's influence on Sidney in Chapter 6, 'Sidney and His Circle', in his fascinating biography of Dee: *John Dee: the World of an Elizabethan Magus*, Routledge and Kegan Paul, London, 1972, pp. 126–59. See Suggestions for Further Reading.
44. *The Art of Memory*, p. 262.
45. French, *John Dee*, p. 130; Yates, *The Art of Memory*, p. 284.
46. Gouws, p. 45.
47. *Miscellaneous Prose of Sir Philip Sidney*, ed. Katherine Duncan-Jones and Jan van Dorsten, OUP, 1973, p. 127.
48. Gouws, pp. 42–6.
49. minute: detail
50. Gouws, p. 46.
51. III. p. 166.
52. Gouws, p. 18.
53. whilome: formerly
54. diuin'd: made divine
55. Mi Wieri, Veni, veni, de vita periclitor et te cupio. – Nec vivus nec mortuus ero ingratus. Plura non possum sed obnixe oro ut festines. Arnemi. Tuus Ph. Sidney. III. p. 283. (My translation in text.)
56. See Gouws, p. 214 n.
57. Gouws, pp. 77–8.
58. Gouws, p. 186nn.
59. Gouws, p. 11.
60. Gouws, p. 77.
61. For the English version Sidney and Greville would have known, see E. E. Henley (ed.) *Plutarch's Lives of the Noble Grecians and Romans Englished by Sir Thomas North*, anno 1579, Tudor Translations, 1895, vol. IV p. 349.
62. Gouws, p. 27.

NOTE ON THE TEXT

The text of the present edition is based on that of 1598, with the exceptions of *Two Pastoralls*, first printed in 1602, and Psalms from *The Psalms of David*, of which there is no early edition. The original spelling has been kept. The fluidity of Elizabethan spelling often serves to call attention to puns and other word-play; a poetic technique obliterated by modern, rigid orthography. Italicisation and capitalisation of proper and abstract nouns have been made as far as possible consistent. The punctuation has been slightly modified throughout where this might clarify meaning and remove ambiguity. Details specifically relevant to the presentation of individual texts will be found in the title endnotes.

DEFENCE OF POESIE, ASTROPHIL AND STELLA AND OTHER WRITINGS

THE LADY OF MAY[*]

Her most excellent Majesty walking in Wanstead Garden, as she passed downe into the grove, there came suddenly among the traine one apparelled like an honest man's wife of the countrey, where crying out for justice, and desiring all the Lords and Gentlemen to speake a good word for her, she was brought to the presence of her Majestie, to whom, upon her knees, she offred a supplication, and used this speech.

The *Suiter*

Most faire Lady, for other your titles of state statlier persons shall give you, and thus much mine own eies are witnesses of, take here the complaint of me, poor wretch, as deeplie plunged in miserie, as I wish you the highest point of happinesse.

One only daughter I have, in whom I had placed all the hopes of my good hap, so well had she with her good parts recompensed my paine of bearing her, and care of bringing her up: but now, alas, that she is come to the time that I should reape my full comfort of her, so is she troubled with that notable matter, which we in countrey call matrimony, as I cannot chuse but feare the losse of her wits, at least of her honesty. Other women thinke they may be unhappily combred with one maister husband; my poore daughter is oppressed with two, both loving her, both equally liked of her, both striving to deserve her. But now, lastly (as this jealousie for sooth is a vile matter) each have brought their partakers with them, and are, at this present, without your presence redresse it, in some bloody controversie; now sweete Lady, helpe; your owne way guides you to the place where they encomber her. I dare stay here no longer, for our men say in the countrey, the sight of you is infectious.

And with that she went away a good pace, leaving the supplication with her Majestie, which very formallie contained this.

Supplication

Most Gracious Soveraigne,
To one, whose state is raised over all,
Whose face doth oft the bravest sort enchaunt;
Whose mind is such as wisest minds appall;
Who in one selfe these divers giftes can plant;
   How dare I, wretch, seeke there my woes to rest,
   Where eares be burnt, eyes dazled, harts opprest?

Your state is great, your greatnesse is our shield;
Your face hurts oft, but still it doth delight,
Your mind is wise, your wisedome makes you mild,
Such planted gifts enrich even beggars' sight:
   So dare I, wretch, my bashfull feare subdue,
   And feede mine eares, mine eyes, my hart in you.

Herewith, the woman-suiter being gone, there was heard in the woods a confused noyse, and forthwith there came out six sheapheards, with as many fosters, haling and pulling to whether side they should draw the Lady of May, who seemed to incline neither to the one nor the other side. Among them was Maister Rhombus,* *a schoolmaister of a village thereby, who, being fully perswaded of his own learned wisedome, came thither, with his authority to part their fray; where, for aunswer, he received many unlearned blowes. But the* Queen *comming to the place where she was seene of them, though they knew not her estate, yet something there was which made them startle aside and gaze upon her: till old father* Lalus* *stepped forth (one of the substantiallest shepheards) and making a legge or two, said these words.*

Lalus the Old Shepheard

May it please your benignity to give a litle superfluous intelligence to that, which with the opening of my mouth, my tongue and teeth shall deliver unto you. So it is, right worshipful audience, that a certain she creature, which we shepheards call a woman, of a minsicall countenance, but, by my white Lambe, not three quarters so beautious as yore selfe, hath disanulled the braine pan of two of our featioust yong men. And wil you wot how? By my mother *Kit's* soule, with a certaine fransicall maladie they call Love: when I was a yong man they called it flat follie. But here is a substantiall schoole-maister can better disnounce the whole foundation of the matter, although, in sooth, for all his loquence, our young men were nothing dutious to his clerkeship.

Come on, come on, Maister schoolemaister, be not so bashlesse, we say, that the fairest are ever the gentlest: tell the whole case, for you can much better vent the points of it than I.

Then came forward Maister Rhombus, and, with many speciall graces, made this learned oration. *

Now the thumderthumping *Jove* transfund his dotes into your excellent formositie, which have with your resplendent beames thus segregated the enmitie of these rurall animals: I am *Potentissima Domina** a schoole maister; that is to say, a Pedagogue, one not a little versed in the disciplinating of the juventall frie, wherein (to my laud I say it) I use such geometricall proportion, as neither wanted mansuetude nor correction: for so it is described, *Parcare Subiectos et debellire superbos.**

Yet hath not the pulchritude of my vertues protected me from the contaminating hands of these plebians; for comming, *solummodo,** to have parted their sanguinolent fray, they yeelded me no more reverence, than if I had been some *Pecorinus Asinus.** I, even I, that am, who am I? *Dixi verbus sapiento satum est.** But what sayd that Trojan *Æneas*, when he sojorned in the surging sulkes of the sandiferous seas, *Haec olim memonasse juvebit.**

Well well, *ad propositos revertebo,** the puritie of the veritie is, that a certain *Pulchra puella profecto** elected and constituted by the integrated detirmination of all this topographical region as the soveraigne Lady of this Dame Maia's month,* has been *quodammodo* hunted, as you would say, pursued by two, a brace, a couple, a cast of yong men, to whom the crafty coward *Cupid* had *inquam,* delivered his dire-dolorous dart.

But here the May Lady *interrupted his speech, saying to him:*

Away away, you tedious foole, your eyes are not worthy to look to yonder Princelie sight; much lesse your foolish tongue to trouble her wise eares.

At which Master Rhombus *in a great chafe cried out:*

O *Tempori,* O *Moribus!** in profession a childe; in dignitie a woman; in yeares a Lady, *in caeteris* a maid; should thus turpifie the reputation of my doctrine, with the reputation of a foole, O *Tempori,* O *Moribus!*

But here again the May Lady *saying to him:*

Leave off, good Latine foole, and let me satisfie the long desire I have had to feede mine eyes with the only sight this age hath graunted to the world.

The poore scholemaister went his way backe, and the Lady kneeling downe said in this manner:

Do not think (sweete and gallant Lady) that I do abase myself thus much unto you because of your gay apparell, for what is so brave as the naturall beauty of the flowers? nor because a certain Gentleman* hereby seekes to do you all the honour he can in his house; that is not the matter, he is but our neighbour, and these be our own groves; nor yet because of your great estate, since no estate can be compared to be the Lady of the whole moneth of May, as I am. So that since both this place and this time are my servants, you may be sure I would looke for reverence at your hands if I did not see something in your face which makes me yeeld to you; the troth is, you excell me in that wherein I desire most to excell, and that makes me give this homage unto you, as the beautifullest Lady these woods have ever received. But now, as old father *Lalus* directed me, I will tel you my fortune, that you may be judge of my mishaps and others' worthinesse. Indeed so it is, that I am a faire wench or else I am deceived, and therefore by the consent of all our neighbours have bene chosen for the absolute Lady of this mery moneth. With me have bene (alas I am ashamed to tell it) two yong men, the one a forrester named *Therion,** the other *Espilus** a shepheard very long even in love; forsooth I like them both, and love neither: *Espilus* is the richer, but *Therion* the livelier. *Therion* doth me many pleasures as stealing me venison out of these forrests, and many other such like prettie and prettier services, but withal he grows to such rages, that sometimes he strikes me, sometimes he rails at me. This shepheard *Espilus*, of a mild disposition, as his fortune hath not been to do me great service, so he hath never done me any wrong, but feeding his sheepe, sitting under some sweete bush, sometimes they say he records my name in doleful verses. Now the question I am to ask you, fair Ladie, is, whether the many deserts and many faults of *Therion*, or the very small deserts and no faults of *Espilus* be to be preferred. But before you give your judgement (most excellent Ladie) you shall heare what each of them can say for themselves in their rurall songs.

Thereupon Therion *challenged* Espilus *to sing with him, speaking these six verses.*

Therion

Come *Espilus*, come now declare thy skill,
Shew how they canst deserve so brave desire;
Warme well thy wits, if thou wilt win her will,
For water cold did never promise fire:
    Great sure is she, on whom our hopes do live,
    Greater is she who must the judgement give.

Espilus

Two thousand sheepe I have as white as milke,
Though not so white as is thy lovely face,
The pasture rich, the wooll as soft as silke,
All this I give, let me possesse thy grace;

But Espilus, *as if he had been inspired with the Muses, began forthwith to sing, whereto his fellow shepheards set in with their recorders, which they bare in their bags like pipes, and so of Therion's did the forresters, with the cornets they wore bout their neckes like huntinghornes in baudrickes.*

Espilus

Tune up my voice, a higher note I yeeld,
To high conceipts the sone must needes be high;
More high than stars, more firme then flintie field
Are all my thoughts, in which I live or die:
    Sweete soule, to whom I vowed am as slave,
    Let not wild woods so great a treasure have.

Therion

The highest note comes oft from basest mind,
As shallow brookes to yeeld the greatest sound;
Seeke other thoughts thy life or death to find;
Thy stars be fal'n, plowed is thy flintie ground;
    Sweete soule, let not a wretch that serveth sheepe
    Among his flocke so sweete a treasure keepe.

Espilus

Two thousand sheepe I have as white as milke
Though not so white as is thy lovely face,
The pasture rich, the wooll as soft as silke;
All this I give, let me possesse thy grace;
    But still take heede, least thou thy selfe submit
    To one that hath no wealth, and wants his wit.

Therion

Two thousand deere in wildest woods I have,
Them can I take, but you I cannot hold:
He is not poore who can his freedom save,
Bound but to you, no wealth but you I would:
    But take this beast, if beasts you feare to misse,
    For of his beasts the greatest beast he is.

Espilus, kneeling to the Queene,

Judge you to whom all beautie's force is lent.

Therion

Judge you of Love, to whom all Love is lent.

But as they waited for the judgement her Majestie should give of their deserts, the shepheards and foresters grew to a great contention, whether of their fellowes had sung better, and so whether the estate of shepheards or forresters were the more worshipfull. The speakers were Dorcas* *an old shepheard, and* Rixus* *a young foster, betweene whom the schoole-maister* Rhombus *came in as moderator.*

Dorcas, the Shepheard

Now al the blessings of my old grandam (silly *Espilus*) light upon thy shoulders for this honiecomb singing of thine; now of my honestie, al the bels of the towne could not have sung better; if the proud hert of the harlotrie lie not downe to thee now, the sheepes' rot catch her, to teach her that a faire woman hath not her fairenesse to let it grow rustish.

Rixus the Foster

O *Midas** why art thou not alive now to lend thine eares to this drivle? By the precious bones of a hunts-man, he knowes not the bleaying of a calfe from the song of a nightingale; but if yonder great Gentlewoman be as wise as she is faire, *Therion*, thou shalt have the prize, and thou, old *Dorcas*, with young master *Espilus*, shall remain tame fooles, as you be.

Dorcas

And with cap and knee be it spoken, it is your pleasure, *Rixus*, to be a wild foole?

Rixus

Rather than a sheepish dolt.

Dorcas

It is much refreshing to my bowels, you have made your choise; for my share, I will bestow your leavings upon one of your fellowes.

Rixus

And art thou not ashamed, old foole, to liken *Espilus* a shepheard to *Therion* of the noble vocation of hunts-men, in the presence of such a one as even with her eye only can give thee cruel punishment?

Dorcas

Hold thy peace, I will neither meddle with her nor her eyes, they sayne in our towne they are dangerous both; neither wil I liken

Therion to my boy *Espilus*, since one is a thievish proller, and
the other is quiet as a lambe that new came from sucking.

Rhombus the Schoole-maister

*Heu, Ehem, hei Insipidum, Inscitum vulgorum et populorum!**
Why, you brute Nebulons, have you not had my *Corpusculum**
so long among you, and cannot yet tell how to edifie a
argument? Attend and throw your eares to me, for I am
gravidated with child, till I have endoctrinated your plumbeous
cerebrosities. First you must divisionate your point, *quasi* you
should cut a cheese into two particles, for thus must I uniforme
my speech to your obtuse conceptions; for *prius dividendum
oratio antequam definiedum; exemplum gratia** either *Therion*
must conquer this Dame Maia's Nimphe, or *Espilus* must
overthrow her, and that *secundum* their dignity, which must
also be subdivisionated into three equal *species*, either according
to the penetrancie of their singing, or the meliority of their
functions, or lastly the superancy of their merits. *De* singing
satis. *Nunc* are you to argumentate of the qualifying of their
estate first, and then whether hath more infernally, I mean more
deeply, deserved.

Dorcas

O poor *Dorcas*, poor *Dorcas*, that I was not set in my young
dayes to schoole, that I might have purchased the understanding
of maister *Rhombus*' misterious speeches. But yet thus much I
concerne of them, that I must even give up what my conscience
doth find in the behalfe of the shepheards, O sweete hony milken
Lommes, and is their any so flintie a hart, that can find about
him to speake against them, that have the charge of such good
soules as you be, among whom is no envy, and all obedience;
where it is lawfull for a man to be good if he list, and hath no
outward cause to draw him from it; where his eye may be busied
in considering the works of nature, and the hart quietly rejoyced
in the honest using them. If templation, as Clerks say, be the
most excellent, which is so fit a life for Templars as this, neither
subject to violent oppression, nor servile flatterie? How many
Courtiers, thinke you, have I heard under our field, in bushes,
making their woefull complaints; some, of the greatnes of their
Mistresse's estate, which dazled their eyes and yet burned their

harts; some, of the extremitie of her beauty mixed with extreame cruelty; some of her too much wit, which made all their loving labours folly. O how often have I heard one name sound in many mouthes, making the vales witnesses of their doleful agonies! So that with long lost labour, finding their thoughts bare no other wooll but despaire, of yong Courtiers they grew old shepheards. Well, sweete Lams, I will ende with you as I began: he that can open his mouth against such innocent soules, let him be hated as much as a filthy fox; let the tast of him be worse then mustie cheese; the sound of him be more dreadful than the howling of a wolfe; his sight more odible than a toade in one's porreage.

Rixus

Your life indeede hath some goodnesse.

Rhombus the School-maister

O Tace, tace, or all the fat wil be ignified; first let me delucidate the very intrinsicall maribone of the matter. He doth use a certaine rhetoricall invasion into the point, as if in deed he had conference with his Lams, but the troth is he doth equitate you in the meane time, maister Rixus, for thus he sayth, that sheepe are good. Ergo the shepheard is good, an Enthememe a loco contingentibus,* as my finger and my thumb are contingentes: againe he sayth, who liveth well, is likewise good, but shepheards live well, ergo they are good: a Syllogism in Darius king of Persia, a conjugatis*; as you would say, a man couple to his wife, two bodies, but one soule; but do you but acquiescate to my exhortation, and you shall extinguish him. Tell him his major is a knave, his minor is a foole, and his conclusion both. Et ecce homo blancatum quasi lilium.*

Rixus

I was saying the shepheards life had some goodnesse in it, because it borrowed of the countrey quietnesse something like ours': but that is not all, for ours' besides that quiet part, doth both strengthen the body and raise up the mind with this gallant sort of activity. O sweete contentation, to see the long life of the hurtlesse trees: to see how in streight growing up, though never so high, they hinder not their fellowes; they only enviously trouble which are crookedly bent. What life is to be compared to ours' where the very growing things are ensamples of goodnesse? We have no hopes but we may quickly go about them, and going about them, we soone obtaine them; not like those that have long followed one (in truth) most excellent chace,* do now at length perceive she could never be taken: but if that she stayd at any time near the pursuers, it was never meant to tarry with them, but only to take breath to fly further from them. He therefore that doubts that our life doth not far excell all others, let him doubt that the well deserving and painfull *Therion* is not to be preferred before the idle *Espilus*; which is as much as to say, that the Roes are not swifter than Sheepe, nor the Stags more goodly than Gotes.

Rhombus

Bene, bene, nunc de propositione prepositus;* that is as much as to say, as well, well, now of the proposed question, that was, whether the many great services, and many great faults of *Therion*, or the few small services, and no faults of *Espilus*, be to be preferred; incepted or accepted the former.

The *May Lady*

No, no; your ordinarie braines shall not deale in that matter: I have already submitted it to one, whose sweete spirit hath passed through greater difficulties; neither will I that your blockheards lie in her way.

Therefore, O Lady, worthy to see the accomplishment of your desires, since all your desires be most worthy of you, vouchsafe our eares such happinesse, and me that particular favor, as that you will judge whether of these be more worthy of me, or whether I be worthy of them: and this I will say, that in judging me, you judge more than me in it.

This being said, it pleased her Majesty to judge that Espilus *did the better deserve her: but what words, what reasons she used for it, this paper, which carrieth so base names, is not worthy to containe. Sufficeth it, that upon the judgement given, the shepheards and forresters made a full consort of their cornets and recorders, and then did* Espilus *sing this song, tending to the greatnesse of his owne joy, and yet to the comfort of the other side, since they were overthrowne by a most worthy adversarie. The song contained two short tales, and thus it was.*

Espilus

Sylvanus long in love, and long in vaine,
At length obtained the point of his desire,
When being askt, now that he did obtaine
His wished weale, what more he could require;
   'Nothing', sayd he, 'for most I joy in this,
   That Goddesse mine, my blessed being sees.'

Therion

When wanton *Pan*, deceiv'd with Lion's skin,*
Came to the bed, where wound for kisse he got,
To wo and shame the wretch did enter in,
Till this he took for comfort of his lot:
   'Poor Pan', he sayd, 'although thou beaten be,
   It is no shame, since *Hercules* was he.'

Espilus

Thus joyfully in chosen tunes rejoyce,
That such a one* is witnesse of my hart,
Whose cleerest eyes I blisse, and sweetest voyce,
That see my good, and judgeth my desert:

Therion

Thus wofully I in wo this salve do find,
My foule mishap came yet from fairest mind.*

The musike fully ended, the May Lady *took her leave in this sort:*

Lady, your selfe, for other titles do rather diminish than add unto you, I and my litle companie* must now leave you: I should do you wrong to beseech you to take our follies well, since your bountie is such, as to pardon greater faults. Therefore I will wish you good night, and praying to God according to the title I possess that, as hitherto it hath excellently done, so hence forward the flourishing of May may long remaine in you, and with you.

FINIS

CERTAINE SONETS*

1

Since shunning paine, I ease can never find,
Since bashfull dread seekes where he knowes me harmed;
Since will is won, and stopped eares* are charmed;
Since force doth faint, and sight doth make me blind;

Since loosing long, the faster still I bind;   5
Since naked sence can conquer reason armed;
Since heart in chilling feare with yce is warmed:
In fine, since strife of thought but marres the mind,

I yeeld, O *Love*, unto thy loathed yoke,
Yet craving law of armes, whose rule doth teach,   10
That hardly usde, who ever prison broke
In justice quit, of honour made no breach:
  Whereas if I a gratefull gardien have,
  Thou art my Lord, and I thy vowed slave.

2

When *Love* puft up with rage of hy disdaine,
Resolv'd to make me patterne of his might,
Like foe, whose wits inclin'd to deadly spite,
Would often kill to breed more feeling paine,

He would, not arm'd with beautie, only raigne   5
On those affectes which easily yeeld to sight,
But vertue sets so high, that reason's light,
For all his strife can onlie bondage gaine.

So that I live to pay a mortall fee,
Dead palsie sicke of all my chiefest parts: 10
Like those whom dreames make uglie monsters see,
And can crie helpe with nought but grones and starts:

Longing to have, having no wit to wish,
To starving minds such is God *Cupid's* dish.

3

*To the tune of Non credo gia che piu infelice amante**

The fire to see my wrongs for anger burneth;
The aire in raine for my affliction weepeth;
The sea to ebbe for griefe his flowing turneth;
The earth with pitie dull the center keepeth:*
   Fame is with wonder blazed;   5
   Times runnes away for sorrow;
   Place standeth still amazed
To see my night of evils, which hath no morow.
     Alas, all onely she no pitie taketh,
      To know my miseries, but chaste and cruell   10
     My fall her glorie maketh;
      Yet still her eyes give to my flames their fuell.

Fire burne me quite, till sense of burning leave me;
Aire let me draw no more thy breath in anguish;
Sea drownd in thee, of tedious life bereave me;   15
Earth take this earth, wherein my spirits languish.
   Fame say I was not borne;
   Time haste my dying hower;
   Place see my grave uptorne;
Fire, aire, sea, earth, fame, time, place, shew your power.   20
     Alas, from all their helps I am exiled,
      For hers am I, and death feares her displeasure.
     Fie death, thou are beguiled,
      Though I be hers, she makes of me no treasure.

4

To the same tune

The Nightingale as soone as Aprill bringeth
Unto her rested sense a perfect waking,
While late bare earth, proud of new clothing springeth,
Sings out her woes, a thorne her song-booke making:
   And mournfully bewailing,   5
   Her throate in tunes expresseth

What griefe her breast oppresseth,
For *Thereus'* force on her chaste will prevailing.
  O *Philomela* faire,* O take some gladnesse,
  That here is juster cause of plaintfull sadnesse;   10
  Thine earth now springs, mine fadeth,
  Thy thorne without, my thorne my heart invadeth.

Alas she hath no other cause of anguish
But *Thereus'* love, on her by strong hand wrokne,
Wherein she suffring all her spirits' languish,   15
Full womanlike complaines her will was brokne.
  But I who dayly craving,
  Cannot have to content me,
  Have more cause to lament me,
  Since wanting is more woe then too much having.   20
  O *Philomela* faire, O take some gladnesse,
  That here is juster cause of plaintfull sadnesse:
  Thine earth now springs, mine fadeth:
  Thy thorne without, my thorne my heart invadeth.

15

Uppon the Devyse of a Seeled* Dove*, with this worde of
   Petrarch: Non mi vuol e non mi trahe d'Impaccio*

Like as the Dove which seeled up doth flie,
  Is neither freed, nor yet to service bound,
But hopes to gaine some helpe by mounting hie,
  Till want of force do force her fall to ground;

Right so my minde, caught by his guiding eye   5
  And thence cast off, where his sweete hurt he found,
Hath neither leave to live, nor doome to dye,
  Nor held in evill, nor suffered to be sound,

But with his wings of fancies up he goes,
  To hie conceits whose fruits are oft but small,   10
Till wounded, blind, and wearied Spirites, lose
  Both force to flie and knowledge where to fall.
   O happie Dove if she no bondage tried:*
   More happie I, might I in bondage bide.

16a

Edward Dyer*

Prometheus* *when first from heaven hie,*
He brought downe fire, ere then on earth not seene,
   Fond of Delight, a Satyre standing by,
   Gave it a kisse, as it like sweete had beene.

Feeling forthwith the other burning power,   5
   Wood with the smart, with showts and shryking shrill,
He sought his ease in river, field, and bower,
   But for the time his griefe went with him still.

So silly I, with that unwonted sight
   In humane shape, an Angell from above,   10
Feeding mine eyes, the impression there did light
   That since I runne and rest as pleaseth love.
     The difference is, the Satire's lippes, my hart,
     He for a while, I evermore have smart.

16

A Satyre once did runne away for dread,*
   With sound of horne, which he him selfe did blow,
Fearing and feared thus from himselfe he fled,
   Deeming strange evill in that he did not know.

Such causeless feares when coward minds to take,   5
   It makes them flie that which they faine would have:
As this poore beast who did his rest forsake,
   Thinking not why, but how himselfe to save.

Even thus might I, for doubts which I conceave
   Of mine owne wordes, my owne good hap betray,   10
And thus might I for feare of may be, leave
   The sweete pursute of my desired pray.
     Better like I thy Satyre, deerest *Dyer,*
     Who burnt his lips to kisse faire shining fire.

18

In wonted walkes, since wonted fancies change,
   Some cause there is, which of strange cause doth rise;
For in each thing wherto mine eye doth range,
   Part of my paine me seemes engraved lyes.

The Rockes which were of constant mind the marke 5
   In clyming steepe, now hard refusall show;
The shading woods seeme now my Sunne to darke,
   And stately hills disdaine to looke so low.

The restfull Caves now restlesse visions give,
   In Dales I see each way a hard assent: 10
Like late mowne meades, late cut from joy I live.
   Alas sweete Brookes do in my teares augment:
      Rockes, woods, hilles, caves, dales, meads, brookes, answere me;
      Infected mindes infect each thing they see.

19

If I could thinke how these my thoughts to leave,
   Or thinking still my thoughts might have good end:
   If rebell sence would reason's law receave;
   Or reason foyld would not in vaine contend:
      Then might I thinke what thoughts were best to thinke: 5
      Then might I wisely swimme or gladly sinke.

If either you would change your cruell hart,
   Or cruell (still) time did your beautie staine:
   If from my soule this love would once depart,
   Or for my love some love I might obtaine, 10
      Then might I hope a change or ease of minde,
      By your good helpe, or in my selfe to finde.

But since my thoughts in thinking still are spent,
   With reason's stride, by senses overthrowne,
   You fairer still, and still more cruell bent, 15
   I loving still a love that loveth none,
      I yeeld and strive, I kisse and curse the paine:
      Thought, reason, sense, time, you, and I, maintaine.

20

A Farewell

Oft have I musde, but now at length I finde,
   Why those that die, men say they do depart:
Depart, a word so gentle to my minde,
   Weakly did seeme to paint death's ougly dart.

But now the starres with their strange course do binde   5
    Me one to leave, with whome I leave my hart.
I heare a crye of spirits faint and blinde,
    That parting thus my chiefest part I part.

Part of my life, the loathed part to me,
    Lives to impart my wearie clay some breath   10
But that good part, wherein all comforts be,
    Now dead, doth shew departure is a death:
        Yea worse then death, death parts both woe and joy,
        From joy I part still living in annoy.

21

Finding those beames, which I must ever love,
    To marre my minde, and with my hurt to please,
I deemd it best some absence for to prove,
    If further place might further me to ease.

Myne eyes thence drawne, where lived all their light,   5
    Blinded forthwith in darke dispaire did lye,
Like to the Molde with want of guiding sight,
    Deepe plunged in earth, deprived of the skie.

In absence blind, and wearied with that woe,
    To greater woes by presence I returne,   10
Even as the flye, which to the flame doth goe,
    Pleased with the light, that his small corse doth burne:
        Faire choice I have, either to live or dye
        A blinded Molde, or else a burned flye.

30

Ring out your belles, let mourning shewes be spread,
    For *Love* is dead:
        All *Love* is dead, infected
        With plague of deepe disdaine:
        Worth as nought worth rejected,   5
        And *Faith* faire scorne doth gaine.
            From so ungratefull fancie,
            From such a femall franzie,

From them that use men thus,
Good *Lord* deliver us.   10

Weepe neighbours, weepe, do you not heare it said,
    That *Love* is dead?
        His death-bed peacock's follie,
        His winding sheete is shame,
        His will false-seeming holie,   15
        His sole exec'tour blame.
            From so ungratefull fancie,
            From such a femall franzie,
            From them that use men thus,
            Good *Lord* deliver us.   20

Let Dirge be sung, and Trentals rightly read,*
    For *Love* is dead:
        Sir *Wrong* his tombe ordaineth;
        My mistresse' Marble hart,
        Which Epitaph containeth,   25
        'Her eyes were once his dart'.
            From so ungratefull fancie,
            From such a femall franzie,
            From them that use men thus,
            Good *Lord* deliver us.   30

Alas, I lie: rage hath this errour bred,
    Love is not dead,
        Love is not dead, but sleepeth
        In her unmatched mind:
        Where she his counsell keepeth,   35
        Till due desert she find.
            Therefore from so vile fancie,
            To call such a wit a franzie,
            Who love can temper thus,
            Good *Lord* deliver us.   40

                        31

Thou blind man's marke, thou foole's selfe chosen snare,
Fond fancie's scum, and dregs of scattred thought,
Band of all evils, cradle of causelesse care,
Thou web of will, whose end is never wrought;*

Desire, desire I have too dearely bought, 5
With price of mangled mind thy worthlesse ware,
Too long, too long asleepe thou hast me brought,
Who should my mind to higher things prepare.

But yet in vaine thou hast my ruine sought,
In vaine thou madest me to vaine things aspire, 10
In vaine thou kindlest all thy smokie fire;

For vertue hath this better lesson taught,
Within my selfe to seeke my onelie hire:
Desiring nought but how to kill desire.

32

Leave me O *Love*, which reachest but to dust,
And thou my mind aspire to higher things:
Grow rich in that which never taketh rust:
What ever fades, but fading pleasure brings.

Draw in thy beames, and humble all thy might 5
To that sweet yoke, where lasting freedomes be:
Which breakes the clowdes and opens forth the light
That doth both shine and give us sight to see.

O take fast hold, let that light be thy guide,
In this small course which birth drawes out to death, 10
And thinke how evill becommeth him to slide
Who seeketh heav'n, and comes of heav'nly breath.
    Then farewell world, thy uttermost I see,
    Eternall *Love* maintaine thy life in me.

*Splendidis longum valedico nugis.**

ASTROPHIL AND STELLA

1

Loving in truth, and faine in verse my love to show,
That she (deare She) might take some pleasure of my paine:
Pleasure might cause her reade, reading might make her know,
Knowledge might pitie winne, and pitie grace obtaine,
  I sought fit words to paint the blackest face of woe,   5
Studying inventions fine, her wits to entertaine:
Oft turning others' leaves, to see if thence would flow
Some fresh and fruitfull showers upon my sunne-burn'd braine.
  But words came halting forth, wanting *Invention*'s stay,
Invention, Nature's child, fled step-dame *Studie's* blowes,   10
And others' feete still seem'd but strangers in my way.
Thus great with child to speake, and helplesse in my throwes,
  Biting my trewand pen, beating my selfe for spite,
  'Foole,' said my Muse to me, 'looke in thy heart and write.'*

2

Not at first sight, nor with a dribbed shot*
  Love gave the wound, which while I breathe will bleed:
  But knowne worth did in mine* of time proceed,
Till by degrees it had full conquest got.
I saw and liked, I liked but loved not,   5
  I loved, but straight did not what *Love* decreed:
  At length to *Love's* decrees, I forc'd, agreed,
Yet with repining at so partiall lot.
  Now even that footstep of lost libertie
Is gone, and now like slave-borne *Muscovite*,   10
I call it praise to suffer Tyrannie;*
And now employ the remnant of my wit
  To make my selfe beleeve, that all is well,
  While with a feeling skill I paint my hell.

3

self-conscious poet

Let daintie wits crie on the Sisters nine,
That bravely maskt, their fancies may be told:
Or *Pindare's* Apes, flaunt they in phrases fine,
Enam'ling with pied flowers their thoughts of gold:
    Or else let them in statelier glorie shine,   5
Ennobling new found Tropes with problemes old:*
Or with strange similies enrich each line,
Of herbes or beastes, which *Inde* or *Afrike* hold.*
    For me in sooth, no Muse but one I know:
    Phrases and Problemes from my reach do grow,   10
And strange things cost too deare for my poore sprites.
    How then? even thus: in *Stella's* face I reed,
    What Love and Beautie be, then all my deed
But copying is, what in her *Nature* writes.

suggests of artificiality vo depth of emotion

4

Vertue alas, now let me take some rest,
Thou setst a bate betweene my will and wit,
If vaine love have my simple soule opprest,
Leave what thou likest not, deale not thou with it.
    Thy scepter use in some old *Catoe's* brest;*   5
Churches or schooles are for thy seate more fit:
I do confesse, pardon a fault confest,
My mouth too tender is for thy hard bit.*
    But if that needs thou wilt usurping be
    The litle reason that is left in me,   *remnant of my wit*   10
And still th'effect of thy perswasions prove:
    I sweare, my heart such one shall shew to thee,
    That shrines in flesh so true a Deitie,   *Goddess*
That *Vertue*, thou thy selfe shalt be in love.

5

It is most true, that eyes are form'd to serve
The inward light: and that the heavenly part
Ought to be king, from whose rules who do swerve,
Rebels to *Nature*, strive for their owne smart.
    It is most true, what we call *Cupid's* dart,   5
An image is, which for our selves we carve;

just an image

And, fooles, adore in temple of our hart, *again worship*
Till that good God make Church and Churchman starve.
    True, that true Beautie Vertue is indeeed,
Whereof this Beautie can be but a shade,   10
Which elements with mortall mixture breed:*
True, that on earth we are but pilgrims made,
    And should in soule up to our countrey* move:
True, and yet true that I must *Stella* love. *No choice*

6

Some Lovers speake when they their Muses entertaine,
Of hopes begot by feare, of wot not what desires: *useful to quote.*
Of force of heav'nly beames, infusing hellish paine:
Of living deaths, deare wounds, faire stormes and freesing fires:* *Mocking*
    Some one his song in *Jove*, and *Jove's* strange tales attires,   5 *clichés*
Broadred with buls and swans, powdred with golden raine:*
Another humbler wit to shepheard's pipe retires,*
Yet hiding royall bloud full oft in rurall vaine.
    To some a sweetest plaint, a sweetest stile affords,
    While teares powre out his inke, and sighs breathe out his words:
His paper, pale dispaire, and paine his pen doth move.   11
    I can speake what I feele, and feele as much as they,
    But thinke that all the Map of my state I display,
When trembling voice brings forth that I do *Stella* love.
simple unadorned assertion

7

When *Nature* made her chiefe worke, *Stella's* eyes,
In colour blacke, why wrapt she beames so bright?
Would she in beamie blacke, like painter wise,*
Frame daintiest lustre, mixt of shades of light?
    Or did she else that sober hue devise,   5
In object best to knit and strength our sight,
Least if no vaile those brave gleames did disguise,
They sun-like should more dazle then delight?
    Or would she her miraculous power show,
That whereas blacke seemes Beautie's contrary,   *Stella's eyes* 10
She even in blacke doth make all beauties flow?*
    Both so and thus, she minding *Love* should be
    Placed ever there, gave him this mourning weed,
    To honor all their deaths, who for her bleed.   *A's pain.*

8

Love borne in *Greece*, of late fled from his native place,*
    Forc'd by a tedious proofe, that Turkish hardned hart,* *Montagu*
    Is no fit marke to pierce with his fine pointed dart:
And pleasd with our soft peace, staid here his flying race.
But finding these North clymes do coldly him embrace,   5
    Not usde to frozen clips, he strave to find some part,
    Where with most ease and warmth he might employ his art:
At length he perch'd himself in *Stella's* joyfull face,
    Whose faire skin, beamy eyes, like morning sun on snow,
Deceiv'd the quaking boy, who thought from so pure light,   10
Effects of lively heat must needs in nature grow.
But she most faire, most cold, made him thence take his flight
    To my close heart, where while some firebrands he did lay,
    He burnt unwares his wings, and cannot fly away.*

*hint of
blame,
bitterness*

*Light-hearted myth-
making*

9

*Queene *Vertue's* court, which some call *Stella's* face,*
    Prepar'd by *Nature's* choisest furniture,
    Hath his front built of Alablaster pure;
Gold is the covering of that stately place.
The doore by which sometimes comes forth her Grace,   5
    Red Porphir is, which locke of pearle makes sure:
    Whose porches rich (which name of cheekes endure)
Marble mixt red and white do enterlace.
    The windowes now through which this heav'nly guest
Looks over the world, and can find nothing such,   10
Which dare claime from those lights the name of best,
Of touch they are that without touch doth touch,*
    Which *Cupid's* selfe from Beautie's myne did draw:
    Of touch they are, and poore I am their straw.

irresistable

10

a little scornful.

Reason, in faith thou art well serv'd, that still
Wouldst brabling be with sence and love in me:
I rather wisht thee clime the Muses' hill,
Or reach the fruite of *Nature's* choisest tree,*
    Or seeke heavn's course, or heavn's inside to see: 5
Why shouldst thou toyle our thornie soile to till?

colloquialism

*Love takes away
reason cliche*

plain-speaking implication → military metaphors — also avoidance of love clichés + affectations.

Leave sense, and those which sense's objects be:
Deale thou with powers of thoughts, leave love to will.
  But thou wouldst needs fight both with love and sence,
With sword of wit, giving wounds of dispraise,   10
Till downe-right blowes did foyle thy cunning fence:
For soone as they strake thee with *Stella's* rayes,
  Reason thou kneel'dst, and offeredst straight to prove
  By reason good, good reason her to love.

11

  In truth, O *Love*, with what a boyish kind
    Thou doest proceed in thy most serious wayes:
    That when the heav'n to thee his best displayes,
  Yet of that best thou leav'st the best behind,
  For like a child that some faire booke doth find,   5
    With guilded leaves or colourd velume playes,
    Or at the most on some fine picture stayes,
  But never heeds the fruit of writer's mind:
    So when thou saw'st in *Nature's* cabinet
  Stella, thou straight lookst babies in her eyes,*   10
  In her cheeke's pit thou didst thy pitfould set,
  And in her breast bopeepe or couching lyes,
    Playing and shining in each outward part:
    But, foole, seekst not to get into her hart.

12

Cupid, because thou shin'st in *Stella's* eyes,
  That from her lockes, thy day-nets,* none scapes free,
  That those lips swell, so full of thee they bee,
That her sweete breath makes oft thy flames to rise,
  That in her breast thy pap well sugred lies   5
  That her Grace gracious makes thy wrongs, that she
  What words so ere she speake perswades for thee,
That her cleare voyce lifts thy fame to the skies.
  Thou countest *Stella* thine, like those whose powers
Having got up a breach by fighting well,   10
Crie, 'Victorie, this faire day all is ours.'
O no, her heart is such a Cittadell,
  So fortified with wit, stor'd with disdaine,
  That to win it, is all the skill and paine.

She's the castle / citadel now.

13

Phœbus was Judge betweene *Jove, Mars,* and *Love,*
　　Of those three gods, whose armes the fairest were:
　　Jove's golden shield did Eagle sables beare,
Whose talents held young *Ganimed** above:
But in Vert field *Mars* bare a golden speare,　　　　　　5
　　Which through a bleeding heart his point did shove:
　　Each had his creast, *Mars* caried *Venus'* glove,
Jove on his helme the thunderbolt did reare.*
Cupid then smiles, for on his crest there lies
　　Stella's faire haire, her face he makes his shield,　　　10
　　Where roses gueuls are borne in silver field.*
Phœbus drew wide the curtaines of skies
　　To blaze these last, and sware devoutly then,
　　The first, thus matcht, were scantly Gentlemen.*

14

Alas have I not paine enough my friend,*
　　Upon whose breast a fiercer Gripe doth tire
　　Then did on him who first stale downe the fire,*
While *Love* on me doth all his quiver spend,
But with your Rubarb words* yow must contend　　　　5
　　To grieve me worse, in saying that Desire
　　Doth plunge my wel-form'd soule even in the mire
Of sinfull thoughts, which do in ruine end?
　　If that be sinne which doth the maners frame,
Well staid with truth in word and faith of deed,　　　　10
Readie of wit and fearing nought but shame:
If that be sinne which in fixt hearts doth breed
　　A loathing of all loose unchastitie,
　　Then Love is sinne, and let me sinfull be.

15

You that do search for everie purling spring,
　　Which from the ribs of old *Parnassus* flowes,*
　　And everie floure, not sweet perhaps, which growes
Neare therabouts, into your Poesie wring;
You that do Dictionarie's methode bring　　　　　　5
　　Into your rimes, running in ratling rowes;*

You that poore *Petrarch's* long deceased woes,*
With new-borne sighes and denisend wit do sing;
   You take wrong waies, those far-fet helpes be such,
   As do bewray a want of inward tuch:
And sure at length stolne goods do come to light.
   But if (both for your love and skill) your name
   You seeke to nurse at fullest breasts of *Fame*,*
Stella behold, and then begin to endite.

[handwritten margin note: contrast with]   10
[handwritten margin note: frequent idea]

16

In nature apt to like when I did see
   Beauties, which were of manie carrets fine,
   My boiling sprites did thither soone incline,
And, *Love*, I thought that I was full of thee:
But finding not those restlesse flames in me,   5
   Which others said did make their soules to pine:
   I thought those babes of some pinne's hurt did whine,
By my love judging what *Love's* paine might be.
   But while I thus with this yong Lyon plaid;*
Mine eyes (shall I say curst or blest) beheld   10
Stella; now she is nam'd, need more be said?
In her sight I a lesson new have speld,
   I now have learn'd *Love* right, and learn'd even so,
   As who by being poisond doth poison know.

[handwritten margin note: Love will eat his flock]   10
[handwritten margin note: love's suffering again emphasised]

17

His mother deare *Cupid* offended late,
   Because that *Mars*, growne slacker in her love,
   With pricking shot he did not throughly move,
To keepe the pace of their first loving state.*
The boy refusde for feare of *Marse's* hate,   5
   Who threatned stripes, if he his wrath did prove:
   But she in chafe him from her lap did shove,
Brake bow, brake shafts, while *Cupid* weeping sate:
   Till that his grandame *Nature* pittying it,
Of *Stella's* browes made him two better bowes,   10
And in her eyes of arrowes infinit.
O how for joy he leapes, O how he crowes,
   And straight therewith, like wags new got to play,
   Fals to shrewd turnes, and I was in his way.

[handwritten margin note: Defends his noble love, even as he represents it as hell.]

18

With what sharpe checkes I in my selfe am shent,
    When into *Reason's* audite I do go:
    And by just counts my selfe a banckrout know
Of all those goods, which heav'n to me hath lent:
Unable quite to pay even *Nature's* rent,
    Which unto it by birthright I do ow:
    And which is worse, no good excuse can show,
But that my wealth I have most idly spent.
    My youth doth waste, my knowledge brings forth toyes,
My wit doth strive those passions to defend,   10
Which for reward spoile it with vaine annoyes.
I see my course to lose my selfe doth bend:
    I see and yet no greater sorow take,
    Then that I lose no more for *Stella's* sake.

19

On *Cupid's* bow how are my heart-strings bent,
    That see my wracke, and yet embrace the same?
    When most I glorie, then I feele most shame:
I willing run, yet while I run, repent.
My best wits still their owne disgrace invent: 5
    My verie inke turnes straight to *Stella's* name;
    And yet my words, as them my pen doth frame,
Avise themselves that they are vainely spent.
    For though she passe all things, yet what is all
That unto me, who fare like him that both   10
Lookes to the skies, and in a ditch doth fall?
O let me prop my mind, yet in his growth
    And not in Nature for best fruits unfit:*
    'Scholler,' saith *Love,* 'bend hitherward your wit.'

[handwritten margin note: still uncertain about the power/value of his love & his verse. Glory/humiliation]

20

Flie, fly, my friends,* I have my death wound; fly,
See there that boy, that murthring boy I say,
Who like a theefe, hid in darke bush doth ly,
Till bloudie bullet get him wrongfull pray.
    So Tyran he no fitter place could spie,   5
    Nor so faire levell in so secret stay,

[handwritten margin note: honorable death, treacherous murder]
[handwritten note beside line 4: hunted]

As that sweete blacke which vailes the heav'nly eye:
There himselfe with his shot he close doth lay:
 Poore passenger, passe now thereby I did,
And staid pleasd with the prospect of the place,   10
While that blacke hue from me the bad guest hid:
But straight I saw motions of lightning' grace,
 And then descried the glistring of his dart:
 But ere I could flie thence, it pierc'd my heart.

21

Your words my friend* (right healthfull caustiks) blame
 My young mind marde, whom *Love* doth windlas so,
 That mine owne writings like bad servants show
My wits, quicke in vaine thoughts, in vertue lame:
That *Plato* I read for nought, but if he tame   5
 Such coltish gyres, that to my birth I owe
Nobler desires, least else that friendly foe,
Great *Expectation*, weare a traine of shame.
 For since mad March great promise made of me,
If now the May of my yeares much decline,   10
What can be hoped my harvest time will be?
Sure you say well, your wisdome's golden mine
 Dig deepe with learning's spade, now tell me this,
 Hath this world ought so faire as *Stella* is?

22

In highest way of heav'n the Sunne did ride,
 Progressing then from faire twinnes' gold'n place:*
 Having no scarfe of clowds before his face,
But shining forth of heate in his chiefe pride;
When some faire Ladies, by hard promise tied,   5
 On horsebacke met him in his furious race,
 Yet each prepar'd, with fanne's wel-shading grace,
From that foe's wounds their tender skinnes to hide.
Stella alone with face unarmed marcht,
 Either to do like him, which open shone,   10
 Or carelesse of the wealth because her owne:
Yet were the hid and meaner beauties parcht,
 Her's daintiest bare went free; the cause was this,
 The Sunne which others burn'd, did her but kisse.

23

The curious wits, seeing dull pensivenesse
  Bewray it selfe in my long setled eyes,
  Whence those same fumes of melancholy rise,
With idle paines, and missing ayme, do guesse.
Some that know how my spring I did addresse,   5
  Deeme that my Muse some fruit of knowledge plies:
  Others, because the Prince my service tries,*
Thinke that I thinke state errours to redresse.
  But harder Judges judge ambition's rage,
(Scourge of it selfe, still climing slipprie place),
Holds my young braine captiv'd in golden cage.
O fooles, or over-wise, alas the race
  Of all my thoughts hath neither stop nor start,
  But only *Stella's* eyes and *Stella's* hart.

24

Rich fooles there be, whose base and filthy hart
Lies hatching still the goods wherein they flow:
And damning their owne selves to *Tantal's* smart,*
Wealth breeding want, more blist, more wretched grow.
  Yet to those fooles heav'n such wit doth impart,   5
As what their hands do hold, their heads do know,
And knowing, love, and loving, lay apart
As sacred things, far from all daunger's show.
  But that rich foole, who by blind *Fortune's* lot
The richest gemme of Love and life enjoyes,   10
And can with foule abuse such beauties blot;*
Let him, deprived of sweet but unfelt joyes,
  (Exil'd for ay from those high treasures, which
  He knowes not) grow in only follie rich.*

25

The wisest scholler of the wight most wise
By *Phœbus'* doome,* with sugred sentence sayes,
That *Vertue*, if it once met with our eyes,
Strange flames of *Love* it in our soules would raise;
  But for that man with paine this truth descries,   5
While he each thing in sense's ballance wayes,

And so nor will, nor can, behold those skies
Which inward sunne to Heroicke minde displaies,
   Vertue of late, with vertuous care to ster
Love of her selfe, takes *Stella's* shape, that she   10
To mortall eyes might sweetly shine in her.
It is most true, for since I her did see,
   Vertue's great beautie in that face I prove,
   And find th'effect, for I do burne in love.

26

Though dustie wits dare scorne Astrologie,*
And fooles can thinke those Lampes of purest light,
Whose numbers, wayes, greatenesse, eternitie,
Promising wonders, wonder do invite,
   To have for no cause birthright in the skie,   5
But for to spangle the blacke weeds of night:
Or for some brawle, which in that chamber hie,
They should still daunce to please a gazer's sight.
   For me, I do *Nature* unidle know,
And know great causes, great effects procure: 10
And know those Bodies high raigne on the low.*
And if these rules did faile, proofe makes me sure,
   Who oft fore-judge my after-following race,
   By only those two starres in *Stella's* face.

27

Because I oft in darke abstracted guise,
   Seeme most alone in greatest companie,
   With dearth of words, or answers quite awrie,
To them that would make speech of speech arise,
They deeme, and of their doome the rumour flies,   5
   That poison foule of bubling pride doth lie
   So in my swelling breast that only I
Fawne on my self, and others do despise:
   Yet pride I thinke doth not my soule possesse,
Which lookes too oft in his unflattring glasse: 10
But one worse fault, Ambition, I confesse,
That makes me oft my best friends overpasse,
   Unseene, unheard, while thought to highest place
   Bends all his powers, even unto *Stella's* grace.

28

You that with allegorie's curious frame,
  Of other's children changelings use to make,*
  With me those paines for God's sake do not take:
I list not dig so deepe for brasen fame.* *devalves fame*
When I say 'Stella', I do meane the same   5
  Princesse of Beautie, for whose only sake
  The raines of *Love* I love, though never slake,
And joy therein, though Nations count it shame.
  I beg no subject to use eloquence,
Nor in hid wayes to guide Philosophie: 10
Looke at my hands for no such quintessence;*
But know that I in pure simplicitie,
  Breathe out the flames which burne within my heart,
  Love onely reading unto me this art.

29

Like some weake Lords, neighbord by mighty kings,
  To keepe themselves and their chiefe cities free,
  Do easly yeeld, that all their coasts may be
Ready to store their campes of needfull things:
So *Stella's* heart, finding what power *Love* brings,   5
  To keepe it selfe in life and liberty,
  Doth willing graunt, that in the frontiers he
Use all to helpe his other conquerings:
And thus her heart escapes, but thus her eyes
  Serve him with shot, her lips his heralds arre: 10
  Her breasts his tents, legs his triumphall carre:
Her flesh his food, her skin his armour brave,
And I, but for because my prospect lies
Upon that coast, am giv'n up for a slave.

She is the dominating force.

30

Whether the *Turkish* new-moone* minded be
  To fill his hornes this yeare on *Christian* coast;
  How *Poles'* right king meanes, without leave of hoast,*
To warme with ill-made fire* cold *Moscovy*;
If *French* can yet three parts* in one agree;   5
  What now the *Dutch* in their full diets* boast;

Shows how much he is in love, but also shows how divorced he is becoming from important concerns in real world

How *Holland* hearts, now so good townes* be lost,
Trust in the shade of pleasing *Orange* tree;*
    How *Ulster* likes of that same golden bit,
Wherewith my father once made it halfe tame;*   10
If in the *Scottishe* Court be weltring yet;
These questions busie wits to me do frame;
    I, cumbred with good maners, answer do,
    But know not how, for still I thinke of you.*

Compliment back-handed

31

With how sad steps, O Moone, thou climb'st the skies,
    How silently, and with how wanne a face,
    What, may it be that even in heav'nly place
That busie archer his sharpe arrowes tries?
Sure, if that long with *Love* acquainted eyes   5
    Can judge of Love thou feel'st a Lover's case;
    I reade it in thy lookes, thy languisht grace,
To me that feele the like, thy state descries.
    Then ev'n of fellowship, O Moone, tell me
Is constant Love deem'd there* but want of wit? *Irony*   10
Are Beauties there as proud as here they be?
Do they above love to be lov'd, and yet
    Those Lovers scorne whom that *Love* doth possesse?
    Do they call *Vertue* there ungratefulnesse?*

32

*Morpheus,** the lively sonne of deadly *Sleepe,*
    Witnesse of life to them that living die:
    A Prophet oft, and oft an historie,
A Poet eke, as humours fly or creepe,*
Since thou in me so sure a power doest keepe,   5
    That never I with clos'd-up sense do lie,
    But by thy worke my *Stella* I descrie,
Teaching blind eyes both how to smile and weepe,
    Vouchsafe of all acquaintance this to tell,
Whence hast thou Ivorie, Rubies, pearle and gold,   10
To shew her skin, lips, teeth and head so well?
'Foole,' answers he, 'no *Indes* such treasures hold,
    But from thy heart, while my sire* charmeth thee,
    Sweet *Stella's* image I do steale to mee.'

again

33

I might, unhappie word, O me, I might,
And then would not, or could not see my blisse:
Till now, wrapt in a most infernall night,
I find how heav'nly day, wretch, I did misse.
    Hart rent thy selfe, thou doest thy selfe but right,   5
No lovely *Paris* made thy *Hellen* his:*
No force, no fraud, robd thee of thy delight,
Nor *Fortune* of thy fortune author is:
    But to my selfe my selfe did give the blow,*
While too much wit (forsooth) so troubled me,   10
That I respects for both our sakes must show:
And yet could not by rising Morne foresee
    How faire a day was neare, O punisht eyes,
    That I had bene more foolish or more wise.

[margin, handwritten: blames himself / contrast with Wyatt —*]*

34

Come let me write, 'And to what end?' To ease
    A burthned hart. 'How can words ease, which are
    The glasses of thy dayly vexing care?'
Oft cruell fights well pictured forth do please.
'Art not asham'd to publish thy disease?   5
    Nay, that may breed my fame, it is so rare.
    'But will not wise men thinke thy words fond ware?'
Then be they close, and so none shall displease.
    'What idler thing, then speake and not be hard?'
What harder thing then smart, and not to speake?   10
Peace, foolish wit, with wit my wit is mard.
Thus write I while I doubt to write, and wreake
    My harmes on Ink's poore losse, perhaps some find
    Stella's great powrs, that so confuse my kind.

[margin, handwritten: Doubts again ... Enjambment ... makes speaker / tone more / believable (intimate / tone) / realistic.*]*

35

What may words say, or what may words not say,
Where truth it selfe must speake like flatterie?
Within what bounds can one his liking stay,
Where Nature doth with infinite agree?
    What *Nestor's* counsell* can my flames alay,   5
Since *Reason's* selfe doth blow the cole in me?

And ah what hope, that hope should once see day,
Where *Cupid* is sworne page to *Chastity*?
Honour is honour'd, that thou doest possesse
   Him as thy slave, and now long needy *Fame*   10
   Doth even grow rich, naming my *Stella's* name.*
Wit learnes in thee perfection to expresse,
   Not thou by praise, but praise in thee is raisde:
   It is a praise to praise, when thou art praisde.

36

Stella, whence doth this new assault arise,
A conquerd, yelden, ransackt heart to winne?
Whereto long since, through my long battred eyes,
Whole armies of thy beauties entred in.
   And there long since, *Love* thy Lieutenant lies,   5
My forces razde, thy banners raisd within:
Of conquest, do not these effects suffice,
But wilt new warre upon thine owne begin?
   With so sweete voice, and by sweete *Nature* so,
In sweetest strength, so sweetly skild withall,   10
In all sweete stratagems sweete *Arte* can show,
That not my soule, which at thy foot did fall,
   Long since forc'd by thy beames, but stone nor tree
   By *Sence's* priviledge,* can scape from thee.

[handwritten margin note: Again, he's conquered.]

37

My mouth doth water, and my breast doth swell,
   My tongue doth itch, my thoughts in labour be:
   Listen then Lordings with good eare to me,
For of my life I must a riddle tell.
Towardes *Aurora's* Court a Nymph doth dwell,*   5
   Rich in all beauties which man's eye can see:
   Beauties so farre from reach of worlds, that we
Abase her praise, saying she doth excell:
   Rich in the treasure of deserv'd renowne,
Rich in the riches of a royall hart,   10
Rich in those gifts which give th'eternall crowne;
Who though most rich in these and everie part,
   Which make the patents of true worldly blisse,
   Hath no misfortune, but that Rich* she is.

[handwritten margin note: Supernatural]

[handwritten note at bottom: Better off with me]

38

This night while sleepe begins with heavy wings
   To hatch mine eyes, and that unbitted thought
   Doth fall to stray, and my chiefe powres are brought
To leave the scepter of all subject things,
The first that straight my fancie's error brings   5
   Unto my mind, is *Stella's* image, wrought
   By *Love's* owne selfe, but with so curious drought,
That she, me thinks, not onely shines but sings.*
   I start, looke, hearke, but what in closde up sence
Was held, in opend sense it flies away,*   10
Leaving me nought but wailing eloquence.
I, seeing better sights in sight's decay,
   Cald it anew, and wooed sleepe againe:
   But him her host that unkind guest had slaine.

[handwritten margin note: Ah, paradox]

39

Come sleepe, O sleepe, the certaine knot of peace,
The baiting place of wit, the balme of woe,
The poore man's wealth, the prisoner's release,
Th'indifferent Judge betweene the high and the low;
   With shield of proofe shield me from out the prease   5
Of those fierce darts, dispaire at me doth throw:
O make in me those civill warres to cease;
I will good tribute pay if thou do so.*
   Take thou of me smooth pillowes, sweetest bed,
A chamber deafe to noise, and blind to light: 10
A rosie garland,* and a wearie hed:
And if these things, as being thine by right,
   Move not thy heavy grace, thou shalt in me,
   Livelier then else-where, *Stella's* image see.*

[handwritten margin note: Part of the feeling not reason idea]

40

As good to write as for to lie and grone:
   O *Stella* deare, how much thy power hath wrought,
   That hast my mind, none of the basest, brought
My still kept course, while others sleepe, to mone.
Alas, if from the height of *Vertue's* throne,   5
   Thou canst vouchsafe the influence of a thought

Upon a wretch, that long thy grace hath sought;
Weigh then how I by thee am overthrowne:
   And then, thinke thus, although thy beautie be
   Made manifest by such a victorie,   10
Yet noblest Conquerours do wreckes avoid.
   Since then thou hast so farre subdued me,
   That in my heart I offer still to thee,
O do not let thy Temple be destroyd.

41

Having this day my horse, my hand, my launce
   Guided so well, that I obtain'd the prize,
   Both by the judgement of the *English* eyes,
And of some sent from that sweet enemie *Fraunce*,*
Horsemen my skill in horsmanship advaunce: 5
   Towne-folkes my strength; a daintier judge applies
   His praise to sleight, which from good use doth rise;
Some luckie wits impute it but to chaunce;
   Others, because of both sides I do take
My bloud from them, who did excell in this,*   10
Thinke *Nature* me a man of armes did make.
How farre they shoote awrie! the true cause is,
   Stella lookt on, and from her heav'nly face
   Sent forth the beames, which made so faire my race.

42

O eyes, which do the Spheares of beautie move,
Whose beames be joyes, whose joyes all vertues be,
Who while they made *Love* conquer, conquer *Love*,
The schooles where *Venus* hath learn'd Chastitie.
   O eyes, where humble lookes most glorious prove,   5
Only lov'd Tyrants, just in cruelty,
Do not, O do not from poore me remove,
Keepe still my Zenith, ever shine on me.
   For though I never see them, but straight wayes
My life forgets to nourish languisht sprites;   10
Yet still on me, O eyes, dart downe your rayes:
And if from Majestie of sacred lights,*
   Oppressing mortall sense, my death proceed,
   Wrackes Triumphs be, which *Love* (high set) doth breed.

43

Faire eyes, sweet lips, deare heart, that foolish I
Could hope by *Cupid's* helpe on you to pray,
Since to himselfe he doth your gifts apply,
As his maine force, choise sport, and easefull stay.
    For when he will see who dare him gainesay,   5
Then with those eyes he lookes, lo by and by
Each soule doth at *Love's* feet his weapons lay,
Glad if for her he give them leave to die.
    When he will play, then in her lips he is,
Where blushing red, that *Love's* selfe them doth love,   10
With either lip he doth the other kisse:
But when he will for quiet's sake remove
   From all the world, her heart is then his rome,
   Where well he knowes, no man to him can come.

44

My words I know do well set forth my mind,
   My mind bemones his sense of inward smart;
   Such smart may pitie claime of any hart,
Her heart, sweete heart, is of no Tygre's kind:
And yet she heares, and yet no pity I find;   5
   But more I crie, lesse grace she doth impart,
   Alas, what cause is there so overthwart,
That Noblenesse it selfe makes thus unkind?
   I much do guesse, yet find no truth save this,
That when the breath of my complaints doth tuch   10
Those daintie dores unto the Court of blisse,*
The heav'nly nature of that place is such,
   That once come there, the sobs of mine annoyes
   Are metamorphosd straight to tunes of joyes.

45

Stella oft sees the verie face of wo
   Painted in my beclowded stormie face:
   But cannot skill to pitie my disgrace,
Not though thereof the cause her selfe she know:
Yet hearing late a fable, which did show
   Of Lovers never knowne, a grievous case,

Pitie thereof gate in her breast such place
That, from that sea deriv'd, teares' spring did flow.
   Alas, if Fancy drawne by imag'd things,
Though false, yet with free scope more grace doth breed   10
Then servant's wracke, where new doubts honor brings;
Then thinke my deare, that you in me do reed
   Of Lover's ruine some sad Tragedie:
   I am not I, pitie the tale of me. *

Carries ironies, altho' in 'Defence' he considers this possibility

46

I curst thee oft, I pitie now thy case,
   Blind-hitting boy, since she that thee and me
   Rules with a becke, so tyrannizeth thee,
That thou must want or food, or dwelling place.
For she protests to banish thee her face,   5
   Her face? O *Love*, a Rogue thou then shouldst be,
   If *Love* learne not alone to love and see,
Without desire to feed of further grace.
   Alas poore wag, that now a scholler art
To such a schoole-mistresse, whose lessons new   10
Thou needs must misse, and so thou needs must smart.
Yet Deare, let me this pardon get of you,
   So long (though he from booke myche do desire)
   Till without fewell you can make hot fire.

recurring trope, a book to be learnt from, ? to study etc. + gain inspiration

47

What, have I thus betrayed my libertie?
   Can those blacke beames such burning markes engrave
   In my free side? or am I borne a slave,
Whose necke becomes such yoke of tyranny?
Or want I sense to feele my miserie?   5
   Or sprite, disdaine of such disdaine to have?
   Who for long faith, tho dayly helpe I crave,
May get no almes but scorne of beggerie.
   Vertue awake, Beautie but beautie is,
I may, I must, I can, I will, I do   10
Leave following that, which it is gaine to misse.
Let her go: soft, but here she comes. Go to,
   Unkind, I love you not: O me, that eye
   Doth make my heart give to my tongue the lie.

?

a bit frantic

48

Soule's joy, bend not those morning starres from me,
    Where *Vertue* is made strong by *Beautie's* might,
    Where *Love* is chastnesse, *Paine* doth learne delight,
And *Humblenesse* growes one with *Majestie*.
What ever may ensue, O let me be   5
    Copartner of the riches of that sight:
    Let not mine eyes be hel-driv'n from that light:
O looke, O shine, O let me die and see.
    For though I oft my selfe of them bemone,
    That through my heart their beamie darts be gone,   10
Whose curelesse wounds even now most freshly bleed:
    Yet since my death-wound is already got,
    Deare Killer, spare not thy sweet cruell shot:
A kind of grace it is to slay with speed.

49

I on my horse, and *Love* on me doth trie
    Our horsmanships, while by strange worke I prove
    A horsman to my horse, a horse to *Love*;
And now man's wrongs in me, poore beast, descrie.
The raines wherewith my Rider doth me tie,   5
    Are humbled thoughts, which bit of Reverence move,
    Curb'd in with Feare, but with guilt bosse above
Of Hope, which makes it seeme faire to the eye.
    The Wand is Will, thou, Fancie, Saddle art,
Girt fast by Memorie, and while I spurre   10
My horse, he spurres with sharpe Desire my hart:
He sits me fast, how ever I do sturre:
    And now hath made me to his hand so right,*
    That in the Manage myselfe takes delight.

50

Stella, the fulnesse of my thoughts of thee
Cannot be staid within my panting breast,
But they do swell and struggle forth of me,
Till that in words thy figure be exprest.
    And yet as soone as they so formed be,   5
According to my Lord *Love's* owne behest;

With sad eyes I their weake proportion see,
To portrait that which in this world is best.
  So that I cannot chuse but write my mind,
And cannot chuse but put out what I write,
While those poore babes their death in birth do find:
And now my pen these lines had dashed quite,
  But that they stopt his furie from the same,
  Because their forefront bare sweet *Stella's* name.

51

Pardon mine eares, both I and they do pray,
  So may your tongue still fluently proceed,
  To them that do such entertainment need,
So may you still have somewhat new to say.
On silly me do not the burthen lay,
  Of all the grave conceits your braine doth breed;
  But find some *Hercules* to beare, in steed
Of *Atlas* tyr'd,* your wisedome's heav'nly sway.
  For me, while you discourse of courtly tides.
Of cunningst fishers in most troubled streames,
Of straying wayes, when valiant errour guides:
Meane while my heart confers with *Stella's* beames,
  And is even irkt that so sweet Comedie,
  But such unsuted speech* should hindred be.

52

A strife is growne betweene *Vertue* and *Love*,
  While each pretends that *Stella* must be his:
  Her eyes, her lips, her all, saith *Love* do this,
Since they do weare his badge, most firmely prove.
But *Vertue* thus that title doth disprove,
  That *Stella* (O deare name) that *Stella* is
  That vertuous soule, sure heire of heav'nly blisse:
Not this faire outside, which our hearts doth move.
  And therefore, though her beautie and her grace
Be *Love's* indeed, in *Stella's* selfe he may
By no pretence claime any maner place.
Well *Love*, since this demurre our sute doth stay,
  Let *Vertue* have that *Stella's* selfe; yet thus,
  That *Vertue* but that body graunt to us.

53

In *Martiall* sports I had my cunning tride,
  And yet to breake more staves did me addresse:
  While with the people's shouts I must confesse,
Youth, lucke, and praise, even fild my veines with pride.
When *Cupid*, having me his slave describe   5
  In *Marse's* liverie, prauncing in the presse:
  'What now sir foole,' said he, 'I would no lesse,
Looke here, I say.' I look'd, and *Stella* spide,
  Who hard by made a window send forth light.
My heart then quak'd, then dazled were mine eyes,   10
One hand forgott to rule, th'other to fight.
Nor trumpets' sound I heard, nor friendly cries;
  My Foe came on, and beat the aire for me,
  Till that her blush taught me my shame to see.

Losing his manliness?

54

Because I breathe not love to everie one,
  Nor do not use set colours for to weare,
  Nor nourish speciall lockes of vowed haire,
Nor give each speech a full point of a grone,
The courtly Nymphs, acquainted with the mone   5
  Of them, who in their lips *Love's* standerd beare;
  'What he?' say they of me, 'now I dare sweare,
He cannot love: no, no, let him alone.'
  And thinke so still, so *Stella* know my mind,
Professe in deed I do not *Cupid's* art;   10
But you faire maides, at length this true shall find,
That his right badge is but worne in the hart:
  Dumbe Swannes, not chatring Pies, do Lovers prove,
  They love indeed, who quake to say they love.

disdain for affektation, mere mannerisms. How true.

55

Muses, I oft invoked your holy ayde,*
  With choisest flowers my speech to engarland so;
  That it, despisde in true but naked shew,
Might winne some grace in your sweet grace arraid.
And oft whole troupes of saddest words I staid,   5
  Striving abroad a foraging to go,

Seldom invokes Muse. Not taken to heart (abstraction) (back)

about himself, not about her image

Untill by your inspiring I might know,
How their blacke banner might be best displaid.
　But now I meane no more your helpe to trie,
Nor other sugring of my speech to prove,   10
But on her name incessantly to crie:
For let me but name her whom I do love,
　So sweete sounds straight mine eare and heart do hit,
　That I well find no eloquence like it.

56

Fy, schoole of *Patience*, Fy, your lesson is
　Far far too long to learne it without booke:*
　What, a whole weeke without one peece of looke,
And thinke I should not your large precepts misse?*
When I might reade those letters faire of blisse,   5
　Which in her face teach vertue, I could brooke
　Somewhat thy lead'n counsels, which I tooke
As of a friend that meant not much amisse:
　But now that I, alas, do want her sight,
What, dost thou thinke that I can ever take   10
In thy cold stuffe a flegmatike delight?*
No, *Patience*, if thou wilt my good, then make
　Her come, and heare with patience my desire,
　And then with patience bid me beare my fire.

57

Wo, having made with many fights his owne
　Each sence of mine, each gift, each power of mind,
　Growne now his slaves, he forst them out to find
The thorowest words, fit for woe's selfe to grone,
Hoping that when they might find *Stella* alone,   5
　Before she could prepare to be unkind,
　Her soule, arm'd but with such a dainty rind,
Should soone be pierc'd with sharpnesse of the mone.
　She heard my plaints, and did not only heare,
But them (so sweete is she) most sweetly sing,*   10
With that faire breast making woe's darknesse cleare:
A pretty case! I hoped her to bring
　To feele my griefes, and she with face and voice
　So sweets my paines, that my paines me rejoyce.

58

Doubt there hath bene, when with his golden chaine
   The Oratour so farre men's harts doth bind,*
   That no pace else their guided steps can find,
But as he them more short or slacke doth raine,
Whether with words this soveraignty he gaine,   5
   Cloth'd with fine tropes, with strongest reasons lin'd,
   Or else pronouncing grace, wherewith his mind
Prints his owne lively forme in rudest braine.
   Now judge by this: in piercing phrases late,
   Th' anatomy of all my woes I wrate,   10
Stella's sweete breath the same to me did reed,
   O voice, O face, maugre my speeche's might,
   Which wooed wo, most ravishing delight
Even those sad words even in sad me did breed.

59

Deare, why make you more of a dog then me?*
   If he do love, I burne, I burne in love:
   If he waite well, I never thence would move:
If he be faire, yet but a dog can be.
Litle he is, so litle worth is he;   5
   He barks, my songs thine owne voyce oft doth prove:*
   Bid'n, perhaps he fetcheth thee a glove,
But I unbid, fetch even my soule to thee.
   Yet while I languish, him that bosome clips,
   That lap doth lap, nay lets, in spite of spite,   10
This sowre-breath'd mate tast of those sugred lips.
   Alas, if you graunt only such delight
   To witlesse things, then *Love* I hope (since wit
Becomes a clog) will soone ease me of it.

60

When my good Angell guides me to the place,
   Where all my good I do in *Stella* see,
   That heav'n of joyes throwes onely downe on me
Thundred disdaines and lightnings of disgrace:
But when the ruggedst step of Fortune's race   5
   Makes me fall from her sight, then sweetly she

With words, wherein the Muses' treasures be,
Shewes love and pitie to my absent case.
　Now I, wit-beaten long by hardest Fate,
So dull am, that I cannot looke into　　　　　　　　　　10
The ground of this fierce *Love* and lovely *Hate*:
Then some good body tell me how I do,
　　Whose presence, absence, absence presence is;
　　Blist in my curse, and cursed in my blisse.

61

Oft with true sighes, oft with uncalled teares,
Now with slow words, now with dumbe eloquence
I *Stella's* eyes assayll, invade her eares;
But this at last is her sweet breath'd defence:
　That who indeed infelt affection beares,　　　　　　5
So captives to his Saint both soule and sence,
That wholly hers, all selfnesse he forbeares,
Thence his desires he learnes, his live's course thence.
　Now since her chast mind hates this love in me,
　　With chastned mind, I straight must shew that she　10
Shall quickly me from what she hates remove.
　O Doctor *Cupid*, thou for me reply,
　Driv'n else to graunt by Angel's sophistrie,*
That I love not, without I leave to love.

62

Late tyr'd with wo, even ready for to pine
With rage of *Love*, I cald my Love unkind;
She in whose eyes *Love*, though unfelt, doth shine,
Sweet said that I true love in her should find.
　I joyed, but straight thus watred was my wine,　　5
That love she did, but loved a *Love* not blind,
Which would not let me, whom she loved, decline
From nobler course, fit for my birth and mind:
　And therefore by her *Love's* authority,
　Willd me these tempests of vaine love to flie,*　　10
And anchor fast my selfe on *Vertue's* shore.
　Alas, if this the only mettall be
　Of *Love*, new-coind to helpe my beggery,
Deare, love me not, that you may love me more.

63

O *Grammer* rules, O now your vertues show;
     So children still reade you with awfull eyes,
     As my young Dove may in your precepts wise
Her graunt to me, by her owne vertue know.
For late with heart most high, with eyes most low,
     I crav'd the thing which ever she denies:
     She lightning *Love*, displaying *Venus*' skies,
Least once should not be heard, twise said, 'No, No.'
     Sing then my Muse, now *Io Pean* sing,*
     Heav'ns envy not at my high triumphing: 10
But *Grammer's* force with sweet successe confirme,
     For *Grammer* sayes (O this deare *Stella* weighe,)
     For *Grammer* sayes (to *Grammer* who sayes nay)
That in one speech two Negatives affirme.*

First song*

Doubt you to whom my Muse these notes entendeth,
Which now my breast orecharg'd to Musicke lendeth?
To you, to you, all song of praise is due,
Only in you my song begins and endeth.

Who hath the eyes which marrie state with pleasure,   5
Who keepes the key of *Nature's* chiefest treasure?
To you, to you, all song of praise is due,
Only for you the heav'n forgate all measure.

Who hath the lips, where wit in fairenesse raigneth,
Who womankind at once both deckes and stayneth?   10
To you, to you, all song of praise is due,
Onely by you *Cupid* his crowne maintaineth.

Who hath the feet, whose step all sweetnesse planteth,
Who else for whom *Fame* worthy trumpets wanteth?
To you, to you, all song of praise is due,   15
Onely to you her Scepter *Venus* granteth.

Who hath the breast, whose milke doth passions nourish,
Whose grace is such, that when it chides doth cherish?
To you, to you, all song of praise is due,
Onelie through you the tree of life doth flourish.   20

Who hath the hand which without stroke subdueth,
Who long dead beautie with increase reneweth?
To you, to you, all song of praise is due,
Onely at you all envie hopelesse rueth.

Who hath the haire which, loosest, fastest tieth,   25
Who makes a man live then glad when he dieth?
To you, to you, all song of praise is due:
Only of you the flatterer never lieth.

Who hath the voyce, which soule from sences sunders,
Whose force but yours the bolts of beautie thunders?   30
To you, to you, all song of praise is due:
Only with you not miracles are wonders.*

Doubt you to whom my Muse these notes intendeth,
Which now my breast orecharg'd to Musicke lendeth?
To you, to you, all song of praise is due: 35
Only in you my song begins and endeth.

64

No more, my deare, no more these counsels trie,
    O give my passions leave to run their race:
    Let Fortune lay on me her worst disgrace,
Let folke orecharg'd with braine against me crie,
Let clouds bedimme my face, breake in mine eye,   5
    Let me no steps but of lost labour trace,
    Let all the earth with scorne recount my case,
But do not will me from my Love to flie.
    I do not envie *Aristotle's* wit,
Nor do aspire to *Cæsar's* bleeding fame,
Nor ought do care, though some above me sit,
Nor hope, nor wishe another course to frame,*
    But that which once may win thy cruell hart:
Thou art my Wit, and thou my Vertue art.

65

Love, by sure proofe I may call thee unkind,
That giv'st no better eare to my just cries:
Thou whom to me such my good turnes should bind,
As I may well recount, but none can prize:

For when, nak'd boy, thou couldst no harbour find   5
In this old world, growne now so too too wise:
I lodg'd thee in my heart, and being blind
By Nature borne, I gave to thee mine eyes.
　Mine eyes, my light, my heart, my life, alas,
If so great services may scorned be: 10
Yet let this thought thy Tygrish courage passe:
That I perhaps am somewhat kinne to thee;
　　Since in thine armes, if learnd fame truth hath spread,
　　Thou bear'st the arrow, I the arrow head.

66

And do I see some cause a hope to feede,
Or doth the tedious burd'n of long wo
In weakened minds, quicke apprehending breed,
Of everie image, which may comfort show?
　I cannot brag of word, much lesse of deed,   5
Fortune wheeles still with me in one sort slow,*
My wealth no more, and no whit lesse my need,
Desire still on the stilts of feare doth go.
　And yet amid all feares a hope there is
Stolne to my heart, since last faire night, nay day,   10
Stella's eyes sent to me the beames of blisse,
Looking on me, while I lookt other way:
　　But when mine eyes backe to their heav'n did move,
　　They fled with blush, which guiltie seem'd of love.

67

Hope, art thou true, or doest thou flatter me?
　Doth Stella now begin with piteous eye,
　The ruines of her conquest to espie:
Will she take time, before all wracked be?
Her eyes-speech is translated thus by thee: 5
　But failst thou not in phrase so heav'nly hie?*
　Looke on againe, the faire text better trie: again.
What blushing notes doest thou in margine see?
　What sighes stolne out, or kild before full borne?
Hast thou found such and such like arguments?   10
Or art thou else to comfort me forsworne?
Well, how so thou interpret the contents,

I am resolv'd thy errour to maintaine,
Rather then by more truth to get more paine.

68

Stella, the onely Planet of my light,
    Light of my life, and life of my desire,
    Chiefe good, whereto my hope doth only aspire,
World of my wealth, and heav'n of my delight.
Why doest thou spend the treasures of thy sprite,   5
    With voice more fit to wed *Amphion's* lyre,*
    Seeking to quench in me the noble fire,
Fed by thy worth, and kindled by thy sight?
    And all in vaine, for while thy breath most sweet,
With choisest words, thy words with reasons rare,   10
Thy reasons firmly set on *Vertue's* feet,
Labour to kill in me this killing care:
    O thinke I then, what paradise of joy
    It is, so faire a *Vertue* to enjoy.

69

O joy, to high for my low stile to show:
    O blisse, fit for a nobler state then me:
    Envie, put out thine eyes, least thou do see
What Oceans of delight in me do flow.
My friend, that oft saw through all maskes my wo,*   5
    Come, come, and let me powre my selfe on thee;
    Gone is the winter of my miserie,
My spring appeares, O see what here doth grow.
    For *Stella* hath with words where faith doth shine,
Of her high heart giv'n me the monarchie: 10
I, I, O I may say, that she is mine.
And though she give but thus conditionly
    This realme of blisse, while vertuous course I take,
    No kings be crown'd, but they some covenants make.

70

My Muse may well grudge at my heav'nly joy,
    If still I force her in sad rimes to creepe:
    She oft hath drunke my teares, now hopes to enjoy
Nectar of Mirth, since I *Jove's* cup do keepe:*
    Sonets be not bound prentise to annoy:*   5
    Trebles sing high, as well as bases deepe:

Paint figure again.

Griefe but *Love's* winter liverie is, the Boy
   Hath cheekes to smile, as well as eyes to weepe.
     Come then my Muse, shew thou height of delight
In well raisde notes, my pen the best it may   10
Shall paint out joy, though but in blacke and white.
Cease eager Muse, peace pen, for my sake stay,
     I give you here my hand for truth of this,
     Wise silence is best musicke unto blisse.

CENTRAL

part imitation

71

Who will in fairest booke of *Nature* know,
   How *Vertue* may best lodg'd in beautie be,
   Let him but learne of *Love* to reade in thee,
Stella, those faire lines, which true goodnesse show.
There shall he find all vices' overthrow,   5
   Not by rude force, but sweetest soveraigntie
   Of reason, from whose light those night-birds* flie:
That inward sunne in thine eyes shineth so.
   And not content to be *Perfection*'s heire
Thy selfe, doest strive all minds that way to move,   10
Who marke in thee what is in thee most faire.
So while thy beautie drawes the heart to love,
   As fast thy *Vertue* bends that love to good:
   'But ah,' *Desire* still cries, 'give me some food.'

72

Desire, though thou my old companion art,
   And oft so clings to my pure *Love*, that I
   One from the other scarcely can descrie,
While each doth blow the fier of my hart;
Now from thy fellowship I needs must part,   5
   Venus is taught with *Dian's* wings to flie:*
   I must no more in thy sweet passions lie;
Vertue's gold now must head my *Cupid's* dart.*
   Service and Honor, wonder with delight,
Feare to offend, will worthie to appeare,   10
Care shining in mine eyes, faith in my sprite,
These things are left me by my only Deare;
   But thou *Desire*, because thou wouldst have all,
   Now banisht art, but yet alas how shall?

Second song

Have I caught my heav'nly jewell,
Teaching sleepe most faire to be?
Now will I teach her that she,
When she wakes, is too too cruell.

Since sweet sleep her eyes hath charmed,   5
The two only darts of *Love*:
Now will I with that boy prove
Some play, while he is disarmed.

Her tongue waking still refuseth,
Giving frankly niggard No: 10
Now will I attempt to know,
What No her tongue sleeping useth.

See the hand which waking gardeth,
Sleeping, grants a free resort:
Now will I invade the fort;   15
Cowards *Love* with losse rewardeth.

But O foole, thinke of the danger,
Of her just and high disdaine:
Now will I alas refraine,
Love feares nothing else but anger.   20

Yet those lips so sweetly swelling,
Do invite a stealing kisse:
Now will I but venture this,
Who will read must first learne spelling.

Oh sweet kisse, but ah she is waking,
Lowring beautie chastens me: 25
Now will I away hence flee:
Foole, more foole, for no more taking.*

73

Love still a boy, and oft a wanton is,
School'd onely by his mother's tender eye:
What wonder then if he his lesson misse,
When for so soft a rod deare play he trie?
　And yet my Starre, because a sugred kisse   5
In sport I suckt, while she asleepe did lie,

Doth lowre, nay, chide; nay, threat for only this:
Sweet, it was saucie *Love*, not humble I.*
  But no 'scuse serves, she makes her wrath appeare
In *Beautie*'s throne, see now who dares come neare   10
Those scarlet judges, threatning bloudy paine?*
    O heav'nly foole, thy most kisse-worthie face,
    Anger invests with such a lovely grace,
That *Anger*'s selfe I needs must kisse againe.

74

I never dranke of *Aganippe* well,*
Nor ever did in shade of *Tempe* sit:*
And Muses scorne with vulgar braines to dwell,
Poore Layman I, for sacred rites unfit.
    Some do I heare of Poets' furie tell,   5
But (God wot) wot not what they meane by it:*
And this I sweare by blackest brooke of hell,
I am no pick-purse of another's wit.
    How falles it then, that with so smooth an ease
My thoughts I speake, and what I speake doth flow   10
In verse, and that my verse best wits doth please?
Guesse we the cause: 'What, is it thus?' Fie no:
    'Or so?' Much lesse: 'How then?' Sure thus it is:
    My lips are sweet, inspired with *Stella's* kisse.

75

Of all the kings that ever here did raigne,
Edward named fourth, as first in praise I name,
Not for his faire outside, nor well lined braine,
Although lesse gifts impe feathers oft* on *Fame*,
    Nor that he could young-wise, wise-valiant frame   5
His Sire's revenge, joyn'd with a kingdome's gaine:
And gain'd by *Mars*, could yet mad *Mars* so tame,
That Ballance weigh'd what sword did late obtaine,
    Nor that he made the Flouredeluce so 'fraid,
Though strongly hedg'd of bloudy *Lyon*'s pawes,   10
That wittie *Lewis* to him a tribute paid.
Nor this, nor that, or any such small cause,
    But only for this worthy knight durst prove
    To lose his Crowne, rather then faile his Love.*

76

She comes, and streight therewith her shining twins do move
   Their rayes to me, who in her tedious absence lay
Benighted in cold wo, but now appeares my day,
The onely light of joy, the onely warmth of *Love*.
She comes with light and warmth, which like *Aurora** prove   5
   Of gentle force, so that mine eyes dare gladly play
   With such a rosie morne, whose beames most freshly gay
Scortch not, but onely do darke chilling sprites remove.
   But lo, while I do speake, it groweth noone with me,
Her flamie glistring lights increase with time and place: 10
My heart cries 'Ah', it burnes, mine eyes now dazled be:
No wind, no shade can coole, what helpe then in my case,
   But with short breath, long lookes, staid feet and walking hed,
   Pray that my sunne go downe with meeker beames to bed.

77

Those lookes, whose beames be joy, whose motion is delight,
That face, whose lecture shewes what perfect beautie is:
That presence, which doth give darke hearts a living light:
That grace, which *Venus* weepes that she her selfe doth misse:
   That hand, which without touch holds more then *Atlas** might;
Those lips, which make death's pay a meane price for a kisse: 6
That skin, whose passe-praise hue scorns this poore terme of white:
Those words, which do sublime the quintessence of blisse:
   That voyce, which makes the soule plant himselfe in the eares:
That conversation sweet, where such high comforts be,
As consterd in true speech, the name of heav'n it beares,
Makes me in my best thoughts and quietst judgement see,
   That in no more but these I might be fully blest:
   Yet ah, my Mayd'n Muse doth blush to tell the best.

78

O How the pleasant aires of true love be
   Infected by those vapours, which arise
   From out that noysome gulfe, which gaping lies
Betweene the jawes of hellish *Jealousie*,
A monster, other's harme, selfe-miserie,   5
   Beautie's plague, Vertue's scourge, succour of lies:

Who his owne joy to his owne hurt applies,
And onely cherish doth with injurie.
   Who since he hath, by *Nature*'s speciall grace,
   So piercing pawes, as spoyle when they embrace,   10
So nimble feet as stirre still, though on thornes:
   So manie eyes ay seeking their owne woe,
   So ample eares as never good newes know:
Is it not evill that such a Devill wants hornes?*

[margin, handwritten: lack of proportion?]

[margin, handwritten: Devil/husband/jealousy]

79

Sweet kisse, thy sweets I faine would sweetly endite,
   Which even of sweetnesse sweetest sweetner art:
   Pleasingst consort, where each sence holds a part,
Which, coupling Doves, guides *Venus*' chariot right.*
Best charge, and bravest retrait in *Cupid's* fight,   5
   A double key, which opens to the heart,
   Most rich, when most his riches it impart:
Neast of young joyes, schoolmaster of delight,
   Teaching the meane, at once to take and give
The friendly fray, where blowes both wound and heale,   10
The prettie death, while each in other live,
Poore hope's first wealth, ostage of promist weale,
   Breakefast of *Love*, but lo, lo, where she is,
   Cease we to praise, now pray we for a kisse.

80

Sweet swelling lip, well maist thou swell in pride,
   Since best wits thinke it wit thee to admire;
   Nature's praise, Vertue's stall, *Cupid's* cold fire,
Whence words, not words, but heav'nly graces slide.
The new *Pernassus*, where the Muses bide,   5
   Sweetner of musicke, wisedome's beautifier:
   Breather of life, and fastner of desire,
Where Beautie's blush in Honour's graine is dide.
   Thus much my heart compeld my mouth to say,
   But now spite of my heart my mouth will stay,   10
Loathing all lies, doubting this Flatterie is:
   And no spurre can his resty race renew,
   Without how farre this praise is short of you,
Sweet lip, you teach my mouth with one sweet kisse.

81

O kisse, which doest those ruddie gemmes impart,
Or gemmes, or frutes of new-found *Paradise*,
Breathing all blisse and sweetning to the heart,
Teaching dumbe lips a nobler exercise.
   O kisse, which soules, even soules together ties*
By linkes of *Love*, and only *Nature*'s art:
How faine would I paint thee to all men's eyes,
Or of thy gifts at least shade out some part.
   But she forbids, with blushing words, she sayes,
   She builds her fame on higher seated praise: 10
But my heart burnes, I cannot silent be.
   Then since (deare life) you faine would have me peace,
   And I, mad with delight, want wit to cease,
Stop you my mouth with still still kissing me.

82

Nymph of the gard'n, where all beauties be:
   Beauties which do in exellencie passe
   His who till death lookt in a watrie glasse,*
Or hers whom naked the *Trojan* boy did see.*
Sweet gard'n Nymph, which keepes the Cherrie tree,*   5
   Whose fruit doth farre th'*Esperian* tast* surpasse:
   Most sweet-faire, most faire-sweet, do not alas,
From comming nere those Cherries banish me:
   For though full of desire, emptie of wit,
Admitted late by your best-graced grace,   10
I caught at one of them a hungrie bit;
Pardon that fault, once more graunt me the place,
   And I do sweare even by the same delight,
   I will but kisse, I never more will bite.

83

Good brother *Philip*,* I have borne you long,
   I was content you should in favour creepe,
   While craftily you seem'd your cut to keepe,
As though that faire soft hand did you great wrong.
I bare (with Envie) yet I bare your song,   5
   When in her necke you did Love ditties peepe;

In Lillies' neast, where *Love's* selfe lies along.
   What, doth high place ambitious thoughts augment?
Is sawcinesse reward of curtesie?   10
Cannot such grace your silly selfe content,
But you must needs with those lips billing be?
   And through those lips drinke Nectar from that toong;
   Leave that sir *Phip*, least off your necke be wroong. *violence*

Third song

If *Orpheus*' voyce had force to breathe such musicke's love
Through pores of sencelesse trees, as it could make them move:*
If stones good measure daunc'd, the *Theban* walles to build,
To cadence of the tunes, which *Amphyon's* lyre did yeeld,*
More cause a like effect at leastwise bringeth: *climax main* 5
O stones, O trees, learne hearing, *Stella* singeth. *dance*

If Love might sweet'n so a boy of shepheard' brood,
To make a Lyzard dull to taste Love's daintie food:
If Eagle fierce could so in *Grecian* Mayd delight,
As his light was her eyes, her death his endlesse night:*   10
Earth gave that Love, heav'n I trow Love refineth:
O birds, O beasts, looke Love, lo, *Stella* shineth.

The birds, beasts, stones and trees feele this, and feeling *Love*:
And if the trees, nor stones stirre not the same to prove,
Nor beasts, nor birds do come unto this blessed gaze,   15
Know, that small Love is quicke, and great Love doth amaze:
They are amaz'd, but you with reason armed,
O eyes, O eares of men, how are you charmed!

84

Highway since you my chiefe *Pernassus* be,*
   And that my Muse to some eares not unsweet,
   Tempers her words to trampling horses feet,
More oft then to a chamber melodie;
Now blessed you, beare onward blessed me   5
   To her, where I my heart safeliest shall meet.
   My Muse and I must you of dutie greet
With thankes and wishes, wishing thankfully.
   Be you still faire, honourd by publike heed,
By no encrochment wrongd, nor time forgot: 10

Nor blam'd for bloud, nor sham'd for sinfull deed.
And that you know, I envy you no lot
    Of highest wish, I wish you so much blisse,
    Hundreds of yeares you *Stella's* feet may kisse.

85

I see the house, my heart thy selfe containe,
    Beware full sailes drowne not thy tottring barge:
    Least joy, by Nature apt sprites to enlarge,*
Thee to thy wracke beyond thy limits straine.
Nor do like Lords, whose weake confused braine,   5
    Not pointing to fit folkes each undercharge,
    While everie office themselves will discharge,
With doing all, leave nothing done but paine.
    But give apt servants their due place, let eyes
See Beautie's totall summe summ'd in her face: 10
Let eares heare speech, which wit to wonder ties,
Let breath sucke up those sweetes, let armes embrace
    The globe of weale, lips *Love's* indentures make:
    Thou but of all kingly Tribute take.

worth to be tribute to Kelly.

Fourth song*

Onely joy, now here you are,
Fit to heare and ease my care:
Let my whispering voyce obtaine,
Sweete reward for sharpest paine:
Take me to thee, and thee to me.   5
'No, no, no, no, my Deare, let be.'

Night hath closd all in her cloke,
Twinckling starres Love-thoughts provoke:
Danger hence good care doth keepe,
Jealousie it selfe doth sleepe:
Take me to thee, and thee to me.   10
'No, no, no, no, my Deare, let be.'

Better place no wit can find,
Cupid's yoke to loose or bind:
These sweet flowers on fine bed too,
Us in their best language woo: 15

Only the she's given a voice.

A voice of denial.

A voice of rejecting.

Take me to thee, and thee to me,
'No, no, no, no, my Deare, let be.'

This small light the Moone bestowes,
Serves thy beames but to disclose,   20
So to raise my hap more hie;
Feare not else, none can us spie:
Take me to thee, and thee to me.
'No, no, no, no, my Deare, let be.'

That you herd was but a Mouse,   25
Dumbe sleepe holdeth all the house;
Yet a sleep, me thinkes they say,
Yong folkes, take time while you may:
Take me to thee, and thee to me.
'No, no, no, no, my Deare, let be.'   30

Niggard Times threats, if we misse
This large offer of our blisse,
Long stay ere he graunt the same:
Sweet then, while each thing doth frame:
Take me to thee, and thee to me.   35
'No, no, no, no, my Deare, let be.'

Your faire mother is a bed,
Candles out, and curtains spread:
She thinkes you do letters write:
Write, but let me first endite: 40
Take me to thee, and thee to me.
'No, no, no, no, my Deare, let be.'

Sweet alas, why strive you thus?
Concord better fitteth us:
Leave to *Mars* the force of hands,   45
Your power in your beautie stands:
Take me to thee, and thee to me.
'No, no, no, no, my Deare, let be.'

Wo to me, and do you sweare
Me to hate but I forbeare?
Cursed be my destines all,
That brought me so high to fall:
Soone with my death I will please thee.
'No, no, no, no, my Deare, let be.'

86

Alas, whence came this change of lookes? If I
  Have chang'd desert, let mine owne conscience be
  A still felt plague, to selfe condemning me:
Let wo gripe on my heart, shame loade mine eye.
But if all faith, like spotlesse Ermine* ly   5
  Safe in my soule, which only doth to thee
  (As his sole object of felicitie)
With wings of *Love* in aire of wonder flie,
  O ease your hand, treate not so hard your slave:
In justice paines come not till faults do call;   10
Or if I needs (sweet Judge) must torments have,
Use something else to chast'n me withall,
  Then those blest eyes, where all my hopes do dwell,
  No doome should make one's heav'n become his hell.

*Fift song**

While favour fed my hope, delight with hope was brought,
Thought waited on delight, and speech did follow thought:
Then grew my tongue and pen records unto they glory:
I thought all words were lost, that were not spent of thee:
I thought each place was darke but where thy lights would be,   5
And all eares worse then deafe, that heard not out thy storie.

I said, thou wert most faire, and so indeed thou art:
I said, thou wert most sweet, sweet poison to my heart:
I said, my soule was thine (O that I then had lyed)
I said, thine eyes were starres, thy breasts the milk'n way,   10
Thy fingers *Cupid's* shafts, thy voyce the Angels' lay:
And all I said so well, as no man it denied.

But now that hope is lost, unkindnesse kils delight,
Yet thought and speech do live, though metamorphosd quite:
For rage now rules the reynes, which guided were by Pleasure.   15
I thinke now of thy faults, who late thought of thy praise,
That speech falles now to blame, which did thy honour raise,
The same key op'n can, which can locke up a treasure.

Thou then whom partiall heavens conspir'd in one to frame,
The proofe of Beautie's worth, th'enheritrix of fame,   20
The mansion seat of blisse, and just excuse of Lovers;

See now those feathers pluckt, wherewith thou flewst most high:
See what clouds of reproch shall darke thy honour's skie,
Whose owne fault casts him downe, hardly high seat recovers.

And O my Muse, though oft you luld her in your lap,   25
And then, a heav'nly child, gave her Ambrosian pap:
And to that braine of hers your hidnest gifts infused,*
Since she disdaining me, doth you in me disdaine:
Suffer not her to laugh, while both we suffer paine:
Princes in subjects wrongd, must deeme themselves abused.   30

Your Client poore my selfe, shall *Stella* handle so?
Revenge, revenge, my Muse, Defiance' trumpet blow:
Threat'n what may be done, yet do more then you threat'n.
Ah, my sute granted is, I feele my breast doth swell:
Now child, a lesson new you shall begin to spell: 35
Sweet babes must babies have, but shrewd gyrles must be beatn'n.

Thinke now no more to heare of warme fine odourd snow,
Nor blushing Lillies, nor pearles' ruby-hidden row,
Nor of that golden sea, whose waves in curles are brok'n:
But of thy soule, so fraught with such ungratefulnesse,   40
As where thou soone mightst helpe, most faith dost most oppresse,
Ungratefull who is cald, the worst of evils is spok'n.

Yet worse then worst, I say thou art a theefe, a theefe?
Now God forbid. A theefe, and of worst theeves the cheefe:
Theeves steal for need, and steale but goods, which paine recovers,
But thou rich in all joyes, doest rob my joyes from me,   46
Which cannot be restor'd by time nor industrie:
Of foes the spoile is evill, far worse of constant lovers.

Yet gentle *English* theeves do rob, but will not slay;
Thou *English* murdring theefe, wilt have harts for thy pray: 50
The name of murdrer now on thy faire forehead sitteth:
And even while I do speake, my death wounds bleeding be:
Which (I protest) proceed from only cruell thee,
Who may and will not save, murder in truth committeth.

But murder, private fault, seems but a toy to thee,   55
I lay then to thy charge unjustest Tyrannie,
If Rule by force without all claime a Tyran showeth,
For thou doest lord my heart, who am not borne thy slave,
And which is worse, makes me most guiltlesse torments have,

A rightfull Prince by unright deeds a Tyran groweth.   60

Lo you grow proud with this, for tyrans make folke bow:
Of foule rebellion then I do appeach thee now;
Rebell by *Nature*'s law, rebell by law of reason,
Thou, sweetest subject, wert borne in the realme of *Love*,
And yet against thy Prince thy force dost dayly prove: 65
No vertue merits praise, once toucht with blot of Treason.

But valiant Rebels oft in fooles' mouthes purchase fame:
I now then staine thy white with vagabunding shame,
Both Rebell to the Sonne, and Vagrant from the Mother;
For wearing *Venus*' badge, in every part of thee,   70
Unto *Dianae's* traine thou runaway didst flee:*
Who faileth one, is false, though trusty to another.

What, is not this enough? nay farre worse commeth here;
A witch I say thou art, though thou so faire appeare;
For I protest, my sight never thy face enjoyeth,   75
But I in me am chang'd, I am alive and dead:
My feete are turn'd to rootes, my hart becommeth lead,
No witchcraft is so evill, as which man's mind destroyeth.

Yet witches may repent, thou art far worse then they,
Alas, that I am forst such evill of thee to say,   80
I say thou art a Devill, though clothd in Angel's shining:
For thy face tempts my soule to leave the heav'n for thee,
And thy words of refuse, do powre even hell on mee:
Who tempt, and tempted plague, are Devils in true defining.

You then ungratefull thiefe, you murdring Tyran you,   85
You Rebell run away, to Lord and Lady untrue,
You witch, you Divill, (alas) you still of me beloved,
You see what I can say; mend yet your froward mind,
And such skill in my Muse you reconcil'd shall find,
That all these cruell words your praises shall be proved.   90

Sixt song

O you that heare this voice,
O you that see this face,
Say whether of the choice
Deserves the former place:

Feare not to judge this bate,   5
For it is void of hate.

This side doth Beauty take,
For that doth Musike speake,
Fit oratours to make
The strongest judgements weake: 10
The barre to plead their right,
Is only True Delight,

Thus doth the voice and face,
These gentle Lawyers, wage,
Like loving brothers' case   15
For father's heritage,
That each, while each contends,
It selfe to other lends.

For Beautie beautifies,
With heavenly hew and grace,   20
The heavenly harmonies;
And in this faultlesse face,
The perfect beauties be
A perfect harmony.

Musicke more liftly swels   25
In speeches nobly placed:
Beauty as farre excels,
In action aptly graced:
A friend each party drawes,
To countenance his cause: 30

Love more affected seemes
To Beautie's lovely light,
And wonder more esteemes
Of Musick's wondrous might:
But both to both so bent,   35
As both in both are spent.

Musike doth witnesse call
The eare, his truth to trie:
Beauty brings to the hall,
The judgement of the eye,   40
Both in their objects such,
As no exceptions tutch.

The Common Sence,* which might
Be Arbiter of this,
To be forsooth upright,
To both sides partiall is:
He layes on this chiefe praise,
Chiefe praise on that he laies.

Then Reason, Princesse hy,
Whose throne is in the mind,   50
Which Musicke can in sky
And hidden beauties find,
Say whether thou wilt crowne,
With limitlesse renowne.

? Seems to just break off

Seventh song

Whose senses in so evill consort, their stepdame *Nature* laies,
That ravishing delight in them most sweete tunes do not raise;
Of if they do delight therein, yet are so cloyed with wit,
As with sententious lips to set a title vaine on it: 4
O let them heare these sacred tunes, and learne in wonder's schooles,
To be, in things past bounds of wit, fooles, if they be not fooles.

Who have so leaden eyes, as not to see sweet beautie's show,
Or seeing, have so wodden wits, as not that worth to know;
Or knowing, have so muddy minds, as not to be in love;
Or loving, have so frothy thoughts, as easly thence to move: 10
O let them see these heavenly beames, and in faire letters reede
A lesson fit, both sight and skill, love and firme love to breede.

Heare then, but then with wonder heare; see but adoring see,
No mortall gifts, no earthly fruites, now here descended be:
See, do you see this face? nay image of the skies,   15
Of which the two life-giving lights are figured in her eyes:
Heare you this soule-invading voice, and count it but a voice?
The very essence of their tunes, when Angels do rejoyce.

Eighth song*

In a grove most rich of shade,
Where birds wanton musicke made,
May then yong his pide weedes showing,
New perfumed with flowers fresh growing,

Astrophil with *Stella* sweete,   5
Did for mutuall comfort meete, ⊛ *dramatic fantasising*
Both within themselves oppressed,
But each in the other blessed.

Him great harmes had taught much care,
Her faire necke a foule yoke bare, * *of marriage*   10
But her sight his cares did banish,
In his sight her yoke did vanish.

Wept they had, alas the while,
But now teares themselves did smile,
While their eyes by love directed,   15
Enterchangeably reflected.

Sigh they did, but now betwixt
Sighs of woes were glad sighs mixt,
With armes crost, ⊛ yet testifying
Restlesse rest, and living dying.   20

Their eares hungry of each word,
Which the deere tongue would afford,
But their tongues restrained from walking,
Till their harts had ended talking.

But when their tongues could not speake,   25
Love it selfe did silence breake;
Love did set his lips asunder,
Thus to speake in love and wonder:

'*Stella* soveraigne of my joy,
Faire triumpher of annoy,   30
  Stella starre of heavenly fier,
  Stella loadstar of desier.

'*Stella*, in whose shining eyes,
Are the lights of *Cupid's* skies,
Whose beames, where they once are darted,   35
Love therewith is streight imparted.

'*Stella*, whose voice when it speakes,
Senses all asunder breakes;
Stella, whose voice when it singeth,
Angels to acquaintance bringeth.   40

'*Stella*, in whose body is
Writ each character of blisse,
Whose face all, all beauty passeth,
Save thy mind which yet surpasseth.

'Graunt, O graunt, but speech alas,   45
Failes me fearing on to passe,
Graunt, O me, what am I saying?
But no fault there is in praying.

'Graunt, O deere, on knees I pray,
(Knees on ground he then did stay)   50
That not I, but since I love you,
Time and place for me may move you.

'Never season was more fit,
Never roome more apt for it;
Smiling ayre allowes my reason,   55
These birds sing: "Now use the season."

'This small wind which so sweet is,
See how it the leaves doth kisse,
Ech tree in his best attiring,
Sense of love to love inspiring.   60

'Love makes earth the water drink,
Love to earth makes water sinke;
And if dumbe things be so witty,
Shall a heavenly grace want pitty?'

There his hands in their speech, faine   65
Would have made tongue's language plaine;
But her hands his hands repelling,
Gave repulse all grace excelling.

Then she spake; her speech was such,
As not eares but hart did tuch: 70
While such wise she love denied,
As yet love she signified.

'*Astrophil*' sayd she, 'my love
Cease in these effects to prove:
Now be still, yet still beleeve me,   75
Thy griefe more then death would grieve me.

'If that any thought in me,
Can tast comfort but of thee,
Let me, fed with hellish anguish,
Joylesse, hopelesse, endlesse languish.   80

'If those eyes you praised, be
Half so deere as you to me,
Let me home returne, starke blinded
Of those eyes, and blinder minded.

'If to secret of my hart,   85
I do any wish impart,
Where thou art not formost placed,
Be both wish and I defaced.

'If more may be sayd, I say,
All my blisse in thee I lay;   90
If thou love, my love content thee,
For all love, all faith is meant thee.

'Trust me while I thee deny,
In my selfe the smart I try,
Tyran honour doth thus use thee,   95
Stella's selfe might not refuse thee.

'Therefore, Deere, this no more move,
Least, though I leave not thy love,
Which too deep in me is framed,
I should blush when thou art named.'   100

Therewithall away she went,
Leaving him so passion rent,
With what she had done and spoken,
That therewith my song is broken.

Ninth song

Go my flocke,* go get you hence,
Seeke a better place of feeding,
Where you may have some defence
From the stormes in my breast breeding,
And showers from mine eyes proceeding.   5

Leave a wretch, in whom all wo
Can abide to keepe no measure,

Merry flocke, such one forgo,
Unto whom mirth is displeasure,
Only rich in mischiefe's treasure.   10

Yet alas before you go,
Heare your wofull maister's story,
Which to stones I els would show:
Sorrow onely then hath glory,
When tis excellently sory.   15

Stella fiercest shepherdesse,
Fiercest but yet fairest ever;
Stella whom O heavens do blesse,
Tho against me shee persever,
Tho I blisse enherit never.   20

Stella hath refused me,
Stella who more love hath proved,
In this caitife hart to be,
Then can in good eawes be moved
Toward Lamkins best beloved.   25

Stella hath refused me,
Astrophil that so wel served,
In this pleasant spring must see
While in pride flowers be preserved,
Himselfe onely winter-sterved.   30

Why alas doth she then sweare,
That she loveth me so dearely,
Seing me so long to beare
Coles of love that burne so clearly;
And yet leave me helplesse meerely?   35

Is that love? forsooth I trow,
If I saw my good dog grieved,
And a helpe for him did know,
My love should not be beleeved,
But he were by me releeved.   40

No, she hates me, wellaway,
Faining love, somewhat to please me:
For she knowes, if she display
All her hate, death soone would seaze me,

And of hideous torments ease me.   45

Then adieu, deere flocke adieu:
But alas, if in your straying
Heavenly *Stella* meete with you,
Tell her in your piteous blaying,
Her poore slave's unjust decaying.   50

87

When I was forst from *Stella* ever deere,
Stella food of my thoughts, hart of my hart,
Stella whose eyes make all my tempests cleere,
By iron lawes of duty to depart:
  Alas I found, that she with me did smart,   5
I saw that teares did in her eyes appeare;
I saw that sighes her sweetest lips did part,
And her sad words my saddest sence did heare.
  For me, I wept to see pearles scattered so,
  I sighd her sighes, and wailed for her wo,   10
Yet swam in joy, such love in her was seene.
  Thus while th' effect most bitter was to me,
  And nothing then the cause more sweet could be,
I had bene vext, if vext I had not beene.

88

Out traytour Absence, darest thou counsell me,
From my deare Captainnesse to run away?
Because in brave array heere marcheth she,
That to win me, oft shewes a present pay?*
  Is faith so weake? Or is such force in thee?   5
When Sun is hid, can starres such beames display?
Cannot heavn's food, once felt, keepe stomakes free
From base desire on earthly cates to pray?
  Tush Absence, while thy mistes eclipse that light,
  My Orphan sence flies to the inward sight,   10
Where memory sets foorth the beames of love.
  That where before hart loved and eyes did see,
  In hart both sight and love now coupled be;
United powers make each the stronger prove.

89

Now that of Absence the most irksome night,
  With darkest shade doth overcome my day;
  Since *Stella's* eyes, wont to give me my day,
Leaving my Hemisphere, leave me in night,
Each day seemes long, and longs for long-staid night,
  The night as tedious, wooes th'approch of day;
  Tired with the dusty toiles of busie day,
Languisht with horrors of the silent night,
Suffering the evils both of the day and night,
  While no night is more darke then is my day,   10
Nor no day hath lesse quiet then my night:
  With such bad mixture of my night and day,
That living thus in blackest winter night,
  I feele the flames of hottest sommer day.

90

Stella thinke not that I by verse seeke fame,
  Who seeke, who hope, who love, who live but thee;
  Thine eyes my pride, thy lips my history:
If thou praise not, all other praise is shame.
Nor so ambitious am I, as to frame,   5
  A nest for my yong praise in Lawrell tree:
  In truth I sweare, I wish not there should be
Graved in mine Epitaph a Poet's name:*
  Ne if I would, could I just title make,
That any laud to me thereof should grow,   10
Without my plumes from others' wings I take.
For nothing from my wit or will doth flow,
  Since all my words thy beauty doth endite,
  And *Love* doth hold my hand, and makes me write.

91

Stella, while now by honour's cruell might,
  I am from you, light of my life, mis-led,
  And that faire you my Sunne, thus overspred
With absence' vaile, I live in Sorowe's night.
If this darke place yet shew like candle light,   5
  Some beautie's peece, as amber colour'd hed,

Milke hands, rose cheeks, or lips more sweet, more red,
Or seeing jets, blacke, but in blacknesse bright.
They please I do confesse, they please mine eyes,
But why? because of you they models be,   10
Models such be wood-globes of glistring skies.
Deere, therefore be not jealous over me,
    If you heare that they seeme my hart to move,
    Not them, O no, but you in them I love.

92

Be your words made (good Sir) of *Indian* ware,
    That you allow me them by so small rate?
    Or do you cutted *Spartanes* imitate?
Or do you meane my tender eares to spare,   5
That to my questions you so totall are,
    When I demaund of *Phenix Stella's* state?
    You say forsooth, you left her well of late.
O God, thinke you that satisfies my care?
    I would know whether she did sit or walke,
How cloth'd, how waited on, sighd she or smilde,   10
Whereof, with whom, how often did she talke,
With what pastime time's journey she beguilde,
    If her lips daignd to sweeten my poore name.
    Say all, and all well sayd, still say the same.

Tenth song*

O deare life, when shall it be,
    That mine eyes thine eyes may see?
    And in them thy mind discover,
    Whether absence have had force   5
    Thy remembrance to divorce,
    From the image of thy lover?

O, if I my self find not,
    After parting ought forgot,
    Nor debard from beautie's treasure,
    Let no tongue aspire to tell,   10
    In what high joyes I shall dwell,
    Only thought aymes at the pleasure.

Thought therefore I will send thee,
  To take up the place for me;
  Long I will not after tary,   15
  There unseene thou maist be bold,
  Those faire wonders to behold,
  Which in them my hopes do cary.

Thought, see thou no place forbeare,
  Enter bravely every where,   20
  Seaze on all to her belonging;
  But if thou wouldst garded be,
  Fearing her beames, take with thee
  Strength of liking, rage of longing.

Thinke of that most gratefull time,   25
  When my leaping hart will clime,
  In my lips to have his biding,
  There those roses for to kisse,
  Which do breath a sugred blisse.
  Opening rubies, pearles deviding.   30

Thinke of my most Princely power,
  When I blessed shall devower,
  With my greedy licorous sences,
  Beauty, musicke, sweetnesse, love
  While she doth against me prove   35
  Her strong darts, but weake defences.

Thinke, thinke of those dalyings,
  When with Dovelike murmurings,
  With glad moning passed anguish,
  We change eyes, and hart for hart,   40
  Each to other do imparte,
  Joying till joy make us languish.

O my *Thought*, my thoughts surcease,
  Thy delights my woes increase,
  My life melts with too much thinking;   45
  Thinke no more but die in me,
  Till thou shalt revived be,
  At her lips my Nectar drinking.

93

O fate, O fault, O curse, child of my blisse,
  What sobs can give words grace my griefe to show?
  What inke is blacke inough to paint my wo?
Through me, wretch me, even *Stella* vexed is.
Yet truth (if Caitif's breath mighte call thee) this   5
  Witnesse with me, that my foule stumbling so,
  From carelesnesse did in no maner grow,
But confus'd with too much care did misse.
  And do I then my selfe this vaine scuse give?
I have (live and I know this) harmed thee,   10
Tho worlds quite me, shall I my selfe forgive?
Only with paines my paines thus eased be,
  That all thy hurts in my hart's wracke I reede;
  I cry thy sighs; my deere, thy teares I bleede.

94

Griefe, find the words, for thou hast made my braine
  So darke with misty vapors, which arise
  From out thy heavy mould, that inbent eyes
Can scarce discerne the shape of mine owne paine.
Do thou then (for thou canst) do thou complaine,   5
  For my poore soule, which now that sicknesse tries,
  Which even to sence, sence of it selfe denies,
Though harbengers of death lodge there his traine.
  Or if they love of plaint yet mine forbeares,
As of a caitife worthy so to die,   10
Yet waile thy selfe, and waile with causefull teares,
That though in wretchednesse thy life doth lie,
Yet growest more wretched then thy nature beares,
By being placed in such a wretch as I.

95

Yet sighs, deere sighs, indeede true friends you are,
  That do not leave your least friend at the wurst,
  But as you with my breast I oft have nurst,
So gratefull now you waite upon my care.
Faint coward joy no longer tarry dare,   5
  Seeing hope yeeld when this wo strake him furst:

Delight protests he is not for the accurst,
Though oft himselfe my mate-in-armes* he sware.
    Nay sorrow comes with such maine rage, that he
Kils his owne children, tears, finding that they   10
By love were made apt to consort with me.
Only true sighs, you do not go away,
    Thanke may you have for such a thankfull part,
    Thanke-worthiest yet when you shall breake my hart.

96

Thought, with good cause thou likest so well the night,
    Since kind or chance gives both one liverie,
    Both sadly blacke, both blackly darkned be,
Night bard from Sun, thou from thy owne Sunne's light;
Silence in both displaies his sullen might,   5
    Slow heavinesse in both holds one degree,
    That full of doubts, thou of perplexity;
Thy teares expresse night's native moisture right.
    In both a mazefull solitarinesse:
In night of sprites the gastly powers stur,   10
In thee or sprites or sprited gastlinesse:
But, but (alas) night's side the ods hath fur,
    For that at length yet doth invite some rest,
    Thou though still tired, yet still doost it detest.

97

Dian that faine would cheare her friend the *Night*,
    Shewes her oft at the full her fairest face,
    Bringing with her those starry Nimphs, whose chace
From heavenly standing hits each mortall wight.*
But ah poore *Night*, in love, with *Phœbus'* light,   5
    And endlesly dispairing of his grace,
    Her selfe (to shew no other joy hath place)
Silent and sad in mourning weedes doth dight:
    Even so (alas) a Lady* *Dian's* peere,
With choise delights and rarest company   10
Would faine drive cloudes from out my heavy cheere.
But wo is me, though joy it selfe were she,
    She could not shew my blind braine waies of joy,
    While I dispaire my Sunne's sight to enjoy.

98

Ah Bed, the field where joye's peace some do see,
    The field where all my thoughts to warre be traind,*
    How is thy grace by my strange fortune staind!
How thy lee shores by my sighes stormed be!
With sweete soft shades thou oft invitest me   5
    To steale some rest, but wretch I am constraind,
    (Spurd with love's spur, though gald and shortly raind
With care's hard hand)* to turne and tosse in thee.
    While the blacke horrors of the silent night,
    Paint woe's blacke face so lively to my sight,   10
That tedious leasure marks each wrinckled line:
    But when *Aurora* leades out *Phœbus*' dance,*
    Mine eyes then only winke, for spite perchance,
That worms should have their Sun, and I want mine.

99

When far spent Night perswades each mortall eye,
    To whom nor art nor nature graunteth light,
    To lay his then marke-wanting shafts of sight,
Clos'd with their quivers in sleep's armory;
With windowes ope then most my mind doth lie,   5
    Viewing the shape of darknesse and delight,
    Takes in that sad hue, which with th'inward night
Of his mazde powers keepes perfit harmony:
    But when birds charme, and that sweete aire, which is
Morne's messenger, with rose enameld skies   10
Cals each wight to salute the floure of blisse;
In tombe of lids then buried are mine eyes,
    Forst by their Lord, who is asham'd to find
    Such light in sense, with such a darkned mind.

100

O teares, no teares, but raine from beautie's skies,
    Making those Lillies and those Roses* grow,
    Which ay most faire, now more then most faire show,
While gracefull pitty beauty beautifies.
O honied sighs, which from that breast do rise,   5
    Whose pants do make unspilling creame to flow,*

Wing'd with whose breath, so pleasing *Zephires* blow,
As can refresh the hell where my soule fries.
  O plaints conserv'd in such a sugred phraise,
  That eloquence it selfe envies your praise,   10
While sobd out words a perfect Musike give.
  Such teares, sighs, plaints, no sorrow is, but joy:
  Or if such heavenly signes must prove annoy,
All mirth farewell, let me in sorrow live.

101

Stella is sicke, and in that sicke bed lies
Sweetnesse, which breathes and pants as oft as she:
And grace, sicke too, such fine conclusions tries,
That sicknesse brags it selfe best graced to be.
  Beauty is sicke, but sicke in so faire guise,   5
  That in that palenesse beautie's white we see;
  And joy, which is inseperate from those eyes;
Stella now learnes (strange case) to weepe in thee.
  Love moves thy paine, and like a faithfull page,
  As thy lookes sturre, runs up and downe to make   10
  All folkes prest at thy will thy paine to asswage
Nature with care sweates for her darling's sake,
    Knowing worlds passe, ere she enough can find
    Of such heaven stuffe, to cloath so heavenly mynde.

102

Where be those Roses gone, which sweetned so our eyes?
  Where those red cheeks, which oft with faire encrease did frame
  The height of honor in the kindly badge of shame?
Who hath the crimson weeds stolne from my morning skies?
How doth the colour vade of those vermillion dies,   5
  Which *Nature*' selfe did make, and selfe engraind the same?
  I would know by what right this palenesse overcame
That hue, whose force my hart still unto thraldome ties?
  Gallein's adoptive sonnes,* who by a beaten way
  Their judgements hackney on, the fault on sicknesse lay,   10
But feeling proofe makes me say they mistake it furre:
  It is but *Love*, which makes his paper perfit white
  To write therein more fresh the story of delight,
While beautie's reddest inke *Venus* for him doth sturre.

103

O happie *Tems*, that didst my *Stella* beare,
I saw thy selfe with many a smiling line
Upon thy cheerefull face, joye's livery weare:
While those faire planets on thy streames did shine.
    The bote for joy could not to daunce forbeare,   5
While wanton winds with beauties so devine
Ravisht, staid not, till in her golden haire
They did themselves (O sweetest prison) twine.
    And faine those *Æols*' youthes* there would their stay
Have made, but forst by *Nature* still to flie,   10
First did with puffing kisse those lockes display:
She so discheveld, blusht; from window I
    With sight thereof cride out; O faire disgrace,
    Let honor' selfe to thee graunt highest place.

104

Envious wits what hath bene mine offence,
    That with such poysonous care my lookes you marke,
    That to each word, nay sigh of mine you harke,
As grudging me my sorrowe's eloquence?
Ah, is it not enough, that I am thence,   5
    Thence, so farre thence, that scarcely any sparke
    Of comfort dare come to this dungeon darke,
Where rigrows exile lockes up all my sense?
    But if I by a happy window passe,
If I but stars upon mine armour beare,   10
Sicke, thirsty, glad (though but of empty glasse:)*
Your morall notes straight my hid meaning teare
    From out my ribs, and puffing prove that I
    Do *Stella* love. Fooles, who doth it deny?

Eleventh song

  'Who is it that this darke night,
  Underneath my window playneth?'
  It is one who from thy sight,
  Being (ah) exild, disdayneth
  Every other vulgar light.   5

[handwritten margin note: speaks again (unnamed?) in his mind?]

'Why, alas, and are you he?
Be not yet those fancies changed?'
Deere when you find change in me,
Though from me you be estranged,
Let my chaunge to ruine be.   10

'Well, in absence this will dy,
Leave to see, and leave to wonder.'
Absence sure will helpe, if I
Can learne, how my selfe to sunder
From what in my hart doth ly.   15

'But time will these thoughts remove:
Time doth worke what no man knoweth.'
Time doth as the subject prove,
With time still th' affection groweth
In the faithfull Turtle dove.*   20

'What if you new beauties see,
Will not they stir new affection?'
I will thinke theye pictures be,
(Image like of Saints' perfection)
Poorely counterfeting thee.   25

'But your reason's purest light,
Bids you leave such minds to nourish?'
Deere, do reason no such spite,
Never doth thy beauty florish
More then in my reason's sight.   30

'But the wrongs love beares, will make
Love at length leave undertaking.'
No, the more fooles it do shake,
In a ground of so firme making,
Deeper still they drive the stake.   35

'Peace, I thinke that some give eare:
Come no more, least I get anger.'
Blisse, I will my blisse forbeare,
Fearing (sweete) you to endanger,
But my soule shall harbour there.   40

'Well, be gone, be gone I say,
Lest that *Argus* eyes perceive you.'*

O unjustest fortune's sway,
Which can make me thus to leave you,
And from lowts to run away.   45

105

Unhappie sight, and hath she vanisht by
   So neere, in so good time, so free a place?
   Dead glasse, doost thou thy object so imbrace,
As what my hart still sees thou canst not spie?
I sweare by her I love and lacke, that I   5
   Was not in fault, who bent thy dazling race
   Onely unto the heav'n of *Stella's* face,
Counting but dust what in the way did lie.
   But cease mine eyes, your tears do witnesse well
That you, guiltlesse thereof, your Nectar mist: 10
Curst be the page from whome the bad torch fell,
Curst be the night which did your strife resist,
   Curst be the Cochman which did drive so fast,
   With no worse curse then absence makes me tast.

106

O absent presence *Stella* is not here;
   False flattering *Hope*, that with so faire a face,
   Bare me in hand, that in this Orphane place,
Stella, I say my *Stella*, should appeare.
What saist thou now, where is that dainty cheere   5
   Thou toldst mine eyes should helpe their famisht case?
   But thou art gone, now that selfe felt disgrace
Doth make me most to wish thy comfort neere.
   But heere I do store of faire Ladies meete,
   Who may with charme of conversation sweete,   10
Make in my heavy mould new thoughts to grow:
   Sure they prevaile as much with me, as he
   That bad his friend, but then new maim'd, to be
Mery with him, and not thinke of his woe.

107

Stella since thou so right a Princesse art
   Of all the powers which life bestowes on me,

That ere by them ought undertaken be,
They first resort unto that soueraigne part;
Sweete, for a while give respite to my hart,   5
   Which pants as though it still should leape to thee:
   And on my thoughts give thy Lieftenancy
To this great cause, which needs both use and art *
   And as a Queene, who from her presence sends
Whom she imployes, dismisse from thee my wit,   10
Till it have wrought what they owne will attends.
On servants' shame oft Maister's blame doth sit;
   O let not fooles in me thy workes reprove,
   And scorning say, 'See what it is to love.'

108

When *Sorrow* (using mine owne fier's might)
   Melts downe his lead into my boyling brest,
   Through that darke fornace to my hart opprest,
There shines a joy from thee my only light;
But soone as thought of thee breeds my delight,   5
   And my yong soule flutters to thee his nest,
   Most rude *Dispaire* my daily unbidden guest,
Clips streight my wings, streight wraps me in his night,
   And makes me then bow downe my head, and say,
Ah what doth *Phœbus*' gold that wretch availe,   10
Whom iron doores do keepe from use of day?
So strangely (alas) thy works in me prevaile,
   That in my woes for thee thou art my joy,
   And in my joyes for thee my only annoy.

THE DEFENCE OF POESIE*

When the right vertuous *Edward Wotton* and I were at the Emperor's Court together, wee gave our selves to learne horsemanship of *John Pietro Pugliano,* one that with great commendation had the place of an Esquire in his stable. And hee, according to the fertilnes of the Italian wit, did not onely afoord us the demonstration of his practise, but sought to enrich our mindes with the contemplations therein which hee thought most precious. But with none I remember mine eares were at any time more loden, then when (either angred with slowe paiment, or mooved with our learner-like admiration) he exercised his speech in the prayse of his facultie. Hee sayd, Souldiours were the noblest estate of mankinde, and horsemen the noblest of Souldiours. Hee sayde they were the Maisters of warre, and ornaments of peace; speedy goers, and strong abiders; triumphers both in Camps and Courts. Nay, to so unbeleeved a poynt hee proceeded, as that no earthly thing bred such wonder to a Prince as to be a good horseman. Skill of government was but a *Pedanteria* in comparison. Then would hee adde certaine prayses, by telling what a peerlesse beast a horse was; the onely serviceable Courtier without flattery, the beast of most beutie, faithfulnes, courage, and such more, that if I had not beene a peece of a Logician before I came to him, I think he would have perswaded mee to have wished my selfe a horse. But thus much at least with his no fewe words hee drave into me, that selfe-love is better then any guilding to make that seeme gorgious wherein our selves are parties. Wherein, if *Pugliano* his strong affection and weake arguments will not satisfie you, I wil give you a neerer example of my selfe, who (I knowe not by what mischance) in these my not old yeres and idelest times, having slipt into the title of a Poet, am provoked to say somthing unto you in the defence of that my unelected vocation, which if I handle with

more good will then good reasons, beare with me, sith the
scholler is to be pardoned that foloweth the steppes of his
Maister. And yet I must say that as I have just cause to make
a pittiful defence of poore Poetry, which from almost the
highest estimation of learning is fallen to be the laughing-   5
stocke of children; so have I need to bring some more
availeable proofes: sith the former is by no man barred of
his deserved credite, the silly latter hath had even the names
of Philosophers used to the defacing of it, with great danger
of civill war among the Muses. And first, truly to al them   10
that professing learning inveigh against Poetry, may justly be
objected, that they goe very neer to ungratfulnes, to seek to
deface that which, in the noblest nations and languages that
are knowne, hath been the first light-giver to ignorance, and
first Nurse, whose milk by little and little enabled them to   15
feed afterwards of tougher knowledges: and will they now
play the Hedghog that, being received into the den, drave
out his host?* or rather the Vipers', that with theyr birth kill
their Parents?* Let learned *Greece* in any of her manifold
Sciences be able to shew me one booke before *Musæus*,   20
Homer, and *Hesiod*,* all three nothing els but Poets. Nay,
let any historie be brought that can say any writers were
there before them, if they were not men of the same skil, as
Orpheus, Linus,* and some other are named: who, having
beene the first of that Country that made pens deliverers of   25
their knowledge to their posterity, may justly chalenge to bee
called their Fathers in learning: for not only in time they had
this priority (although in it self antiquity be venerable) but
went before them, as causes to drawe with their charming
sweetnes the wild untamed wits to an admiration of knowl-   30
edge. So as *Amphion* was sayde to move stones with his
Poetrie to build *Thebes*;* and *Orpheus* to be listened to by
beastes, indeed stony and beastly people.* So among the
Romans were *Livius Andronicus*, and *Ennius*.* So in the
Italian language the first that made it aspire to be a Treasure- 35
house of Science were the Poets *Dante, Boccace*, and
Petrarch. So in our English were *Gower* and *Chawcer*.

After whom, encouraged and delighted with theyr excellent fore-going, others have followed, to beautifie our mother
tongue, as wel in the same kinde as in other Arts. This did   40
so notably shewe it selfe, that the Phylosophers of *Greece*

durst not a long time appeare to the worlde but under the masks of Poets. So *Thales, Empedocles*, and *Parmenides** sange their naturall Phylosophie in verses: so did *Pythagoras* and *Phocylides** their morall counsells: so did *Tirteus** in war matters, and *Solon** in matters of policie: or rather, they, beeing Poets, dyd exercise their delightful vaine in those points of highest knowledge, which before them lay hid to the world. For that wise *Solon* was directly a Poet it is manifest, having written in verse the notable fable of the *Atlantick* Iland, which was continued by *Plato*.*

And truely, even *Plato*, whosoever well considereth, shall find that in the body of his work, though the inside and strength were Philosophy, the skinne as it were and beautie depended most of Poetrie: for all standeth upon Dialogues, wherein he faineth many honest Burgesses of *Athens* to speake of such matters that if they had been sette on the racke, they would never have confessed them. Besides, his poetical describing the circumstances of their meetings, as the well ordering of a banquet, the delicacie of a walke, with enterlacing meere tales, as *Gyges*' Ring,* and others, which who knoweth not to be flowers of Poetrie did never walke into *Apollo's* Garden.

And even Historiographers (although theyr lippes sounde of things doone, and veritie be written in theyr fore-heads) have been glad to borrow both fashion and perchance weight of Poets. So *Herodotus* entituled his Historie by the name of the nine Muses:* and both he and all the rest that followed him either stole or usurped of Poetrie their passionate describing of passions, the many particularities of battailes, which no man could affirme, or, if that be denied me, long Orations put in the mouthes of great Kings and Captaines, which it is certaine they never pronounced. So that, truely, neyther Phylosopher nor Historiographer coulde at the first have entred into the gates of populer judgements, if they had not taken a great pasport of Poetry, which in all Nations at this day, wher learning florisheth not, is plaine to be seene: in all which they have some feeling of Poetry. In *Turkie* besides their lawe-giving Divines, they have no other Writers but Poets. In our neighbour Countrey *Ireland* where truelie learning goeth very bare, yet are theyr Poets held in a devoute reverence. Even among the most barbarous and simple

Indians where no writing is, yet have they their Poets, who make and sing songs, which they call *Areytos*, both of theyr Auncestors deedes and praises of theyr Gods: a sufficient probabilitie that if ever learning come among them, it must be by having theyr hard dull wits softned and sharpened 5 with the sweete delights of Poetrie. For untill they find a pleasure in the exercises of the minde, great promises of much knowledge will little perswade them that knowe not the fruites of knowledge. In *Wales*, the true remnant of the auncient *Brittons*,* as there are good authorities to shewe 10 the long time they had Poets, which they called *Bardes*, so thorough all the conquests of *Romaines, Saxons, Danes*, and *Normans*, some of whom did seeke to ruine all memory of learning from among them, yet doo their Poets, even to this day, last; so as it is not more notable in soone beginning then 15 in long continuing. But since the Authors of most of our Sciences were the *Romans*, and before them the *Greekes*, let us a little stand uppon their authorities, but even so farre as to see what names they have given unto this now scorned skill. 20

Among the Romans a Poet was called *Vates*, which is as much as a Diviner, Fore-seer, or Prophet, as by his conjoyned wordes *Vaticinium* and *Vaticinari* is manifest: so heavenly a title did that excellent people bestow upon this hart-ravishing knowledge. And so farre were they carried into the admir- 25 ation thereof, that they thought in the chaunceable hitting uppon any such verses great foretokens of their following fortunes were placed. Whereupon grew the worde of *Sortes Virgilianae*, when, by suddaine opening *Virgil's* booke, they lighted upon any verse of hys making: whereof the histories 30 of the Emperors lives are full. As of *Albinus*, the Governour of our Iland, who in his childehoode mette with this verse,

Arma amens capio nec sat rationis in armis;*

and in his age performed it:* which although it were a very vaine and godles superstition, as also it was to think that 35 spirits were commaunded by such verses, whereupon this word Charmes, derived of *Carmina*, commeth* – so yet serveth it to shew the great reverence those wits were helde in. And altogether not without ground, since both the Oracles of *Delphos* and *Sibilla's* prophecies were wholy 40 delivered in verses. For that same exquisite observing of number and measure in words, and that high flying liberty of conceit proper to the Poet, did seeme to have some divine force in it.

And may not I presume a little further, to shew the reasonableness of this worde *Vates*? And that the holy *David's Psalmes* are a divine Poem? If I doo, I shall not do it without the testimonie of great learned men, both auncient and moderne: but even the name *Psalmes* will speake for mee, which, being interpreted, is nothing but songes. Then that it is fully written in meeter, as all learned Hebricians agree, although the rules be not yet fully found. Lastly and principally, his handeling his prophecy, which is meerely poetical. For what els is the awaking his musicall instruments; the often and free changing of persons; his notable *Prosopopeias*, when he maketh you, as it were, see God comming in his Maiestie; his telling of the beastes' joyfulnes, and hills leaping, but a heavenlie poesie, wherein almost hee sheweth himselfe a passionate lover of that unspeakable and everlasting beautie to be scene by the eyes of the minde, onely cleered by fayth? But truely nowe having named him, I feare mee I seeme to prophane that holy name, applying it to Poetrie, which is among us throwne downe to so ridiculous as estimation: but they that with quiet judgements will looke a little deeper into it, shall finde the end and working of it such, as beeing rightly applyed, deserveth not to bee scourged out of the Church of God.

But now, let us see how the *Greekes* named it, and howe they deemed of it. The *Greekes* called him a Poet, which name hath, as the most excellent, gone thorough other Languages. It commeth of this word *Poiein*, which is to make: wherein I know not, whether by lucke or wisedome, wee Englishmen have mette with the *Greekes* in calling him a Maker:* which name, how high and incomparable a title it is, I had rather were knowne by marking the scope of other Sciences then by my partiall allegation.

There is no Arte delivered to mankinde that hath not the workes of Nature for his principall object, without which they could not consist, and on which they so depend, as they become Actors and Players, as it were, of what Nature will have set forth. So doth the Astronomer looke upon the

starres, and, by that he seeth, setteth downe what order
Nature hath taken therein. So doe the Geometrician and
Arithmetician in their diverse sorts of quantities.* So doth
the Musitian in times* tel you which by nature agree, which
not. The naturall Philosopher thereon hath his name; and   5
the morrall Philosopher standeth upon the naturall vertues,
vices, and passions of man; and 'followe *Nature*' (saith hee)
'therein, and thou shalt not erre.' The Lawyer sayth what
men have determined. The Historian what men have done.
The Grammarian speaketh onely of the rules of speech; and   10
the Rethorician and Logitian, considering what in nature
will soonest prove and perswade, thereon give artificial rules,
which still are compassed within the circle of a question,
according to the proposed matter. The Phisition waigheth
the nature of a man's bodie, and the nature of things helpeful   15
or hurtefull unto it. And the Metaphisick, though it be in the
seconde and abstract notions, and therefore be counted
supernaturall, yet doth hee indeede builde upon the depth of
nature. Onely the Poet, disdayning to be tied to any such
subjection, lifted up with the vigor of his owne intention,   20
dooth growe in effect into another nature, in making things
either better then Nature bringeth forth, or, quite anewe;
formes such as never were in nature, as the *Heroes, Demi-*
*gods, Cyclops, Chimeras, Furies,** and such like: so as hee
goeth hand in hand with *Nature*, not inclosed within the   25
narrow warrant of her guifts, but freely ranging onely within
the Zodiack of his owne wit.

Nature never set forth the earth in so rich tapistry as divers
Poets have done, neither with so plesant rivers, fruitful trees,
sweet smelling flowers, nor whatsoever els may make the too   30
much loved earth more lovely. Her world is brasen, the Poets
only deliver a golden. But let those things alone and goe to
man, for whom as the other things are, so it seemeth in him
her uttermost cunning is imployed, and knowe whether shee
have brought foorth so true a lover as *Theagines,** so con-   35
stant a friende as *Pylades,** so valiant a man as *Orlando,**
so right a Prince as *Xenophon's Cyrus,** so excellent a man
every way as *Virgil's Aeneas*: neither let this be jestingly
conceived, because the works of the one be essentiall, the
other, in imitation or fiction; for any understanding knoweth   40
the skil of the Artificer standeth in that *Idea* or fore-conceite

of the work, and not in the work it selfe.* And that the Poet
hath that *Idea* is manifest, by delivering them forth in such
excellencie as hee hath imagined them. Which delivering
forth also is not wholie imaginative, as we are wont to say
by them that build Castles in the ayre: but so farre substan- 5
tially it worketh, not onely to make a *Cyrus*, which had been
but a particuler excellencie, as *Nature* might have done, but
to bestow a *Cyrus* upon the worlde, to make many *Cyrus's*,
if they wil learne aright why and how that Maker made him.

Neyther let it be deemed too sawcie a comparison to 10
ballance the highest poynt of mans wit with the efficacie of
Nature: but rather give right honor to the heavenly Maker
of that maker, who, having made man to his owne likenes,
set him beyond and over all the workes of that second
nature,* which in nothing hee sheweth so much as in Poetrie, 15
when with the force of a divine breath he bringeth things
forth far surpassing her dooings, with no small argument to
the incredulous of that first accursed fall of *Adam*:* sith our
erected wit maketh us know what perfection is, and yet our
infected will keepeth us from reaching unto it. But these 30
arguments wil by fewe be understood, and by fewer granted.
Thus much (I hope) will be given me, that the *Greekes* with
some probabilitie of reason gave him the name above all
names of learning. Now let us goe to a more ordinary
opening of him, that the trueth may be more palpable: and 25
so I hope, though we get not so unmatched a praise as the
Etimologie of his names wil grant, yet his very description,
which no man will denie, shall not justly be barred from a
principall commendation.

Poesie therefore is an arte of imitation, for so *Aristotle* 30
termeth it in his word *Mimesis*, that is to say a representing,
counterfetting, or figuring foorth: to speake metaphorically,
a speaking picture: with this end, to teach and delight. Of
this have beene three severall kindes.

The chiefe both in antiquitie and excellencie were they 35
that did imitate the inconceivable excellencies of GOD. Such
were *David* in his *Psalmes, Salomon* in his *Song of Songs* in
his *Ecclesiastes*, and *Proverbs, Moses* and *Debora* in theyr
Hymnes,* and the writer of *Job*; which, beside other, the
learned *Emanuell Tremelius* and *Franciscus Junius* doe enti- 40
tle the poeticall part of the Scripture.* Against these none

will speake that hath the Holie Ghost in due holy reverence. In this kinde, though in a full wrong divinitie, were *Orpheus, Amphion, Homer* in his Hymnes,* and many other, both *Greekes* and *Romaines*; and his Poesie must be used, by whosoever will follow *Saint James* his counsell, in singing Psalmes when they are merry:* and I knowe is used with the fruite of comfort by some, when, in sorrowfull pangs of their death-bringing sinnes, they find the consolation of the never-leaving goodnesse.*

The second kinde is of them that deale with matters Philosophicall; eyther morall, as *Tirteus, Phocilides*, and *Cato*;* or naturall, as *Lucretius*,* and *Virgil's Georgicks*;* or Astronomicall, as *Manilius* and *Pontanus*;* or historical, as *Lucan*:* which who mislike, the faulte is in their judgements, quite out of taste, and not in the sweet foode of sweetly uttered knowledge.

But because thys second sorte is wrapped within the folde of the proposed subject, and takes not the course of his owne invention, whether they properly be Poets or no let Gramarians dispute: and goe to the thyrd, indeed right Poets, of whom chiefly this question ariseth; betwixt whom and these second is such a kinde of difference as betwixt the meaner sort of Painters (who counterfet onely such faces as are sette before them) and the more excellent, who, having no law but wit, bestow that in cullours upon you which is fittest for the eye to see: as the constant though lamenting looke of *Lucretia*, when she punished in her selfe an others fault;* wherein he painteth not *Lucretia* whom he never sawe, but painteth the outwarde beauty of such a vertue. For these third be they which most properly do imitate to teach and delight, and to imitate borrow nothing of what is, hath been, or shall be: but range, onely rayned with learned discretion, into the divine consideration of what may be, and should be. These bee they that, as the first and most noble sorte, may justly bee termed *Vates*, so these are waited on in the excellent languages and best understandings, with the fore described name of Poets: for these indeede doo meerely make to imitate, and imitate both to delight and teach, and delight to move men to take that goodnes in hande, which without delight they would flye as from a stranger; and teach, to make them know that goodnes whereunto they are mooved, which being the noblest scope to which ever any learning was directed, yet want there not idle tongues to barke at them.

These be subdivided into sundry more speciall denominations. The most notable bee the Heroick, Lirick, Tragick, Comick, Satirick, Iambick, Elegiack, Pastorall, and certaine others, some of these being termed according to the matter they deale with, some by the sorts of verses they liked best to write in, for indeede the greatest part of Poets have apparelled their poeticall inventions in that numbrous kinde of writing which is called verse: indeed but apparelled, verse being but an ornament and no cause to Poetry, sith there have beene many most excellent Poets that never versified, and now swarme many versifiers that neede never aunswere to the name of Poets. For *Xenophon*, who did imitate so excellently as to give us *effigiem iusti imperii*, the portraiture of a just Empire under the name of *Cyrus* (as *Cicero* sayth of him), made therein an absolute heroicall Poem;* so did *Heliodorus* in his sugred invention of that picture of love in *Theagines* and *Chariclea*;* and yet both these writ in Prose: which I speak to shew that it is not riming and versing that maketh a Poet, no more then a long gowne maketh an Advocate, who though he pleaded in armor should be an Advocate and no Souldier. But it is that fayning notable images of vertues, vices, or what else, with that delightfull teaching, which must be the right describing note to know a Poet by: although indeed the Senate of Poets hath chosen verse as their fittest rayment, meaning, as in matter they passed all in all, so in maner to goe beyond them: not speaking (table talke fashion or like men in a dreame) words as they chanceably fall from the mouth, but peyzing each sillable of each worde by just proportion according to the dignitie of the subject.

Nowe therefore it shall not bee amisse first to waigh this latter sort of Poetrie by his works, and then by his partes; and if in neyther of these Anatomies hee be condemnable, I hope wee shall obtaine a more favourable sentence. This purifing of wit, this enritching of memory, enabling of judgment, and enlarging of conceyt, which commonly we call learning, under what name soever it com forth, or to what immediat end soever it be directed, the final end is to

lead and draw us to as high a perfection as our degenerate
soules, made worse by theyr clayey lodgings, can be capable
of. This, according to the inclination of man, bred many
formed impressions. For some that thought this felicity
principally to be gotten by knowledge, and no knowledge to   5
be so high and heavenly as acquaintance with the starres,
gave themselves to Astronomie; others, perswading themselves to be Demigods* if they knewe the causes of things,
became naturall and supernaturall Philosophers; some an
admirable delight drew to Musicke; and some the certainty   10
of demonstration to the Mathematickes: but all, one and
other, having this scope – to knowe, and by knowledge to
lift up the mind from the dungeon of the body to the
enjoying his owne divine essence.* But when by the ballance
of experience it was found that the Astronomer looking to   15
the starres might fall into a ditch, that the enquiring Philosopher might be blinde in himselfe, and the Mathematician
might draw foorth a straight line with a crooked hart; then
loe, did proofe, the over ruler of opinions, make manifest
that all these are but serving sciences, which as they have   20
each a private end in themselves, so yet are they all directed
to the highest end of the mistres *Knowledge,* by the *Greekes*
called *Arkitecktonike,* which stands, (as I thinke) in the
knowledge of a man's selfe, in the ethicke and politick
consideration, with the end of well dooing and not of well   25
knowing onely; even as the Sadler's next end is to make a
good saddle, but his farther end to serve a nobler facultie,
which is horsemanship; so the horseman's to souldiery, and
the Souldier not onely to have the skill, but to performe the
practise of a Souldier: so that, the ending end of all earthly   30
learning being vertuous action, those skilles that most serve
to bring forth that have a most just title to bee Princes over
all the rest. Wherein, if wee can shewe, the Poet is worthy to
have it before any other Competitors; among whom as
principall challengers step forth the morrall Philosophers,   35
whom, me thinketh, I see comming towards mee with a
sullen gravity, as though they could not abide vice by day
light, rudely clothed for to witnes outwardly their contempt
of outward things, with bookes in their hands agaynst glory,
whereto they sette theyr names, sophistically speaking   40
against subtility, and angry with any man in whom they see

the foule fault of anger: these men casting larges as they goe
of Definitions, Divisions, and Distinctions,* with a scornefull
interogative doe soberly aske whether it bee possible to finde
any path so ready to leade a man to vertue as that which
teacheth what vertue is? and teacheth it not onely by 5
delivering forth his very being, his causes, and effects; but
also by making known his enemie vice, which must be
destroyed, and his combersome servant Passion, which must
be maistered; by shewing the generalities that contayneth it,
and the specialities that are derived from it; lastly, by 10
playne setting downe, how it extendeth it selfe out of the
limits of a mans own little world* to the government of
families, and maintayning of publique societies.

The Historian scarcely giueth leysure to the Moralist to
say so much, but that he, loden with old Mouse-eaten 15
records, authorising himselfe (for the most part) upon other
histories, whose greatest authorities are built upon the
notable foundation of Heare-say, having much a-doe to
accord differing Writers and to pick trueth out of partiality,
better acquainted with a thousande yeeres ago then with the 20
present age, and yet better knowing how this world goeth
then how his owne wit runneth, curious for antiquities and
inquisitive of novelties, a wonder to young folkes and a
tyrant in table talke, denieth, in a great chafe, that any man
for teaching of vertue, and vertuous actions, is comparable 25
to him. I am *Testis temporum, lux veritatis, vita memoriae,
magistra vitae, nuntia vetustatis.**

'The Phylosopher' (sayth hee) 'teacheth a disputative
vertue, but I doe an active: his vertue is excellent in the
dangerlesse Academie of *Plato*, but mine sheweth foorth her 30
honorable face in the battailes of *Marathon, Pharsalia,
Poitiers*, and *Agincourt*.* Hee teacheth vertue by certaine
abstract considerations, but I onely bid you follow the footing
of them that have gone before you. Olde-aged experience
goeth beyond the fine-witted Phylosopher, but I give the 35
experience of many ages. Lastly, if he make the song-booke,
I put the learners hande to the lute: and if hee be the guide, I
am the light.'

Then woulde hee alledge you innumerable examples,
conferring storie by storie, how much the wisest Senatours 40
and Princes haue beene directed by the credite of history,*

as *Brutus, Alphonsus* of *Aragon*,* (and who not, if need
bee). At length the long lyne of theyr disputation maketh a
poynt in thys, that the one giveth the precept, and the other
the example.

Nowe, whom shall wee finde (sith the question standeth
for the highest forme in the Schoole of learning) to bee
Moderator? Trulie, as mee seemeth, the Poet; and if not a
Moderator, even the man that ought to carrie the title from
them both, and much more from all other serving sciences.
Therefore compare we the Poet with the Historian, and with
the Morrall Phylosopher, and, if hee goe beyond them both,
no other humaine skill can match him. For as for the Divine,
with all reverence it is ever to be excepted, not only for
having his scope as far beyonde any of these as eternitie
exceedeth a moment, but even for passing each of these in
themselves. And for the Lawyer, though *Ius* bee the Daughter
of *Justice*, and Justice the chiefe of Vertues,* yet because hee
seeketh to make men good rather *Formidine poenae* then
Virtutis amore, or, to say righter, dooth not indevour to
make men good, but that their evill hurt not others, having
no care, so hee be a good Cittizen, how bad a man he be.
Therefore, as our wickednesse maketh him necessarie, and
necessitie maketh him honorable, so is hee not in the deepest
trueth to stande in rancke with these who all indevour to
take naughtines away, and plant goodnesse even in the
secretest cabinet of our soules. And these foure are all that
any way deale in that consideration of mens manners, which
beeing the supreme knowledge, they that best breed it
deserve the best commendation.

The Philosopher therefore and the Historian are they
which would win the gole, the one by precept, the other by
example. But both not having both, doe both halte. For the
Philosopher, setting downe with thorny argument the bare
rule, is so hard of utterance, and so mistie to bee conceived,
that one that hath no other guide but him shall wade in him
till hee be olde before he shall finde sufficient cause to bee
honest: for his knowledge standeth so upon the abstract and
generall, that happie is that man who may understand him,
and more happie that can applye what hee dooth understand.
On the other side, the Historian, wanting the precept, is so
tyed, not to what shoulde bee but to what is, to the particuler

truth of things and not to the general reason of things, that hys example draweth no necessary consequence, and therefore a lesse fruitfull doctrine.

Nowe dooth the peerelesse Poet performe both: for whatsoever the Philosopher sayth shoulde be doone, hee giveth a perfect picture of it in some one by whom hee presupposeth it was doone. So as hee coupleth the generall notion with the particuler example. A perfect picture I say, for hee yeeldeth to the powers of the minde an image of that whereof the Philosopher bestoweth but a wordish description: which dooth neyther strike, pierce, nor possesse the sight of the soule so much as that other doth.

For as in outward things, to a man that had never seene an Elephant or a Rinoceros, who should tell him most exquisitely all theyr shapes, cullour, bignesse, and perticular markes, or of a gorgeous Pallace the Architecture, with declaring the full beauties, might well make the hearer able to repeate, as it were by rote, all hee had heard, yet should never satisfie his inward conceits with being witnes to it selfe of a true lively knowledge: but the same man, as soone as hee might see those beasts well painted, or the house wel in moddel, should straightwaies grow, without need of any description, to a judicial comprehending of them: so no doubt the Philosopher with his learned definition, bee it of vertue, vices, matters of publick policie or private government, replenisheth the memory with many infallible grounds of wisdom, which, notwithstanding, lye darke before the imaginative and judging powre, if they bee not illuminated or figured foorth by the speaking picture of Poesie.

*Tullie** taketh much paynes, and many times not without poeticall helpes, to make us knowe the force love of our Countrey hath in us. Let us but heare old *Anchises* speaking in the middest of Troye's flames,* or see *Ulysses* in the fulnes of all *Calipso's* delights bewayle his absence from barraine and beggerly *Ithaca.** Anger, the *Stoicks* say, was a short madnes: let but *Sophocles* bring you *Ajax* on a stage, killing and whipping Sheepe and Oxen, thinking them the Army of *Greeks,** with theyr Chiefetaines *Agamemnon* and *Menelaus,** and tell mee if you have not a more familiar insight into anger then finding in the Schoolemen his *Genus* and Difference. See whether wisdome and temperance in *Ulysses** and *Diomedes*,* valure in *Achilles*,* friendship in *Nisus* and *Euryalus** even to an ignoraunt man carry not an apparent shyning: and, contrarily, the remorse of conscience in *Oedipus*,* the soone repenting pride of *Agamemnon*,* the selfe-devouring crueltie in his Father *Atreus*,* the violence of ambition in the two *Theban* brothers,* the sowre-sweetnes of revenge in *Medea*,* and, to fall lower, the *Terentian Gnato** *and our Chaucer's Pandar** so exprest that we nowe use their names to signifie their trades: and finally, all vertues, vices, and passions so in their own naturall seates layd to the viewe, that wee seeme not to heare of them, but cleerly to see through them. But even in the most excellent determination of goodnes, what Philosopher's counsell can so redily direct a Prince, as the fayned *Cyrus* in *Xenophon*? or a vertuous man in all fortunes, as *Aeneas* in *Virgill*? or a whole Common-wealth, as the way of Sir *Thomas More's Eutopia*?* I say the way, because where Sir *Thomas More* erred, it was the fault of the man and not of the Poet, for that way of patterning a Common-wealth was most absolute, though hee perchaunce hath not so absolutely perfourmed it: for the question is, whether the fayned image of Poesie or the regular instruction of Philosophy hath the more force in teaching: wherein if the Philosophers have more rightly shewed themselves Philosophers then the Poets have obtained to the high top of their profession, as in truth,

> *Mediocribus esse poetis,*
> *Non Di, non homines, non concessere Columnae,**

it is, I say againe, not the fault of the Art, but that by fewe men that Arte can bee accomplished. Certainly, even our Saviour Christ could as well have given the morrall common places of uncharitablnes and humblenes as the divine narration of *Dives* and *Lazarus*;* or of disobedience and mercy, as that heavenly discourse of the lost Child and the gratious Father;* but that hys through-searching wisdom knewe the estate of *Dives*, burning in hell, and of *Lazarus* being in *Abraham's* bosome, would more constantly (as it were) inhabit both the memory and judgment. Truly, for my selfe, mee seemes I see before my eyes the lost Childe's disdainefull prodigality, turned to envie a Swine's dinner: which by the learned Divines are thought not historicall acts, but instructing Parables. For conclusion, I say the Philosopher teacheth, but he teacheth obscurely, so as the learned onely can understande him, that is to say, he teacheth them that are already taught; but the Poet is the foode for the tenderest stomacks, the Poet is indeed the right Popular Philosopher. 5 Whereof *Æsop's* tales give good proofe: whose pretty Allegories, stealing under the formall tales of beastes, make many, more beastly then beasts, begin to heare the sound of vertue from these dumbe speakers.

But now may it be alleged that if this imagining of matters 10 be so fitte for the imagination, then must the Historian needs surpasse, who bringeth you images of true matters, such as indeede were doone, and not such as fantastically or falsely may be suggested to have been doone. Truely, *Aristotle* himselfe, in his discourse of Poesie,* plainely determineth 15 this question, saying that Poetry is *Philosophoteron* and *Spoudaioteron*, that is to say, it is more Philosophicall and more studiously serious then history. His reason is, because Poesie dealeth with *Katholou*, that is to say, with the universall consideration; and the history with *Kathekaston*, 20 the perticuler: 'nowe', sayth he, 'the universall wayes what is fit to bee sayd or done, eyther in likelihood or necessity, (which the Poesie considereth in his imposed names), and the particuler onely marks whether *Alcibiades* did, or suffered, this or that.' Thus farre *Aristotle*: which reason of his 25 (as all his) is most full of reason. For indeed, if the question were whether it were better to have a perticular acte truly or falsly set down, there is no doubt which is to be chosen, no more then whether you had rather have *Vespasian's** picture right as hee was, or at the Painter's pleasure nothing resem- 30 bling. But if the question be for your owne use and learning, whether it be better to have it set downe as it should be, or as it was, then certainely is more doctrinable the fained *Cyrus* in *Xenophon* then the true *Cyrus* in *Justine*,* and the fayned *Aeneas* in *Virgil* then the right *Aeneas* in *Dares* 35 *Phrygius.** As to a Lady that desired to fashion her countenance to the best grace, a Painter should more benefite her to portraite a most sweet face, wryting *Canidia* upon it, then to paynt *Canidia* as she was, who, *Horace* sweareth,* was ful ill favoured. 40

If the Poet doe his part a-right, he will shew you in

Tantalus, * *Atreus*, and such like, nothing that is not to be shunned; in *Cyrus, Aeneas, Ulysses*, each thing to be followed; where the Historian, bound to tell things as things were, cannot be liberall (without hee will be poeticall) of a perfect patterne, but, as in *Alexander* or *Scipio** himselfe, shew dooings, some to be liked, some to be misliked. And then how will you discerne what to followe but by your owne discretion, which you had without reading *Quintus Curtius*?* And whereas a man may say, though in uniuersal consideration of doctrine the Poet prevaileth, yet that the historie, in his saying such a thing was done, doth warrant a man more in that hee shall follow, the aunswere is manifest, that if hee stande upon that 'was' – as if hee should argue, because it rayned yesterday, therefore it shoulde rayne to day – then indeede it hath some advantage to a grose conceite; but if he know an example onlie informes a conjectured likelihood, and so goe by reason, the Poet doth so farre exceede him, as hee is to frame his example to that which is most reasonable, be it in warlike, politick, or private matters, where the Historian in his bare 'was' hath many times that which wee call fortune to over-rule the best wisedome. Manie times he must tell events whereof he can yeelde no cause: or, if hee doe, it must be poetically.

For that a fayned example hath as much force to teach as a true example (for as for to move; it is cleere, sith the fayned may bee tuned to the highest key of passion), let us take one example wherein a Poet and a Historian doe concur. *Herodotus* and *Justine* do both testifie that *Zopirus*, King *Darius'* faithfull servaunt, seeing his Maister long resisted by the rebellious *Babilonians*, fayned himselfe in extreame disgrace of his King: for verifying of which, he caused his own nose and eares to be cut off: and so flying to the *Babylonians*, was received, and for his knowne valour so far credited, that hee did finde meanes to deliver them over to *Darius*. Much like matter doth *Livie* record of *Tarquinius* and his sonne.* *Xenophon* excellently faineth such another strategeme, performed by *Abradates* in *Cyrus* behalfe. Now would I fayne know, if occasion bee presented unto you to serve your Prince by such an honest dissimulation, why you doe not as well learne it of *Xenophon's* fiction as of the others' verity: and truely so much the better, as you shall save your nose by the bargaine; for *Abradates* did not counterfet so far. So then the best of the Historian is subject to the Poet; for whatsoever action, or faction, whatsoever counsell, pollicy, or warre strategem the Historian is bound to recite, that may the Poet (if he list) with his imitation make his own; beautifying it 5 both for further teaching, and more delighting, as it pleaseth him: having all, from *Dante* his heaven to hys hell,* under the authoritie of his penne. Which if I be asked what Poets have done so, as I might well name some, yet say I, and say againe, I speak of the Arte, and not of the Artificer. 10

Nowe, to that which commonly is attributed to the prayse of histories, in respect of the notable learning is gotten by marking the successe, as though therein a man should see vertue exalted and vice punished. Truely that commendation is peculiar to Poetrie, and farre of from History. For indeede 15 Poetrie ever setteth vertue so out in her best cullours, making Fortune her wel-wayting hand-mayd, that one must needs be enamored of her. Well may you see *Ulisses* in a storme, and in other hard plights; but they are but exercises of patience and magnanimitie, to make them shine the more in the neere- 20 following prosperitie. And of the contrarie part, if evill men come to the stage, they ever goe out (as the Tragedie Writer answered to one that misliked the shew of such persons) so manacled as they little animate folkes to followe them. But the Historian, beeing captived to the trueth of a foolish 25 world, is many times a terror from well dooing, and an incouragement to unbrideled wickednes.

For see wee not valiant *Miltiades* rot in his fetters?* The just *Phocion* and the accomplished *Socrates* put to death like Traytors?* The cruell *Severus* live prosperously? The excel- 30 lent *Severus** miserably murthered? *Sylla* and *Marius** dying in theyr beddes? *Pompey* and *Cicero* slain then when they would have thought exile a happinesse? See wee not vertuous *Cato** driven to kyll himselfe? and rebell *Cæsar* so advaunced that his name yet, after 1600 yeares, lasteth in 35 the highest honor? And marke but even *Cæsar's* own words of the fore-named *Sylla* (who in that onely did honestly, to put downe his dishonest tyrannie), *Literas nescivit*, as if want of learning caused him to doe well. Hee meant it not by Poetrie, which, not content with earthly plagues, deviseth 40 new punishments in hel for Tyrants: nor yet by Philosophie, which teacheth *Occidendos esse*; but no doubt by skill in Historie, for that indeede can affoord your *Cipselus, Periander, Phalaris, Dionysius*,* and I know not how many more of the same kennell, that speede well enough in theyr abhominable injustice or usurpation. I conclude, therefore, that hee excelleth Historie, not onely in furnishing the minde with knowledge, but in setting it forward to that which deserveth to be called and accounted good: which setting forward, and moving to wel-doing, indeed setteth the Lawrell crowne upon the Poet as victorious, not onely of the Historian, but over the Phylosopher, howsoever in teaching it may bee questionable.

For suppose it be granted (that which I suppose with great reason may be denied) that the Philosopher, in respect of his methodical proceeding, doth teach more perfectly then the Poet, yet do I thinke that no man is so much *Philophilosophos* as to compare the Philosopher, in moving, with the Poet.

And that moving is of a higher degree then teaching, it may by this appeare, that it is wel nigh the cause and the effect of teaching. For who will be taught, if hee bee not moved with desire to be taught? and what so much good doth that teaching bring forth (I speak still of morrall doctrine) as that it moveth one to doe that which it dooth teach? for, as *Aristotle* sayth, it is not *Gnosis* but *Praxis* must be the fruit. And howe *Praxis* cannot be, without being moved to practise, it is no hard matter to consider.

The Philosopher sheweth you the way, hee informeth you of the particularities, as well of the tediousnes of the way, as of the pleasant lodging you shall have when your journey is ended, as of the many by-turnings that may divert you from your way. But this is to no man but to him that will read him, and read him with attentive, studious painfulnes. Which constant desire, whosoever hath in him, hath already past halfe the hardnes of the way, and therefore is beholding to the Philosopher but for the other halfe. Nay truely, learned men have learnedly thought that where once reason hath so much over-mastred passion as that the minde hath a free desire to doe well, the inward light each minde hath in it selfe is as good as a Philosopher's booke; seeing in nature we know it is wel to doe well, and what is well and what is evill, although not in the words of Arte which Philosophers bestowe upon us. For out of naturall conceit the Philosophers drew it; but to be moved to doe that which we know, or to be moved with desire to knowe, *Hoc opus, hic labor est.*

Nowe therein of all Sciences (I speak still of humane, and according to the humaine conceits) is our Poet the Monarch. For he doth not only show the way, but giveth so sweete a prospect into the way, as will intice any man to enter into it. Nay, he doth, as if your journey should lye through a fayre vineyard, at the first give you a cluster of grapes, that, full of that taste, you may long to passe further. He beginneth not with obscure definitions, which must blur the margent with interpretations, and load the memory with doubtfulnesse; but hee commeth to you with words sent in delightfull proportion, either accompanied with, or prepared for, the well inchaunting skill of Musicke; and with a tale forsooth he commeth unto you, with a tale which holdeth children from play, and old men from the chimney corner. And, pretending no more, doth intende the winning of the mind from wickednesse to vertue: even as the childe is often brought to take most wholsom things by hiding them in such other as have a pleasant tast: which, if one should beginne to tell them the nature of the *Aloes* or *Rubarb** they shoulde receive, woulde sooner take their Phisicke at their eares then at their mouth. So is it in men (most of which are childish in the best things, till they bee cradled in their graves): glad they will be heare the tales of *Hercules, Achilles, Cyrus,* and *Aeneas*; and, hearing them, must needs heare the right description of wisdom, valure, and justice; which, if they had been barely, that is to say Philosophically, set out, they would sweare they bee brought to schoole againe.

That imitation; whereof Poetry is, hath the most conveniency to Nature of all other, in so much that, as *Aristotle* sayth, those things which in themselves are horrible, as cruell battailes, unnaturall monsters, are made in poeticall imitation delightfull. Truely, I have knowen men, that even with reading *Amadis de Gaule** (which God knoweth wanteth much of a perfect Poesie) have found their harts moved to the exercise of courtesie, liberalitie, and especially courage. Who readeth *Aeneas* carrying olde *Anchises* on his back,* that wisheth not it were his fortune to performe so excellent

an acte? Whom doe not the words of *Turnus* move? (the tale
of *Turnus* having planted his image in the imagination):

> *Fugientem haec terra videbit?*
> *Usque adeone mori miserum est?**

Where the Philosophers, as they scorne to delight, so must
they bee content little to move, saving wrangling whether
Vertue bee the chiefe or the onely good, whether the contem-
plative or the active life doe excell: which *Plato* and *Boethius*
well knew, and therefore made Mistres *Philosophy* very
often borrow the masking rayment of Poesie. For even those
harde harted evill men who thinke vertue a schoole name,
and knowe no other good but *indulgere genio*, and therefore
despise the austere admonitions of the Philosopher, and feele
not the inward reason they stand upon, yet will be content
to be delighted, which is al the good felow Poet seemeth to
promise; and so steale to see the forme of goodnes (which
seene they cannot but love) ere themselves be aware, as if
they tooke a medicine of Cherries.* Infinite proofes of the
strange effects of this poeticall invention might be alleged;
onely two shall serve, which are so often remembred, as I
thinke all men knowe them.

The one of *Menenius Agrippa*,* who, when the whole
people of *Rome** had resolutely devided themselves from the
Senate, with apparant shew of utter ruine, though hee were
(for that time) an excellent Oratour, came not among them
upon trust of figurative speeches or cunning insinuations;
and much lesse with farre fet Maximes of Phylosophie,
which (especially if they were Platonick they must have
learned Geometrie before they could well have conceived;*
but forsooth he behaves himselfe like a homely and familiar
Poet. Hee telleth them a tale, that there was a time when all
the parts of the body made a mutinous conspiracie against
the belly, which they thought devoured the fruits of each
others' labour: they concluded they would let so unprofitable
a spender starve. In the end, to be short, (for the tale is
notorious, and as notorious that it was a tale) with punishing
the belly they plagued themselves. This applied by him
wrought such effect in the people, as I never read that ever
words brought forth but then so suddaine and so good an
alteration; for upon reasonable conditions a perfect recon-

cilement ensued.* The other is of *Nathan* the Prophet, who
when the holie *David* had so far forsaken God as to confirme
adulterie with murther, when hee was to doe the tenderest
office of a friende, in laying his owne shame before his eyes,
sent by God to call againe so chosen a servant, how doth he 5
it but by telling of a man whose beloved Lambe was
ungratefullie taken from his bosome?* The applycation most
divinely true, but the discourse it selfe fayned; which made
David (I speake of the second and instrumentall cause)* as
in a glasse to see his own filthines, as that heavenly *Psalme* 10
of mercie* wel testifieth.

By these, therefore, examples and reasons, I think it may
be manifest that the Poet, with that same hand of delight,
doth draw the mind more effectually then any other Arte
doth: and so a conclusion not unfitlie ensueth, that as vertue 15
is the most excellent resting place for all worldlie learning to
make his end of, so Poetrie, beeing the most familiar to teach
it, and most princelie to move towards it, in the most
excellent work is the most excellent workman. But I am
content not onely to decipher him by his workes (although 20
works in commendation or disprayse must ever holde an
high authority), but more narrowly will examine his parts:
so that (as in a man) though al together may carry a presence
ful of majestie and beautie, perchance in some one defectious
peece we may find a blemish. Now in his parts, kindes, or 25
Species (as you list to terme them), it is to be noted that some
Poesies have coupled together two or three kindes, as Tragicall and Comicall, wher-upon is risen the Tragicomicall.
Some in the like manner have mingled Prose and Verse,
as *Sanazzar** and *Boethius.** Some have mingled matters 30
Heroicall and Pastorall. But that commeth all to one in this
question, for, if severed they be good, the conjunction cannot
be hurtfull. Therefore perchaunce forgetting some, and leaving some as needlesse to be remembred, it shall not be amisse
in a worde to cite the speciall kindes, to see what faults may 35
be found in the right use of them.

Is it then the Pastorall Poem which is misliked? (For
perchance, where the hedge is lowest they will soonest leape
over). Is the poore pype* disdained, which sometime out of
Melibeus' mouth can shewe the miserie of people under hard 40
Lords or ravening Souldiours? And again, by *Titirus*, what

blessednes is derived to them that lye lowest from the
goodnesse of them that sit highest?* Sometimes under the
prettie tales of Wolves and Sheepe, can include the whole
considerations of wrong dooing and patience; sometimes
shew that contention for trifles can get but a trifling victorie.   5
Where perchaunce a man may see that even *Alexander* and
Darius, when they strave who should be Cocke of thys
world's dunghill, the benefit they got was that the after-livers
may say,

> *Haec memini et victum frustra contendere Thirsim:*   10
> *Ex illo Coridon, Coridon est tempore nobis.**

Or is it the lamenting Elegiack, which in a kinde hart
would move rather pitty then blame, who bewailes with the
great Philosopher *Heraclitus** the weakenes of mankind and
the wretchednes of the world: who surely is to be praysed,   15
either for compassionate accompanying just causes of lam-
entation, or for rightly paynting out how weake be the
passions of wofulnesse? Is it the bitter but wholsome Iambick,* which rubs the galled minde, in making shame the
trumpet of villanie with bolde and open crying out against   20
naughtines? Or the Satirick, who

> *Omne vafer vitium ridenti tangit amico*

who sportingly never leaveth until hee make a man laugh at
folly, and, at length ashamed, to laugh at himselfe; which he
cannot avoyd, without avoyding the follie; who, while   25

> *circum praecordia ludit,**

giveth us to feele how many head-aches a passionate life
bringeth us to – how, when all is done,

> *Est Ulubris, animus si nos non deficit aequus.**

No, perchance it is the Comick, whom naughtie Playmakers   30
and Stage-keepers have justly made odious. To the argument
of abuse I will answer after. Onely thus much now is to be
said, that the Comedy is an imitation of the common errors
of our life, which he representeth in the most ridiculous and
scornefull sort that may be; so as it is impossible that any   35
beholder can be content to be such a one.

Now, as in Geometry the oblique must bee knowne as

well as the right, and in Arithmetick the odde as well as the even, so in the actions of our life who seeth not the filthines of evill wanteth a great foile* to perceive the beauty of vertue. This doth the Comedy handle so in our private and domestical matters, as with hearing it we get as it were an experience, what is to be looked for of a nigardly *Demeas*,* of a crafty *Davus*,* of a flattering *Gnato*,* of a vaine glorious *Thraso*,* and not onely to know what effects are to be expected, but to know who be such, by the signifying badge given them by the Comedian. And little reason hath any man to say that men learne evill by seeing it so set out: sith, as I sayd before, there is no man living but, by the force trueth hath in nature, no sooner seeth these men play their parts, but wisheth them in *Pistrinum*: although perchance the sack of his owne faults lye so behinde hys back that he seeth not himselfe daunce the same measure; whereto yet nothing can more open his eyes then to finde his own actions contemptibly set forth. So that the right use of Comedy will (I thinke) by no body be blamed, and much lesse of the high and excellent Tragedy, that openeth the greatest wounds, and sheweth forth the ulcers that are covered with tissue; that maketh Kinges feare to be Tyrants, and Tyrants manifest their tyrannical humors; that, with sturring the affects of admiration and commiseration, teacheth the uncertainety of this world, and upon how weake foundations guilden roofes are builded; that maketh us knowe

> *Qui sceptra saevus duro imperio regit,*
> *Timet timentes, metus in authorem redit.**

But how much it can move, *Plutarch* yeeldeth a notable testimonie of the abhominable Tyrant *Alexander Pheraeus*;* from whose eyes a Tragedy, wel made and represented, drewe aboundance of teares, who, without all pitty, had murthered infinite numbers, and some of his owne blood. So as he, that was not ashamed to make matters for Tragedies, yet coulde not resist the sweet violence of a Tragedie. And if it wrought no further good in him, it was that he, in despight of himselfe, withdrewe himselfe from harkening to that which might mollifie his hardened heart.

But it is not the Tragedy they doe mislike: for it were too absurd to cast out so excellent a representation of whatso-

ever is most worthy to be learned. Is it the Liricke that most
displeaseth, who with his tuned Lyre, and wel accorded
voyce, giveth praise, the reward of vertue, to vertuous acts?
who gives morrall precepts, and naturall Problemes,* who
sometimes rayseth up his voice to the height of the heavens,   5
in singing the laudes of the immortall God. Certainly I must
confesse my own barbarousnes: I never heard the olde song
of *Percy* and *Douglas** that I found not my heart moved
more then with a Trumpet; and yet is it sung but by some
blinde Crouder, with no rougher voyce then rude stile;*   10
which being so evill apparrelled in the dust and cobwebbes
of that uncivill age,* what would it worke trymmed in the
gorgeous eloquence of *Pindar*?* In *Hungary** I have seene it
the manner at all Feasts, and other such meetings, to have
songes of their Auncestours' valour; which that right Soul-   15
dier-like Nation think the chiefest kindlers of brave courage.
The incomparable *Lacedemonians* did not only carry that
kinde of Musicke ever with them to the field, but even at
home, as such songs were made, so were they all content to
bee the singers of them, when the lusty men were to tell what   20
they dyd, the olde men what they had done, and the young
men what they wold doe. And where a man may say that
Pindar many times prayseth highly victories of small
moment, matters rather of sport then vertue;* as it may be
aunswered, it was the fault of the Poet, and not of the Poetry;   25
so indeede the chiefe fault was in the tyme and custome of
the *Greekes*, who set those toyes at so high a price that
Phillip of *Macedon** reckoned a horse-race wonne at *Olympus* among hys three fearefull felicities. But as the unimitable
Pindar often did, so is that kinde most capable   30
and most fit to awake the thoughts from the sleep of idlenes,
to embrace honorable enterprises.

There rests the Heroicall, whose very name (I thinke)
should daunt all back-biters; for by what conceit can a
tongue be directed to speak evill of that which draweth with   35
it no lesse Champions then *Achilles, Cyrus, Aeneas, Turnus,
Tideus,** and *Rinaldo*? who doth not onely teach and move
to a truth, but teacheth and moveth to the most high and
excellent truth; who maketh magnanimity and justice shine
throughout all misty fearefulnes and foggy desires; who, if   40
the saying of *Plato* and *Tullie* bee true, that who could see

Vertue would be wonderfully ravished with the love of her beauty:* this man sets her out to make her more lovely in her holyday apparell, to the eye of any that will daine not to disdaine untill they understand. But if any thing be already sayd in the defence of sweete Poetry, all concurreth to the 5 maintaining the Heroicall, which is not onely a kinde, but the best and most accomplished kinde of Poetry. For as the image of each action styrreth and instructeth the mind, so the loftie image of such Worthies most inflameth the mind with desire to be worthy, and informes with counsel how to 10 be worthy. Only let *Aeneas* be worne in the tablet of your memory; how he governeth himselfe in the ruine of his Country; in the preserving his old father, and carrying away his religious ceremonies; in obeying the God's commande- ment to leave *Dido*,* though not onely all passionate kin- 15 denes, but even the humane consideration of vertuous grate- fulnes, would haue craved other of him; how in storms, howe in sports, howe in warre, howe in peace, how a fugitive, how victorious, how besiedged, how besiedging, howe to strangers, howe to allyes, how to enemies, howe to 20 his owne; lastly, how in his inward selfe, and how in his outward government, and I thinke, in a minde not prejudiced with a prejudicating humor, hee will be found in excellencie fruitefull, yea, even as *Horace* sayth,

*Melius Chrysippo et Crantore.**   25

But truely I imagine it falleth out with these Poet-whyp- pers, as with some good women, who often are sicke, but in fayth they cannot tel where. So the name of Poetrie is odious to them, but neither his cause nor effects, neither the sum that containes him nor the particularities descending from 30 him, give any fast handle to their carping disprayse.

Since then Poetrie is of all humane learning the most auncient and of most fatherly antiquitie, as from whence other learnings haue taken theyr beginnings; since it is so universall that no learned nation doth despise it, nor no 35 barbarous nation is without it; sith both *Roman* and *Greek* gave divine names unto it, the one of prophecying, the other of making; and that indeede that name of making is fit for him, considering that where as other Arts retaine themselves within their subject, and receive, as it were, their beeing from 40 it, the Poet onely bringeth his owne stuffe, and dooth not learne a conceite out of a matter, but maketh matter for a conceite. Since neither his description nor his ende contayneth any evill, the thing described cannot be evill; since his effects be so good as to teach goodnes and to delight the learners; since therein (namely in morrall doctrine, the chiefe of all knowledges) hee dooth not onely farre passe the Historian, but, for instructing, is well nigh comparable to the Philosopher, and, for moving, leaves him behind him; Since the Holy Scripture (wherein there is no uncleannes) hath whole parts in it poeticall, and that even our Saviour Christ vouchsafed to use the flowers of it; since all his kindes are not onlie in their united formes but in their severed dissections fully commendable: I think (and think I thinke rightly) the Lawrell crowne appointed for tryumphing Captaines doth worthilie (of al other learnings) honor the Poets tryumph. But because wee have eares aswell as tongues, and that the lightest reasons that may be will seeme to weigh greatly, if nothing be put in the counter-ballance, let us heare, and as well as wee can ponder, what objections may bee made against this Arte, which may be worthy eyther of yeelding or answering.

First, truely I note not onely in these *Misomousoi*,* Poethaters, but in all that kinde of people who seek a prayse by dispraysing others, that they doe prodigally spend a great many wandering wordes in quips and scoffes, carping and taunting at each thing, which, by styrring the Spleene,* may stay the braine from a through beholding the worthines of the subject.

Those kinde of objections, as they are full of very idle easines, since there is nothing of so sacred a majestie but that an itching tongue may rubbe it selfe upon it, so deserve they no other answer, but, in steed of laughing at the jest, to laugh at the jester. Wee know a playing wit can prayse the discretion of an Asse, the comfortablenes of being in debt, and the jolly commoditie of beeing sick of the plague. So of the contrary side, if we will turne *Ovids* verse,*

*Ut lateat virtus proximitate mali,**

that good lye hid in neerenesse of the evill, *Agrippa* will be as merry in shewing the vanitie of Science* as *Erasmus* was

in commending of follie.* Neyther shall any man or matter
escape some touch of these smyling raylers. But for *Erasmus*
and *Agrippa*, they had another foundation then the superfi-
ciall part would promise. Marry, these other pleasant Fault-
finders, who wil correct the Verbe before they understande   5
the Noune, and confute others' knowledge before they confirme
theyr owne, I would have them onely remember that scoffing
commeth not of wisedom. So as the best title in true English
they gette with their merriments is to be called good fooles,
for so have our grave Fore-fathers ever termed that humor-   10
ous kinde of jesters. But that which gyveth greatest scope to
their scorning humors is ryming and versing. It is already
sayde (and, as I think, trulie sayde) it is not ryming and
versing that maketh Poesie. One may bee a Poet without
versing,* and a versifyer without Poetry. But yet presuppose   15
it were inseparable (as indeede it seemeth *Scaliger* judgeth)*
truelie it were an inseparable commendation. For if *Oratio*
next to *Ratio*, Speech next to Reason, bee the greatest gyft
bestowed upon Mortalitie, that can not be praiselesse which
dooth most pollish that blessing of speech, which considers   20
each word, not only (as a man may say) by his forcible
qualitie but by his best measured quantitie, carrying even in
themselves a Harmonie (without, perchaunce, Number,
Measure, Order, Proportion be in our time growne odious).
But lay a side the just prayse it hath, by beeing the onely fit   25
speech for Musick (Musick I say, the most divine striker of
the sences), thus much is undoubtedly true, that if reading
bee foolish without remembring, memorie being the onely
treasurer of knowledge, those words which are fittest for
memory are likewise most convenient for knowledge.   30

Now, that Verse farre exceedeth Prose in the knitting upof
the memory, the reason is manifest; the words (besides theyr
delight, which hath a great affinitie to memory) beeing so set
as one word cannot be lost but the whole worke failes: which
accuseth it selfe, calleth the remembrance backe to it   35
selfe, and so most strongly confirmeth it; besides, one word
so, as it were, begetting another, as, be it in ryme or
measured verse, by the former a man shall have a neere gesse
to the follower: lastly, even they that have taught the Art of
memory have shewed nothing so apt for it as a certaine   40
roome devided into many places well and throughly

knowne.* Now, that hath the verse in effect perfectly, every
word having his naturall seate, which seate must needes
make the words remembred. But what needeth more in a
thing so knowne to all men? Who is it that ever was a
scholler that doth not carry away some verses of *Virgill,*   5
Horace, or *Cato,* which in his youth he learned, and even to
his old age serve him for howrely lessons.

> *Percontatorem fugito nam garrulus idem est:**
> *Dum sibi quisque placet credula turba sumus.**

But the fitnes it hath for memory is notably proved by all   10
delivery of Arts: wherein for the most part, from Grammer
to Logick, Mathematick, Phisick, and the rest, the rules
chiefely necessary to bee borne away are compiled in verses.*
So that, verse being in it selfe sweete and orderly, and beeing
best for memory, the onely handle of knowledge, it must be   15
in jest that any man can speake against it.

Nowe then* goe wee to the most important imputations
laid to the poore Poets: for ought I can yet learne, they are
these. First, that there beeing many other more fruitefull
knowledges, a man might better spend his tyme in them then   20
in this. Secondly, that it is the mother of lyes. Thirdly, that it
is the nurse of abuse, infecting us with many pestilent desires;
with a *Syren's* sweetnes, drawing the mind to the Serpent's
tayle* of sinfull fancy. And heerein, especially, Comedies
give the largest field to eare, as *Chaucer* sayth: howe both in   25
other Nations and in ours, before Poets did soften us, we
were full of courage, given to martiall exercises, the pillers
of manlyke liberty, and not lulled asleepe in shady idlenes
with Poets' pastimes. And lastly, and chiefely, they cry out
with an open mouth, as if they out shot *Robin Hood,** that   30
Plato banished them out of hys Common-wealth.* Truely,
this is much, if there be much truth in it. First to the first:
that a man might better spend his tyme is a reason indeede:
but it doth (as they say) but *petere principium*: for if it be, as
I affirme, that no learning is so good as that which teacheth   35
and moveth to vertue, and that none can both teach and
move thereto so much as Poetry, then is the conclusion
manifest that incke and paper cannot be to a more profitable
purpose employed. And certainly, though a man should
graunt their first assumption, it should followe (me thinkes)   40

very unwillingly, that good is not good because better is
better. But I still and utterly denye that there is sprong out
of earth a more fruitefull knowledge. To the second therefore, that they should be the principall lyars, I aunswere
paradoxically, but, truely, I thinke truely, that of all writers
under the sunne the Poet is the least lier, and, though he
would, as a Poet can scarcely be a lyer. The Astronomer,
with his cousin the Geometrician, can hardly escape, when
they take upon them to measure the height of the starres.
How often, thinke you, doe the Phisitians lye, when they
aver things good for sicknesses, which afterwards send
*Charon** a great number of soules drownd in a potion before
they come to his Ferry? And no lesse of the rest, which take
upon them to affirme. Now, for the Poet, he nothing
affirmes, and therefore never lyeth. For, as I take it, to lye is
to affirme that to be true which is false. So as the other
Artists, and especially the Historian, affirming many things,
can, in the cloudy knowledge of mankinde, hardly escape
from many lyes. But the Poet (as I sayd before) never
affirmeth. The Poet never maketh any circles about your
imagination, to conjure you to beleeve for true what he
writes. Hee citeth not authorities of other histories, but even
for his entry calleth the sweete Muses to inspire into him a
good invention; in troth, not labouring to tell you what is,
or is not, but what should or should not be: and therefore,
though he recount things not true, yet because hee telleth
them not for true, he lyeth not, without we will say that
Nathan lyed in his speech, before alledged, to *David*. Which
as a wicked man durst scarce say, so think I none so simple
would say that *Æsope* lyed in the tales of his beasts: for who
thinks that *Æsope* writ it for actually true were well worthy
to have his name cronicled among the beastes hee writeth of.
What childe is there that, comming to a play, and seeing
Thebes written in great letters upon an olde doore, doth
beleeve that it is *Thebes*? If then a man can arrive, at that
child's age, to know that the Poet's persons and dooings are
but pictures of what should be, and not stories of what has
beene, they will never give the lye to things not affirmatively
but allegorically and figurativelie written. And therefore, as
in Historie, looking for trueth, they goe away full fraught
with falsehood, so in Poesie, looking for fiction, they shal

use the narration but as an imaginative groundplot of a profitable invention.

But heereto is replyed, that the Poets gyve names to men they write of, which argueth a conceite of an actuall truth, and so, not being true, prooveth a falshood. And doth the Lawyer lye then, when under the names of *John of the Stile* and *John of the Nokes* hee puts his case?* But that is easily answered. Theyr naming of men is but to make theyr picture the more lively, and not to builde any historie; paynting men, they cannot leave men namelesse. We see we cannot play at Chesse but that we must give names to our Chesse-men; and yet, mee thinks, hee were a very partiall Champion of truth that would say we lyed for giving a peece of wood the reverend title of a Bishop. The Poet nameth *Cyrus* or *Aeneas* no other way then to shewe what men of theyr fames, fortunes, and estates should doe.

Their third is, how much it abuseth men's wit, trayning it to wanton sinfulnes and lustfull love: for indeed that is the principall, if not the onely abuse I can heare alledged. They say the Comedies rather teach then reprehend amorous conceites. They say the Lirick is larded with passionate Sonnets, the Elegiack weepes the want of his mistresse, and that even to the Heroical *Cupid* hath ambitiously climed. Alas, Love, I would thou couldest as well defende thy selfe as thou canst offende others. I would those, on whom thou doest attend, could eyther put thee away, or yeelde good reason why they keepe thee. But grant love of beautie to be a beastlie fault (although it be very hard, since onely man, and no beast, hath that gyft to discerne beauty). Grant that lovely name of Love to deserve all hatefull reproches (although even some of my Maisters the Phylosophers spent a good deale of theyr lamp-oyle in setting foorth the excellencie of it). Grant, I say, what they wil have granted; that not onely love, but lust, but vanitie, but (if they list) scurrilitie, possesseth many leaves of the Poets' bookes: yet thinke I, when this is granted, they will finde theyr sentence may with good manners put the last words foremost, and not say that Poetrie abuseth mans wit, but that mans wit abuseth Poetrie.

For I will not denie but that mans wit may make Poesie (which should be *Eikastike*, which some learned have defined, figuring forth good things) to be *Phantastike*: which doth, contrariwise, infect the fancie with unworthy objects. As the Painter, that shoulde give to the eye eyther some excellent perspective, or some fine picture, fit for building or fortification, or contayning in it some notable example, as *Abraham* sacrificing his Sonne *Isaak, Judith* killing *Holofernes, David* fighting with *Goliath*,* may leave those, and please an ill-pleased eye with wanton shewes of better hidden matters. But what, shall the abuse of a thing make the right use odious? Nay truely, though I yeeld that Poesie may not onely be abused, but that beeing abused, by the reason of his sweete charming force, it can doe more hurt then any other Armie of words, yet shall it be so far from concluding that the abuse should give reproch to the abused, that contrariwise it is a good reason, that whatsoever, being abused, doth most harme, beeing rightly used (and upon the right use each thing conceiveth his title), doth most good.

Doe wee not see the skill of Phisick (the best rampier to our often-assaulted bodies) beeing abused, teach poyson, the most violent destroyer? Doth not knowledge of Law, whose end is to even and right al things, being abused, grow the crooked fosterer of horrible injuries? Doth not (to goe to the highest) God's word abused breed heresie? and his Name abused become blasphemie? Truely, a needle cannot doe much hurt, and as truely (with leave of Ladies be it spoken) it cannot doe much good. With a sword thou maist kill thy Father, and with a sword thou maist defende thy Prince and Country. So that, as in their calling Poets Fathers of lyes they sayd nothing, so in this theyr argument of abuse they prove the commendation.

They alledge here-with, that before Poets began to be in price our Nation hath set their harts' delight upon action, and not upon imagination: rather doing things worthy to bee written, then writing things fitte to be done. What that before tyme was, I thinke scarcely *Sphinx* can tell,* since no memory is no auncient that hath the precedence of Poetrie. And certaine it is that, in our plainest homelines, yet never was the *Albion* Nation* without Poetrie. Marry, thys argument, though it bee leveld against Poetrie, yet is it indeed a chaine-shot against all learning, or bookishnes, as they commonly terme it. Of such minde were certaine *Gothes*, of

whom it is written that, having in the spoile of a famous
Citie taken a fayre librarie, one hangman (be-like fitte to
execute the fruites of their wits, who had murthered a great
number of bodies), would have set fire in it: 'No,' sayde
another very gravely, 'take heede what you doe, for whyle 5
they are busie about these toyes, wee shall with more leysure
conquer their countries.'

This indeede is the ordinary doctrine of ignorance, and
many wordes sometymes I have heard spent in it: but because
this reason is generally against all learning, as well as Poetrie, 10
or rather, all learning but Poetrie; because it were too large
a digression to handle, or at least to superfluous (since it is
manifest that all government of action is to be gotten by
knowledge and knowledge best by gathering many knowledges, which is reading), I onely, with *Horace*, to him that is 15
of that opinion,

Iubeo stultum esse libenter:*

for as for Poetrie it selfe, it is the freest from thys objection.
For Poetrie is the companion of Camps.

I dare undertake, *Orlando Furioso*,* or honest King 20
Arthur, will never displease a Souldier: but the quiddity of
Ens and *Prima materia* will hardly agree with a Corslet:
and therefore, as I said in the beginning, even Turks and
Tartares are delighted with Poets. *Homer*, a *Greeke*, florished before *Greece* florished. And if to a slight conjecture a 25
conjecture may be opposed, truly it may seeme, that as by
him their learned men tooke almost their first light of
knowledge, so their active men, received their first motions
of courage. Onlie *Alexander's* example may serve,* who by
Plutarch is accounted of such vertue, that Fortune was not 30
his guide but his foote-stoole: whose acts speake for him,
though *Plutarch* did not;* indeede the *Phœnix** of warlike
Princes. This *Alexander* left his Schoolemaster, living *Aristotle*, behinde him, but tooke deade *Homer* with him:* he
put the Philosopher *Callisthenes* to death for his seeming 35
philosophicall, indeed mutinous, stubburnnes;* but the
chiefe thing he ever was heard to wish for was that *Homer*
had been alive. He well found he received more braverie of
minde bye the patterne of *Achilles* then by hearing the
definition of Fortitude: and therefore, if *Cato* misliked *Ful*- 40

vius for carying *Ennius** with him to the fielde, it may be aunswered that, if *Cato* misliked it, the noble *Fulvius* liked it, or els he had not doone it: for it was not the excellent *Cato Uticensis* (whose authority I would much more have reverenced), but it was the former, in truth a bitter punisher 5 of faults, but else a man that had never sacrificed to the *Graces.* Hee misliked and cryed out upon all *Greeke* learning, and yet, being fourscore yeeres olde, began to learne it; belike fearing that *Pluto* understood not Latine.* Indeede, the Romaine lawes allowed no person to be carried to the 10 warres but he that was in the Souldiers role: and therefore, though *Cato* misliked his unmustered person, hee misliked not his worke. And if hee had, *Scipio Nasica,* judged by common consent the best *Romaine,* loved him. Both the other *Scipio* Brothers, who had by their vertues no lesse 15 surnames then of *Asia* and *Affrick,* so loved him that they caused his body to be buried in their Sepulcher.* So as *Cato* his authoritie being but against his person, and that aunswered with so farre greater then himselfe, is heerein of no validitie. 20

But now indeede my burthen is great; now *Plato* his name is layde upon mee, whom, I must confesse, of all Philosophers I have ever esteemed most worthy of reverence, and with great reason, since of all Philosophers he is the most poeticall. Yet if he will defile the Fountaine out of which his 25 flowing streames have proceeded, let us boldly examine with what reasons hee did it. First truly, a man might maliciously object that *Plato,* being a Philosopher, was a naturall enemie of Poets: for indeede, after the Philosophers had picked out of the sweete mysteries of Poetrie the right discerning true 30 points of knowledge, they forthwith, putting it in method, and making a Schoole-arte of that which the Poets did onely teach by a divine delightfulnes, beginning to spurne at their guides, like ungratefull Prentices, were not content to set up shops for themselves, but sought by all meanes to discredit 35 their Maisters. Which by the force of delight beeing barred them,* the lesse they could overthrow them, the more they hated them. For indeede, they found for *Homer* seven Cities strove who should have him for their Citizen; where many Citties banished Philosophers as not fitte members to live 40 among them. For onely repeating certaine of *Euripides'* verses, many *Athenians* had their lives saved of the *Syracu-sans*; when the *Athenians* themselves thought many Philos-ophers unwoorthie to live. Certaine Poets, as *Simonides* and *Pindarus*, had so prevailed with *Hiero* the first, that of a Tirant they made him a just King,* where *Plato* could do so little with *Dionisius*, that he himselfe of a Philosopher was made a slave.* But who should doe thus, I confesse, should requite the objections made against Poets with like cavilla-tion against Philosophers, as likewise one should do that should bid one read *Phædrus* or *Symposium* in *Plato*, or the discourse of love in *Plutarch*,* and see whether any Poet doe authorize abhominable filthines, as they doe.* Againe, a man might aske out of what Common-wealth *Plato* did banish them insooth, thence where he himselfe alloweth communitie of women.* So as belike this banishment grewe not for effeminate wantonnes, since little should poeticall Sonets be hurtfull when a man might have what woman he listed. But I honour philosophicall instructions, and blesse the wits which bred them: so as they be not abused, which is likewise stretched to Poetrie.

Saint Paule himselfe, who (yet for the credite of Poets) alledgeth twise two Poets, and one of them by the name of a Prophet,* setteth a watch-word upon Philosophy, indeede upon the abuse. So dooth *Plato* upon the abuse, not upon Poetrie. *Plato* found fault that the Poets of his time filled the worlde with wrong opinions of the Gods, making light tales of that unspotted essence, and therefore would not have the youth depraved with such opinions. Herein may much be said: let this suffice. The Poets did not induce such opinions, but dyd imitate those opinions already induced. For all the *Greeke* stories can well testifie that the very religion of that time stoode upon many, and many-fashioned, Gods; not taught so by the Poets, but followed according to their nature of imitation. Who list may reade in *Plutarch* the discourses of *Isis* and *Osiris*, of the cause why Oracles ceased,* of the divine providence, and see whether the Theologie of that nation stood not upon such dreames which the Poets indeed supersticiously observed. And truly (since they had not the light of Christ) did much better in it then the Philosophers, who, shaking off superstition, brought in Atheisme. *Plato* therefore (whose authoritie I had much

rather justly construe then unjustly resist) meant not in
general of Poets, in those words of which *Julius Scaliger*
saith, *Qua authoritate barbari quidam atque hispidi abuti
velint ad Poetas e republica exigendos*;* but only meant to
drive out those wrong opinions of the Deitie (whereof now, 5
without further law, Christianity hath taken away all the
hurtful beliefe), perchance (as he thought) nourished by the
then esteemed Poets. And a man need goe no further then to
Plato himselfe to know his meaning: who, in his Dialogue
called *Ion*, giveth high and rightly divine commendation 10
unto Poetrie.* So as *Plato*, banishing the abuse, not the
thing, not banishing it, but giving due honour unto it, shall
be our Patron, and not our adversarie. For indeed I had
much rather (since truely I may do it) shew theyr mistaking
of *Plato* (under whose Lyon's skin they would make an Asse- 15
like braying against Poesie) then goe about to overthrow his
authority, whom the wiser a man is the more just cause he
shall find to have in admiration, especially sith he attributeth
unto Poesie more then my selfe doe, namely, to be a very
inspiring of a divine force, farre above mans wit, as in the 20
aforenamed Dialogue is apparant.

Of the other side, who wold shew the honors have been
by the best sort of judgements granted them, a whole sea of
examples woulde present themselves: *Alexanders, Cæsars,
Scipios*, all favorers of Poets; *Laelius*,* called the Romane 25
Socrates, him selfe a Poet, so as part of *Heautontimorume-
non* in *Terence* was supposed to be made by him. And even
the Greeke *Socrates*, whom *Apollo* confirmed to be the onely
wise man,* is sayde to have spent part of his old tyme in
putting *Æsops*' fables into verses. And therefore, full evill 30
should it become his scholler *Plato* to put such words in his
Maister's mouth against Poets. But what need more? *Aristotle* writes the *Arte of Poesie*: and why, if it should not be
written? *Plutarch* teacheth the use to be gathered of them,
and how if they should not be read? And who reades 35
Plutarch's eyther historie or philosophie shall finde hee
trymmeth both theyr garments with gards of Poesie. But I
list not to defend Poesie with the helpe of her underling
Historiographie. Let it suffise that it is a fit soyle for prayse
to dwell upon; and what dispraise may set upon it, is eyther 40
easily over-come, or transformed into just commendation.

So that, since the excellencies of it may be so easily and so
justly confirmed, and the low-creeping objections so soone
trodden downe; it not being an Art of lyes, but of true
doctrine; not of effeminatenesse, but of notable stirring of
courage; not of abusing mans witte, but of strengthning
mans wit; not banished, but honored by *Plato*; let us rather
plant more Laurels for to engarland the Poets' heads (which
honor of beeing Laureate, as besides them onely tryumphant
Captaines were, is a sufficient authoritie to shewe the price
they ought to be held in) then suffer the ill-favouring breath
of such wrong-speakers once to blowe upon the cleere
springs of Poesie.

But since I have runne so long a careere in this matter, me
thinks, before I give my penne a fulle stop, it shall be but a
little more lost time to inquire why *England* (the Mother of
excellent mindes) should bee growne so hard a step-mother
to Poets, who certainly in wit ought to passe all others; sith
all onely proceedeth from their wit, being indeede makers of
themselves, not takers of others. How can I but exclaime,

*Musa mihi causas memora, quo numine laeso.**

Sweete Poesie, that hath aunciently had Kings, Emperors,
Senators, great Captaines, such as, besides a thousand others,
David, Adrian, Sophocles, Germanicus, not onely to favour
Poets, but to be Poets. And of our nearer times can present
for her Patrons a *Robert*, King of Sicill, the great king *Francis*
of France, King *James* of Scotland.* Such Cardinals as
Bembus and *Bibiena*.* Such famous Preachers and Teachers
as *Beza* and *Melancthon*.* So learned Philosophers as *Fracastorius* and *Scaliger*.* So great Orators as *Pontanus* and
Muretus.* So piercing wits as *George Buchanan*.* So grave
Counsellors as, besides many, but before all, that *Hospitall*
of *Fraunce*,* then whom (I thinke) that Realme never
brought forth a more accomplished judgement, more firmely
builded upon vertue. I say these, with numbers of others, not
onely to read others Poesies, but to Poetise for others
reading. That Poesie, thus embraced in all other places,
should onely finde in our time a hard welcome in England, I
thinke the very earth lamenteth it, and therefore decketh our
soyle with fewer Laurels then it was accustomed. For heer-
tofore Poets have in England also flourished; and, which is

to be noted, even in those times when the trumpet of *Mars* did sounde loudest.* And now that an over-faint quietnes* should seeme to strew the house for Poets, they are almost as good reputation as the *Mountibancks* at *Venice*.* Truly even that, as of the one side it giveth great praise to Poesie, 5 which like *Venus* (but to better purpose) hath rather be troubled in the net with *Mars* then enjoy the homelie quiet of *Vulcan*;* so serves it for a peece of a reason why they are lesse gratefull to idle England, which nowe can scarce endure the payne of a pen. Upon this necessarily followeth, that 10 base men with servile wits undertake it: who think it enough if they can be rewarded of the Printer. And so as *Epaminondas* is sayd, with the honor of his vertue, to have made an office, by his exercising it, which before was contemptible, to become highly respected;* so these, no more but setting 15 their names to it, by their owne disgracefulnes disgrace the most gracefull Poesie. For now, as if all the Muses were gotte with childe, to bring foorth bastard Poets, without any commission they doe poste over the banckes of *Helicon*,* tyll they make the readers more weary then Post-horses; 20 while, in the mean tyme, they,

Queis meliore luto finxit praecordia Titan,*

are better content to suppresse the out-flowing of their wit, then by publishing them to bee accounted Knights of the same Order. But I that, before ever I durst aspire unto the 25 dignitie, am admitted into the company of the Paper-blurrers, doe finde the very true cause of our wanting estimation is want of desert; taking upon us to be Poets in despight of *Pallas*.* Nowe, wherein we want desert were a thankeworthy labour to expresse: but if I knew, I should have 30 mended my selfe. But I, as I never desired the title, so have I neglected the meanes to come by it. Onely, over-mastred by some thoughts, I yeelded an inckie tribute unto them. Marry, they that delight in Poesie it selfe should seeke to knowe what they doe, and how they doe; and, especially, looke 35 themselves in an unflattering Glasse of reason, if they bee inclinable unto it. For Poesie must not be drawne by the eares; it must bee gently led, or rather it must lead. Which was partly the cause that made the auncient-learned affirme it was a divine gift, and no humaine skill: since all other 40

knowledges lie ready for any that hath strength of witte: a
Poet no industrie can make, if his owne *Genius* bee not
carried unto it: and therefore is it an old Proverbe, *Orator
fit, Poeta nascitur.* Yet confesse I alwayes that as the fertilest
ground must be manured, so must the highest flying wit have   5
a *Daedalus** to guide him. That *Daedalus*, they say, both in
this and in other, hath three wings to beare it selfe up into
the ayre of due commendation: that is, Arte, Imitation, and
Exercise. But these, neyther artificiall rules nor imitative
patternes, we much cumber our selves withall. Exercise   10
indeede wee doe, but that very forebackwardly: for where
we should exercise to know, we exercise as having knowne:
and so is oure braine delivered of much matter which never
was begotten by knowledge. For, there being two principal
parts, matter to be expressed by words and words to expresse   15
the matter, in neyther wee use Arts of Imitation rightly. Our
matter is *Quodlibet* indeed, though wrongly perfourming
Ovids verse

*Quicquid conabar dicere, versus erit:**

never marshalling it into an assured rancke, that almost the   20
readers cannot tell where to finde themselves.

Chaucer, undoubtedly, did excellently in hys *Troylus* and
Cresseid; of whom, truly, I know not whether to mervaile
more, either that he in that mistie time could see so clearely,
or that wee in this cleare age walke so stumblingly after   25
him.* Yet had he great wants, fitte to be forgiven in so
reverent antiquity. I account the *Mirrour of Magistrates**
meetely furnished of beautiful parts; and in the Earle of
*Surrie's Liricks** many things tasting of a noble birth, and
worthy of a noble minde. The *Sheapheards Kalender* hath   30
much Poetrie in his Eglogues:* indeede worthy the reading,
if I be not deceived. That same framing of his stile to an old
rustick language* I dare not alowe, sith neyther *Theocritus*
in Greeke, *Virgill* in Latine, nor *Sanazar* in Italian did affect
it. Besides these, doe I not remember to have seene but fewe   35
(to speake boldely) printed, that have poeticall sinewes in
them: for proofe whereof, let but most of the verses bee put
in Prose, and then aske the meaning; and it will be found
that one verse did but beget another, without ordering at the
first what should be at the last; which becomes a confused   40

masse of words, with a tingling sound of ryme, barely accompanied with reason.

Our Tragedies and Comedies (not without cause cried out against),* observing rules neyther of honest civilitie nor skilfull Poetrie, excepting *Gorboduck** (againe, I say, of those that I have seene), which notwithstanding, as it is full of stately speeches and well sounding Phrases, clyming to the height of *Seneca* his stile,* and as full of notable moralitie, which it doth most delightfully teach, and so obtayne the very end of Poesie, yet in troth it is very defectious in the circumstances, which greiveth mee, because it might not remaine as an exact model of all Tragedies. For it is faulty both in place and time, the two necessary companions of all corporall actions. For where the stage should alwaies represent but one place, and the uttermost time presupposed in it should be, both by *Aristotle's* precept* and common reason, but one day, there is both many dayes, and many places, inartificially imagined. But if it be so in *Gorboduck*, how much more in al the rest? where you shal have *Asia* of the one side, and *Affrick* of the other, and so many other under-kingdoms, that the Player, when he commeth in, must ever begin with telling where he is, or els the tale wil not be conceived. Now you shall have three Ladies walke to gather flowers, and then we must beleeve the stage to be a Garden. By and by, we heare newes of shipwracke in the same place, and then wee are to blame if we accept it not for a Rock. Upon the backe of that, comes out a hideous Monster, with fire and smoke, and then the miserable beholders are bounde to take it for a Cave. While in the meantime two Armies flye in, represented with foure swords and bucklers, and then what harde heart will not receive it for a pitched fielde? Now, of time they are much more liberall, for ordinary it is that two young Princes fall in love: after many traverces, she is got with childe, delivered of a faire boy; he is lost, groweth a man, falls in love, and is ready to get another child; and all this in two hours space: which how absurd it is in sence even sence may imagine, and Arte hath taught, and all auncient examples justified, and, at this day, the ordinary Players in *Italie** will not erre in. Yet will some bring in an example of *Eunuchus* in *Terence*,* that containeth matter of two dayes, yet far short of twenty yeeres. True it is, and so was it to be played in two daies, and so fitted to the time it set forth. And though *Plautus** hath in one place done amisse, let us hit with him, and not misse with him. But they will say, how then shal we set forth a story which containeth both many places and many times? And doe they not knowe that a Tragedie is tied to the lawes of Poesie, and not of Historie? Not bound to follow the storie, but, having liberty, either to faine a quite newe matter, or to frame the history to the most tragicall conveniencie. Againe, many things may be told which cannot be shewed, if they knowe the difference betwixt reporting and representing. As, for example, I may speake (though I am heere) of *Peru*, and in speech digresse from that to the description of *Calicut*; but in action I cannot represent it without *Pacolet's* horse:* and so was the manner the Auncients tooke, by some *Nuntius*, to recount thinges done in former time or other place. Lastly, if they wil represent an history, they must not (as *Horace* saith) beginne *Ab ovo*, but they must come to the principall poynt of that one action which they wil represent. By example this wil be best expressed. I have a story of young *Polidorus*, delivered for safetie's sake, with great riches, by his Father *Priamus* to *Polimnestor*, King of *Thrace*, in the Troyan war time. Hee after some yeares, hearing the over-throwe of *Priamus*, for to make the treasure his owne, murthereth the child; the body of the child is taken up by *Hecuba*;* shee the same day findeth a slight to bee revenged most cruelly of the Tyrant: where nowe would one of our Tragedy writers begin, but with the delivery of the childe? Then should he sayle over into *Thrace* and so spend I know not how many years, and travell numbers of places. But where doth *Euripides*? Even with the finding of the body, leaving the rest to be tolde by the spirit of *Polidorus*. This need no further to be inlarged; the dullest wit may conceive it.

But besides these grosse absurdities, how all theyr Playes be neither right Tragedies, nor right Comedies; mingling Kings and Clownes, not because the matter so carrieth it, but thrust in Clownes by head and shoulders, to play a part in majesticall matters, with neither decencie nor discretion: so as neither the admiration and commiseration, nor the right sportfulnes, is by their mongrell Tragy-comedie obtained. I know *Apuleius** did some-what so, but that is a

thing recounted with space of time, not represented in one
moment: and I knowe the Auncients have one or two
examples of Tragi-comedies, as *Plautus* hath *Amphitrio*. But,
if we marke them well, we shall find, that they never or very
daintily, match Horn-pypes and Funeralls.* So falleth it out   5
that, having indeed no right Comedy, in that comicall part of
our Tragedy we have nothing but scurrility, unworthy of any
chast eares, or some extreme shewe of doltishnes, indeed fit
to lift up a loude laughter, and nothing els: where the whole
tract of a Comedy shoulde be full of delight, as the Tragedy   10
shoulde be still maintained in a well raised admiration. But
our Comedians thinke there is no delight without laughter;
which is very wrong, for though laughter may come with
delight, yet commeth it not of delight, as though delight
should be the cause of laughter; but well may one thing   15
breed both together: nay rather in themselves they have, as it
were, a kind of contrarietie: for delight we scarcely doe but
in things that have a conveniencie to our selves or to the
generall nature: laughter almost ever commeth of things
most disproportioned to our selves and nature. Delight hath   20
a joy in it, either permanent or present. Laughter hath onely
a scornful tickling. For example, we are ravished with delight
to see a faire woman, and yet are far from being moved to
laughter. We laugh at deformed creatures, wherein certainely
we cannot delight. We delight in good chaunces, we laugh at   25
mischaunces; we delight to heare the happines of our friends,
or Country, at which he were worthy to be laughed at that
would laugh; we shall, contrarily, laugh sometimes to finde
a matter quite mistaken and goe downe the hill agaynst the
byas, in the mouth of some such men, as for the respect of   30
them one shalbe hartely sorry, yet he cannot chuse but laugh;
and so is rather pained then delighted with laughter. Yet
deny I not but that they may goe well together; for as in
Alexander's picture well set out we delight without laughter,
and in twenty mad Anticks we laugh without delight, so in   35
Hercules, painted with his great beard and furious countenance, in womans attire, spinning at *Omphale's* commandement,* it breedeth both delight and laughter. For the
representing of so strange a power in love procureth delight:
and the scornefulnes of the action stirreth laughter. But I   40
speake to this purpose, that all the end of the comicall part

bee not upon such scornefull matters as stirreth laughter onely, but, mixt with it, that delightful teaching which is the end of Poesie. And the great fault even in that point of laughter, and forbidden plainly by *Aristotle*, is that they styrre laughter in sinfull things, which are rather execrable then ridiculous: or in miserable, which are rather to be pittied then scorned. For what is it to make folkes gape at a wretched Begger, or a beggerly Clowne? Or, against lawe of hospitality, to jest at strangers, because they speake not English so well as wee doe? what do we learne? since it is certain

> *Nil habet infelix paupertas durius in se,*
> *Quam quod ridiculos homines facit.**

But rather a busy loving Courtier, a hartlesse threatening *Thraso*, a selfe-wise-seeming schoolemaister, a wry-trans-formed Traveller:* these if we sawe walke in stage names, which we play naturally, therein were delightfull laughter, and teaching delightfulnes: as in the other the Tragedies of *Buchanan** doe justly bring forth a divine admiration. But I have lavished out too many wordes of this play matter. I doe it because as they are excelling parts of Poesie, so is there none so much used in *England*, and none can be more pittifully abused. Which like an unmannerly Daughter, shew-ing a bad education, causeth her mother *Poesie's* honesty to bee called in question.

Other sorts of Poetry almost have we none, but that Lyricall kind of Songs and Sonnets: which, Lord, if he gave us so good mindes, how well it might be imployed, and with howe heavenly fruite, both private and publique, in singing the prayses of the immortall beauty, the immortall goodnes of that God who giveth us hands to write and wits to conceive; of which we might well want words, but never matter; of which we could turne our eyes to nothing, but we should ever have new budding occasions. But truely many of such writings as come under the banner of unresistable love, if I were a Mistress, would never perswade mee they were in love; so coldely they apply fiery speeches, as men that had rather red lovers' writings, and so caught up certaine swelling phrases, which hang together like a man which once tolde mee the winde was at North West, and by South, because he would be sure to name windes enowe, – then that in truth they feele those passions, which easily (as I think) may be bewrayed by that same forciblenes, or *Energia* (as the *Greekes* cal it), of the writer. But let this bee a sufficient though short note, that we misse the right use of the materiall point of Poesie.

Now, for the out-side of it, which is words, or (as I may tearme it) Diction, it is even well worse. So is that hony-flowing matron *Eloquence* apparelled, or rather disguised, in a Curtisan-like painted affectation: one time with so farre fetched words, that many seeme Monsters, but must seeme strangers to any poore English man; another tyme, with coursing of a letter,* as if they were bound to followe the method of a Dictionary;* an other tyme, with figures and flowers, extreamely winter-starved. But I would this fault were only peculiar to Versifiers, and had not as large possession among Prose-printers, and (which is to be mervailed) among many Schollers, and (which is to be pittied) among some Preachers. Truly I could wish, if at least I might be so bold to wish in a thing beyond the reach of my capacity, the diligent imitators of *Tullie** and *Demosthenes* (most worthy to be imitated) did not so much keep *Nizolian* paper-bookes* of their figures and phrases, as by attentive translation as it were devoure them whole, and make them wholly theirs. For nowe they cast sugar and spice upon every dish that is served to the table; like those *Indians*,* not content to weare eare-rings at the fit and naturall place of the eares, but they will thrust jewels through their nose and lippes, because they will be sure to be fine. *Tullie*, when he was to drive out *Catiline*,* as it were with a Thunder-bolt of eloquence, often used that figure of repitition, *Vivit. vivit? imo in Senatum venit &c.** Indeed, inflamed with a well-grounded rage, he would have his words (as it were) double out of his mouth; and so doe that artificially which we see men doe in choller naturally. And we having noted the grace of those words, hale them in sometime to a familier Epistle, when it were too much choller to be chollerick.

How well store* of *Similiter Cadenses* doth sounde with the gravitie of the Pulpit, I woulde but invoke *Demosthenes'* soule to tell: who with a rare daintinesse useth them. Truly they have made mee thinke of the Sophister, that with too much subtiltie would prove two Egges three, and though he might be counted a Sophister, had none for his labour. So these men bringing in such a kind of eloquence, well may they obtaine an opinion of a seeming finenesse, but perswade few, which should be the ende of their finenesse.   5

Now for similitudes, in certaine printed discourses I thinke all Herbarists, all stories of Beasts, Foules, and Fishes are rifled up, that they come in multitudes to waite upon any of our conceits;* which certainly is as absurd a surfet to the eares as is possible: for the force of a similitude not being to 10 prove anything to a contrary disputer but onely to explaine to a willing hearer, when that is done, the rest is a most tedious pratling, rather over-swaying the memory from the purpose whereto they were applyed then any whit informing the judgement, already eyther satisfied, or by similitudes not 15 to be satisfied. For my part, I doe not doubt, when *Antonius* and *Crassus*,* the great forefathers of *Cicero* in eloquence, the one (as *Cicero* testifieth of them) pretended not to know Arte, the other not to set by it, because with a playne sensiblenes they might win credit of popular eares; which 20 credit is the neerest step to perswasion; which perswasion is the chiefe marke of Oratory: — I doe not doubt (I say) but that they used these knacks very sparingly, which who doth generally use any man may see doth daunce to his owne musicke; and so be noted by the audience more careful to 25 speake curiously then to speake truly.

Undoubtedly (at least to my opinion undoubtedly) I have found in divers small learned courtiers a more sounde stile then in some professors of learning: of which I can guesse no other cause, but that the courtier, following that which by 30 practise hee findeth fittest to nature, therein (though he know it not) doth according to Art, though not by Art: where the other, using Art to shew Art, and not to hide Art (as in these cases he should doe), flyeth from nature, and indeede abuseth Art.   35

But what? Me thinkes I deserve to be pounded for straying from Poetrie to Oratorie: but both have such an affinity in this wordish consideration, that I thinke this digression will make my meaning receive the fuller understanding: which is not to take upon me to teach Poets howe they should doe, 40 but onely, finding my selfe sick among the rest, to shew some

one or two spots of the common infection growne among
the most part of writers: that, acknowledging our selves
somewhat awrie, we may bend to the right use both of
matter and manner. Whereto our language giveth us great
occasion, beeing indeed capable of any excellent exercising 5
of it. I know some will say it is a mingled language. And why
not so much the better, taking the best of both* the other?
Another will say it wanteth Grammer. Nay truly, it hath that
prayse, that it wanteth not Grammer: for Grammer it might
have, but it needes it not; beeing so easie of it selfe, and so 10
void of those cumbersome differences of Cases, Genders,
Moodes, and Tenses,* which I thinke was a peece of the
Tower of Babylon's* curse, that a man should be put to
schoole to learne his mother-tongue. But for the uttering
sweetly and properly the conceits of the minde, which is the 15
end of speech, that hath it equally with any other tongue in
the world: and is particulerly happy in compositions of two
or three words together, neere the Greeke, far beyond the
Latine: which is one of the greatest beauties can be in a
language.* 20

Now, of versifying there are two sorts, the one Ancient,
the other Moderne: the ancient marked the quantitie of each
sillable, and according to that framed his verse; the Moderne
observing onely number (with some regarde of the accent),
the chiefe life of it standeth in that lyke sounding of the 25
words, which wee call Ryme. Whether of these be the most
excellent, would beare many speeches. The Ancient (no
doubt) more fit for Musicke, both words and tune observing
quantity, and more fit lively to expresse divers passions, by
the low or loftie sounde of the well-weighed sillable. The 30
latter likewise, with hys rime, striketh a certaine musicke to
the eare: and, in fine, since it doth delight, though by another
way, it obtaines the same purpose: there beeing in either
sweetnesse, and wanting in neither majesty. Truely the
English, before any other Vulgar language I know, is fit for 35
both sorts: for, for the ancient, the Italian is so full of vowels
that it must ever be cumbred with Elisions;* the Dutch so,
of the other side, with consonants, that they cannot yeeld
the sweet sliding fit for a verse; the French in his whole
language, hath not one word that hath his accent in the last 40
sillable saving two, called Antepenultima; and little more

hath the Spanish: and, therefore, very gracelesly may they use Dactiles.* The English is subject to none of these defects.

Nowe, for the ryme, though wee doe not observe quantity, yet we observe the accent very precisely: which other languages eyther cannot doe or will not doe so absolutely. That *Cæsura*, or breathing place in the middest of the verse, neither Italian nor Spanish have; the French, and we, never almost faile of. Lastly, even the very ryme it selfe the Italian cannot put in the last sillable, by the French named the Masculine ryme, but still in the next to the last, which the French call the Female,* or the next before that, which the Italians terme *Sdrucciola*. The example of the former is *Buono, Suono*, of the *Sdrucciola, Femina, Semina*. The French, of the other side, hath both the Male, as *Bon, Son*, and the Female, as *Plaisé, Taisé*. But the *Sdrucciola* he hath not: where the English hath all three, as *Due, True; Father, Rather; Motion, Potion*;* with much more which might be said, but that I finde already the triflingnes of this discourse is much too much enlarged.

So that since the ever-praise-worthy Poesie is full of vertue-breeding delightfulnes, and voyde of no gifte that ought to be in the noble name of learning: since the blames laid against it are either false or feeble; since the cause why it is not esteemed in *Englande* is the fault of Poet-apes, not Poets; since, lastly, our tongue is most fit to honour Poesie and to bee honored by Poesie, I conjure you all that have had the evill lucke to reade this inke-wasting toy of mine, even in the name of the nine Muses, no more to scorne the sacred mysteries of Poesie, no more to laugh at the name of Poets, as though they were next inheritours to Fooles, no more to jest at the reverent title of a Rymer; but to beleeve, with *Aristotle*, that they were the auncient Treasurers of the *Græcians*' Divinity. To beleeve, with *Bembus*, that they were first bringers in all civilitie;* to beleeve, with *Scaliger*, that no Philosopher's precepts can sooner make you an honest man then the reading of *Virgill*; to beleeve, with *Clauserus*, the translator of *Cornutus*,* that it pleased the heavenly Deitie, by *Hesiod* and *Homer*, under the vaile of fables, to give us all knowledge, – Logick, Rethorick, Philosophy, naturall and morall; and *Quid non*? To beleeve, with me, that there are many mysteries contained in Poetrie, which of purpose were written darkely, least by prophane wits it should bee abused.* To beleeve, with *Landin*, that they are so beloved of the Gods that whatsoever they write proceeds of a divine fury.* Lastly, to beleeve themselves, when they tell you they will make you immortall by their verses.

Thus doing, your name shal flourish in the Printers' shops; thus doing, you shall bee of kinne to many a poeticall Preface;* thus doing, you shall be most faire, most rich, most wise, most all; you shall dwell upon Superlatives. Thus doing, though you be *Libertino patre natus*,* you shall suddenly grow *Herculea proles*,*

> *Si quid mea carmina possunt.**

Thus doing, your soule shal be placed with *Dante's Beatrix*, or *Virgil's Anchises*. But if (fie of such a but) you be borne so neere the dull-making *Cataract* of *Nilus** that you cannot heare the Planet-like Musick* of Poetrie, if you have so earth-creeping a mind that it cannot lift it selfe up to looke to the sky of Poetry, or rather, by a certaine rusticall disdaine, will become such a mome as to be a *Momus** of Poetry; then, though I will not wish unto you the Asse's eares of *Midas*,* nor to bee driven by a Poet's verses (as *Bubonax* was)* to hang himselfe, nor to be rimed to death, as is sayd to be doone in Ireland;* yet thus much curse I must send you in the behalfe of all Poets, that while you live, you live in love, and never get favour for lacking skill of a Sonnet, and when you die, your memory die from the earth for want of an Epitaph.

TWO PASTORALLS

I

*Upon his meeting with his two worthy Friends
and fellow-Poets, Sir Edward Dier,
and Maister Fulke Grevill.* *

Joyne Mates in mirth to me,
Graunt pleasure to our meeting:
Let *Pan* our good God* see,
How gratefull is our greeting.
    Joyne hearts and hands, so let it be,
    Make but one Minde in Bodies three.   5

Ye Hymnes, and singing skill
Of God *Apolloe's* giving,*
Be prest our reedes* to fill,
With sound of musicke living.   10
    Joyne hearts and hands, so let it be,
    Make but one Minde in Bodies three.

Sweete *Orpheus'* Harpe, whose sound
The stedfast mountaynes moved,*
Let heere thy skill abound,   15
To joyne sweete friends beloved.
    Joyne hearts and hands, so let it be,
    Make but one Minde in Bodies three.

My two and I be met,
A happy blessed Trinitie;   20
As three most joyntly set,
In firmest band of Unitie.*
    Joyne hearts and hands, so let it be,
    Make but one Minde in Bodies three.

Welcome my two to me, E.D. F.G. P.S.   25
The number best beloved,*
Within my heart you be

In friendship unremoved.
  Joyne hearts and hands, so let it be,
  Make but one Minde in Bodies three.   30

Give leave your flockes to range,
Let us the while be playing;
Within the Elmy grange,
Your flockes will not be straying.
  Joyne hearts and hands, so let it be,   35
  Make but one Minde in Bodies three.

Cause all the mirth you can,
Since I am now come hether,
Who never joy, but when
I am with you together.   40
  Joyne hearts and hands, so let it be,
  Make but one Minde in Bodies three.

Like Lovers do their Love,
So joy I, in you seeing;
Let nothing mee remove   45
From alwayes with you beeing.
  Joyne hearts and hands, so let it be,
  Make but one Minde in Bodies three.

And as the Turtle-Dove
To mate with whom he liveth,*   50
Such comfort, fervent love
Of you to my hart giveth.
  Joyne hearts and hands, so let it be,
  Make but one Minde in Bodies three.

Now joyned be our hands,   55
Let them be ne'r a sunder,
But linkt in binding bands
By metamorphoz'd wonder.*
  So should our sever'd bodies three
  As one for ever joyned bee.

II

*Disprayse of a Courtly life**

Walking in bright *Phœbus'* blaze
Where with heate oppreste I was,

I got to a shady wood,
Where greene leaves did newly bud.
And of grasse was plenty dwelling,
Deckt with pyde flowers sweetely smelling.   5

In this wood a man I met,*
On lamenting wholy set:
Rewing change of wonted state,
Whence he was transformed late,   10
Once to Shepheards' God retayning,
Now in servile Court remayning.

There he wandring malecontent,
Up and downe perplexed went,
Daring not to tell to mee,
Spake unto a sencelesse tree,   15
One among the rest electing
These same words, or this effecting:

'My old mates I grieve to see,
Voyde of me in field to bee,   20
Where we once our lovely sheepe,
Lovingly like friends did keepe,
Oft each other's friendship proving,
Never striving, but in loving.

'But may Love abiding bee   25
In poore shepheard's base degree?
It belongs to such alone
To whome arte of Love is knowne:*
Seely shepheards are not witting
What in art of Love is fitting.   30

'Nay, what neede the Arte to those,
To whome we our love disclose?
It is to be used then,
When we doe but flatter men:
Friendship true in hart assured,   35
Is by nature's giftes procured.

'Therefore shepheardes wanting skill,
Can Love's duties best fulfill:
Since they know not how to faine,
Nor with Love to cloake Disdaine,   40

Like the wiser sorte, whose learning,
Hides their inward will of harming.

'Well was I, while under shade
Oten Reedes* me musicke made,
Striving with my Mates in Song,*   45
Mixing mirth our Songs among,
Greater was that shepheards' treasure,
Then this false, fine, Courtly pleasure.

'Where, how many Creatures be,
So many pufft in minde I see,   50
Like to *Junoe's* birdes of pride,
Scarce each other can abide,
Friends like to blacke Swannes* appearing,
Sooner these than those in hearing.

'Therefore *Pan*,* if thou mayst be   55
Made to listen unto me,
Grant, I say (if seely man
May make treaty to god *Pan*)
That I, without thy denying,
May be still to thee relying.   60

'Only for my two loves' sake,   *Sir Ed. D. and M.F.G.*
In whose love I pleasure take,
Only two do me delight
With their ever-pleasing sight,
Of all men to thee retaining,   65
Grant me with those two remaining.

'So shall I to thee alwayes
With my reedes, sound mighty praise;
And first Lambe that shall befall
Yearely decke thine Altar shall: 70
If it please thee be reflected,
And I from thee not rejected.'

So I left him in that place,
Taking pitty on his case,
Learning this among the rest,   75
That the meane estate is best,
Better filled with contenting,
Voyde of wishing and repenting.

Psalm VIII*

Domine Dominus

1 O Lord that rul'st our mortall lyne
     How through the World thy Name doth shine:
     That hast of thine unmatched glory
     Upon the heavns engrav'n the story.

2 From sucklings hath Thy honour sproong,   5
     Thy force hath flow'd from Babie's tongue
     Wherby Thou stop'st Thyne Enemy's prating
     Bent to revenge and ever hating.

3 When I upon the Heav'ns do look
     Which all from Thee their Essence took   10
     When Moone and Starrs my thoughtes beholdeth
     Whose life no life but of Thee holdeth,

4 Then think I: Ah, what is this Man,
     Whom that Great God remember can?
     And what the race of him descended   15
     It should be ought of God attended?

5 For though in lesse than Angel's state
     Thou planted hast this earthly mate,*
     Yet hast Thou made even him an owner
     Of glorious Croune, and crouning honour.   20

6 Thou placest him upon all lands
     To rule the works of Thyne own hands,
     And so thou hast all things ordained
     That even his feet have on them raigned.

7 Thou under his Dominion plac't   25
     Both Sheep and Oxen wholy hast,
     And all the Beasts for ever breeding
     Which in the fertile fields be feeding.

8 The Bird, free Burgess of the ayre,   30
     The Fish, of Sea the Native heire,

And what thinges els of waters traceth
The unworn paths, his rule embraceth. *
9   O Lord that rulest our mortall lyne,
How through the World Thy name doth shine.

Psalm XIII *

Usque quo Domine

1   How long, O Lord, shall I forgotten be?
      What? ever?
   How long wilt Thou Thy hidden face from me
      Dissever?

2   How long shall I consult with carefull sprite   5
      In anguish?
   How long shall I with foes' triumphant might
      Thus languish?

3   Behold me, Lord, let to Thy hearing creep
      My crying: 10
   Nay give me eyes, and light, least that I sleep
      In dying.

4   Least my Foe bragg, that in my ruin hee
      Prevailed,
   And at my fall they joy that, troublous, me   15
      Assailed.

5   No, No I trust on Thee, and joy in Thy
      Great Pity.
   Still therfore of Thy Graces shall be my
      Song's Ditty.   20

Psalm XIV

Dixit Insipiens

1   The foolish man by flesh and fancy led
      His guiltie heart with this fond thought hath fed,
         There is no God that raigneth.
   And so thereafter he, and all his mates

Do works which earth corrupt and Heaven hates,   5
    Not one that good remaineth.

2 Even God himself sent down his peircing ey,
    If of this Clayey race* he could espy
      One that his Wisdom learneth:
3 And lo, he finds that all astraying went,   10
    All plung'd in stinking filth, not one well bent,
      Not one, that God discerneth.

4 O madnesse of these folks, thus loosely led,
    These Canibals,* who, as if they were bread
      God's people do devower,   15
5 Nor ever call on God, but they shall quake
    More than they now do bragg, when He shall take
      The just into his power.

6 Indeed the poore, opprest by you, you mock,
    Their counsills are your common jesting stock   20
      But God is their recomfort.
7 Ah, when from Syon shall the saver come,
    That Jacob freed by Thee may glad become
      And Israel full of comfort?

Psalm XXIII

Dominus regit me

1 The lord the lord my shepheard is,
    And so can never I
      Tast misery.
2 He rests me in green pasture his
    By waters still and sweet   5
      He guides my feet.

3 He me revives; leads me the way
    Which righteousness doth take,
      For his name's sake.
4 Yea tho I should thro vallys stray   10
    Of death's dark shade I will
      No whit feare ill.

For thou, Deare Lord, Thou me besetst,
  Thy rodd, and Thy staffe be
    To comfort me.   15
5 Before me Thou a table setst,
  Ev'en when foe's envious ey
    Doth it espy.

With oyle Thou dost annoynt my head,
  And so my cup dost fill   20
    That it doth spill.
6 Thus, thus shall all my days be fede,
  This mercy is so sure
    It shall endure,
And long, yea long, abide I shall,   25
  There where the Lord of all
    Doth hold his hall. *

Psalm XXIV

Domini est terra

1 The earth is God's, and what the Globe of earth containeth,
  And all who in that Globe do dwell;
2 For by his power the land upon the Ocean raigneth,
  Through him the floods to their beds fell.
3   Who shall climb to the hill, which God's own hill is named,
     Who shall stand in his Holy place?   6
4   He that hath hurtless hands, whose inward heart is framed
     All pureness ever to embrace;
Who shunning vanity, and works of vaineness leaving,
  Vainly doth not puff up his mind;   10
Who never doth deceive, and much lesse his deceaving
  With perjury doth falsly bind.

5 A blessing from the Lord, from God of his salvation,
  Sweet Righteousness shall he receive;
6 Jacob this is thy seed, God-seeking generation,   15
  Who search of God's face never leave.
7   Lift up your heads you Gates, and you doores ever biding,
     In comes the King of glory bright.
8   Who is this glorious King in might and power riding?
     The lord whose strength makes battails fight. *   20

9   Lift up your heads you gates, and you doores ever-biding,
          In comes the King of glory bright.
10   Who is this Glorious King? The lord of armyes guiding,
          Even He the King of glory hight.

Psalm XLII*

[*Quemadmodum*]

1   As the chafed hart which brayeth
      Seeking some refreshing brook,
      So my soul in panting playeth,
      Thirsting on my God to look.
2   My soul thirsts indeed in me   5
          After ever-living Thee;
          Ah, when comes my blessed being,
          Of Thy face to have a seing?

3   Day and night my teares out flowing
      Have been my ill-feeding food,   10
      With their dayly questions throwing:
      'Where is now Thy God so good?'
4   My heart melts remembring so,
          How in troops I wont to go,
          Leading them his prayses singing,   15
          Holy daunce to God's house bringing.

5   Why art Thou, my soul, so sorry
      And in me so much dismaid?
      Wait on God, for yet his glory
      In my song shall be display'd.   20
6   When but with one look of his
          He shall me restore to blisse:
          Ah my soul it self appaleth,
          In such longing thoughts it falleth.

      For my mind on my God bideth,   25
      Ev'n from Hermon's dwelling led,
      From the grounds where Jordan slideth
      And from Mizzar's hilly head.
7   One deep with noyse of his fall,
          Other deeps of woes doth call,   30

While my God with wasting wonders
On me, wretch, his tempest thunders.

All Thy floods on me abounded,
Over me all Thy waves went;
Yet thus still my hope is grounded,   35
8 That Thy anger being spent,
   I by day thy love shall tast,
   I by night shall singing last,
   Praying, prayers still bequeathing
   To my God that gave me breathing.   40

9 I will say: O Lord, my tower,
Why am I forgott by Thee?
Why should grief my heart devower,
While the foe oppresseth me?
10   Those vile scoffes of naughty ones   45
   Wound and rent me to the bones,
   When foes ask with foule deriding,
   'Where hath now your God his biding?'

11 Why art thou my soul so sorry
And in me so much dismaid?   50
Wait on God, for yet his glory
In my song shall be displayed.
   To him my thanks shall be said
   Who is still my present aid,
   And in fine my soul be raysed;   55
   God is my God, by me praysed.

Psalm XLIII*

Iudica me Deus

1 Judge of all, judge me
And Protector bee
   Of my Cause, oppressed
By most cruel sprites,
Save me from bad wights   5
   In false colours dressed.

2 For, my God, Thy sight
Giveth me my might,

    Why then hast Thou left me?
    Why walk I in woes   10
    While prevayling foes
      Have of joyes bereft me?

3 Send Thy truth and light.
    Let them guide me right
      From the paths of folly,   15
    Bringing me to Thy
    Tabernacle high
      In Thy hill most holy.

4 To God's Altars tho
    Will I boldly go   30
      Shaking off all sadnes,
    To that God that is
    God of all my blisse,
      God of all my gladness.

    Then lo, then I will   25
    With sweet musick's skill
      Gratefull meaning show Thee,
    Then God, yea my God,
    I will sing abroad
      What great thanks I ow Thee.   30

5 Why art thou my soul
    Cast down in such dole?
      What ayles thy discomfort?
    Wait on God, for still
    Thank my God I will,
      Sure aid, present comfort.   35

GLOSSARY

The Lady of May

p. 4 **fosters**: foresters
p. 4 **superfluous**: overflowing
p. 4 **minsicall**: dainty
p. 4 **disanulled**: emptied
p. 4 **featioust**: most accomplished
p. 4 **fransicall**: frantic
p. 5 **disnounce**: explain
p. 5 **loquence**: eloquence
p. 5 **vent**: express
p. 5 **transfund**: pour out
p. 5 **dotes**: gifts
p. 5 **formositie**: beauty
p. 5 **juventall frie**: youthful young
p. 5 **mansuetude**: kindness
p. 5 **sanguinolent**: bloodthirsty
p. 5 **sulkes**: furrows
p. 5 **sandiferous**: sand-bearing
p. 5 **quodammodo**: in a certain manner
p. 5 **inquam**: I say
p. 6 **chafe**: fury
p. 6 **turpifie**: besmirch
p. 6 **doctrine**: learning
p. 6 **brave**: glorious
p. 7 *verses*: lines
p. 7 **desire**: object of desire
p. 8 *baudrickes*: shoulder belts
p. 9 **silly**: simple
p. 9 **harlotrie**: flirt
p. 9 **bleaying**: lowing
p. 10 **proller**: prowler
p. 10 **Nebulons**: worthless creatures

p. 10 **edifie**: construct
p. 10 **gravidated**: heavily pregnant
p. 10 **endoctrinated**: instructed
p. 10 **plumbeous**: leaden
p. 10 **cerebrosities**: brains
p. 10 **divisionate**: subdivide
p. 10 *quasi*: as if
p. 10 **uniforme**: suit
p. 10 **secundum**: secondly
p. 10 **dignity**: worth
p. 10 *species*: kinds
p. 10 **meliority**: superiority
p. 10 **functions**: occupations
p. 10 *De . . . satis*: Enough about . . .
p. 10 *Nunc*: Now
p. 10 **qualifying**: defining
p. 10 **whether**: which
p. 10 **purchased**: attained
p. 11 **concerne**: understand
p. 11 **Lommes**: lambs
p. 11 **templation**: contemplation
p. 11 **Clerks**: learned men
p. 11 **Templars**: those given to contemplation
p. 11 **odible**: hateful
p. 11 *Tace*: be silent
p. 11 **ignified**: set on fire
p. 11 **delucidate**: make clear
p. 11 **intrinsicall**: inner
p. 11 **maribone**: marrow-bone
p. 11 **invasion**: entry
p. 11 **equitate**: (over)-ride
p. 12 *Ergo*: therefore
p. 12 **contingentes**: close
p. 12 **acquiescate**: agree
p. 12 *major*: major point
p. 12 *minor*: secondary point
p. 12 **contentation**: satisfaction
p. 12 **hurtlesse**: harmless
p. 12 **ensamples**: examples
p. 12 **painfull**: painstaking

p. 12 **incepted:** former (beginning with the first, i.e. Therion)
p. 14 **blisse:** bless

Certaine Sonets

p. 15 **gratefull gardien:** kindly gaoler
p. 15 **affectes:** passions
p. 15 **mortall:** deadly
p. 15 **Dead palsie sick of:** paralysed in
p. 16 **blazed:** emblazoned
p. 17 **wrokne:** committed
p. 18 *Wood:* mad
p. 20 **Molde:** mole
p. 20 **corse:** body
p. 20 **faire scorne:** a fair lady's scorn
p. 20 **franzie:** frenzy
p. 21 **due desert:** one who deserves her
p. 21 **temper:** moderate
p. 21 **marke:** target
p. 21 **Band:** gathering

Astrophil and Stella

p. 23 **leaves:** pages
p. 23 **sunne-burn'd:** parched
p. 23 **trewand:** idle
p. 24 **daintie:** delicate
p. 24 **maskt:** disguised
p. 24 **Apes:** mimics
p. 24 **Tropes:** figures of speech
p. 24 **reed:** read
p. 24 **bate:** dispute
p. 24 **vaine:** useless
p. 24 **inward light:** reason
p. 25 **Broadred:** embroidered
p. 26 **clips:** embraces
p. 26 **furniture:** embellishment
p. 26 **Porphir:** porphyry
p. 26 **windowes:** (her eyes)
p. 26 **touch:** jet
p. 26 **brabling:** quarrelling

p. 26 **Muses' hill:** Parnassus
p. 27 **fence:** swordplay
p. 27 **strake:** struck
p. 27 **kind:** nature
p. 27 **pitfould:** trap
p. 27 **bopeepe:** hide-and-seek
p. 27 **breach:** way through
p. 28 **armes:** heraldic blazons
p. 28 **talents:** claws
p. 28 **Vert:** green
p. 28 **gueuls:** red (gules)
p. 28 **blaze:** display
p. 28 **scantly:** hardly
p. 28 **Gripe:** vulture
p. 29 **denisend:** naturalised
p. 29 **far-fet:** far-fetched
p. 29 **inward tuch:** natural ability
p. 29 **endite:** express
p. 29 **carrets:** carats.
p. 29 **stripes:** blows
p. 29 **chafe:** anger
p. 29 **wags:** boys
p. 29 **shrewd turnes:** mischievous tricks
p. 30 **checkes:** reproaches
p. 30 **shent:** ashamed
p. 30 **banckrout:** bankrupt
p. 30 **toyes:** trifles
p. 30 **wracke:** ruin
p. 30 **Avise:** warne
p. 30 **bullet:** bird-bolt
p. 30 **Tyran:** tyrant
p. 30 **levell:** aim
p. 31 **passenger:** passer-by
p. 31 **healthfull caustiks:** corrosive medicines
p. 31 **marde:** hampered
p. 31 **windlas:** encircle
p. 31 **but if:** unless
p. 31 **coltish gyres:** youthful cavorting
p. 31 **least:** lest
p. 31 **weare a traine of:** lead to
p. 31 **race:** course

p. 31 **unarmed:** uncovered
p. 32 **Bewray:** betray
p. 32 **blist:** blessed
p. 33 **inward sunne:** the light of reason
p. 33 **ster:** stir up
p. 33 **weeds:** garments
p. 33 **brawle:** dance
p. 34 **raines:** reins
p. 34 **slake:** loose
p. 34 **but for:** only
p. 34 **prospect:** situation
p. 34 *Dutch*: Germans
p. 35 *Holland*: Dutch
p. 35 **weltring:** political disorder
p. 35 *Indes*: Indies
p. 36 **rent:** rend
p. 36 **fond ware:** worthless goods
p. 36 **idler:** more useless
p. 36 **hard:** heard
p. 36 **wreake:** inflict
p. 36 **cole:** coal
p. 37 **yelden:** surrendered
p. 37 **razde:** destroyed
p. 37 **crowne:** (of heavenly blessedness)
p. 38 **hatch:** close up
p. 38 **unbitted:** unrestrained
p. 38 **error:** straying
p. 38 **drought:** draftsmanship
p. 38 **decay:** failing (in sleep)
p. 38 **it:** Stella's image
p. 38 **baiting:** feeding
p. 38 **indifferent:** equal
p. 38 **prease:** heavy assault
p. 39 **wreckes:** retribution
p. 39 **daintier:** more perceptive
p. 39 **sleight:** skill
p. 39 **use:** practice
p. 39 **race:** course
p. 39 **Spheares:** planets
p. 39 **remove:** go
p. 39 **Keepe . . . Zenith:** stay directly overhead

p. 39 **straight wayes:** immediately
p. 40 **rome:** room
p. 40 **kind:** nature
p. 40 **annoyes:** griefs
p. 40 **skill:** understand how
p. 40 **disgrace:** misfortune
p. 40 **fable:** fiction
p. 41 **Then:** than
p. 41 **wracke:** ruin
p. 41 **becke:** gesture
p. 41 **Rogue:** vagabond
p. 41 **wag:** boy
p. 41 **myche:** play truant
p. 41 **burning markes:** brands
p. 42 **beamie:** shining
p. 42 **raines:** reins
p. 42 **guilt bosse:** gilded knob ornamenting the bit
p. 42 **Wand:** whip
p. 42 **do sturre:** am fractious
p. 42 **Manage:** exercise (as in modern dressage)
p. 42 **staid:** kept
p. 43 **put out:** erase
p. 43 **dashed:** crossed out
p. 43 **silly:** simple
p. 43 **errour:** wandering
p. 43 **maner:** kind of
p. 43 **demurre:** objection
p. 43 **sute:** law-suit
p. 44 **rule:** control
p. 44 **courtly Nymphs:** court ladies
p. 44 **so:** providing that
p. 44 **Pies:** magpies
p. 44 **staid:** kept from
p. 44 **a foraging:** roving in search of provisions
p. 45 **peece of look:** glance
p. 45 **brooke:** endure
p. 45 **dainty rind:** delicate skin
p. 45 **mone:** complaint
p. 46 **tropes:** figure of speech
p. 46 **pronouncing grace:** delivery
p. 46 **rudest:** least subtle

p. 46 **anatomy:** analysis
p. 46 **wrate:** wrote
p. 46 **reed:** expound
p. 46 **clog:** hindrance
p. 47 **lovely:** loving
p. 47 **selfnesse:** thought of self
p. 47 **live's:** life's
p. 47 **Doctor:** teacher
p. 48 **awfull:** awe-struck
p. 48 **graunt to me:** gift to me
p. 48 **state with pleasure:** dignity with delight
p. 48 **stayneth:** puts (all others) in the shade
p. 49 **disgrace:** mishap
p. 50 **courage:** heart
p. 50 **apprehending:** understanding
p. 50 **stilts:** crutches
p. 50 **take time:** pause
p. 51 **doth only aspire:** does alone aspire
p. 52 **Boy:** Cupid
p. 52 **raisde:** loud
p. 53 **Lowring:** frowning
p. 53 **his mother's:** Venus'
p. 54 **lowre:** frown
p. 54 **vulgar:** common
p. 54 **Flouredeluce:** fleur de lys: the arms of France
p. 54 **bloudy Lyon's:** red lion, the arms of Scotland
p. 54 *Lewis*: Louis XI of France
p. 54 **Prove:** risk
p. 55 **twins:** eyes
p. 55 **staid:** halting
p. 55 **walking hed:** wandering mind
p. 55 **lecture:** lesson
p. 55 **sublime:** extract
p. 55 **consterd:** construed
p. 56 **consort:** harmony
p. 56 **retrait:** retreat
p. 56 **ostage:** hostage
p. 56 **Honour's graine:** imperial purple colour
p. 56 **resty:** sluggish
p. 57 **your cut to keepe:** behave properly
p. 58 **neast:** nest

p. 58 **amaze:** stun

p. 58 **Tempers:** fits

p. 59 **undercharge:** delegated task

p. 59 **weale:** joy

p. 59 **indentures:** contracts

p. 60 **Niggard:** miserly

p. 60 **endite:** compose

p. 60 **but:** unless

p. 61 **gripe on:** rend (like a vulture)

p. 61 **reynes:** reins

p. 61 **partiall:** unfair

p. 62 **Ambrosian pap:** divine nourishment

p. 62 **babies:** dolls

p. 62 **shrewd:** spiteful

p. 62 **paine:** trouble

p. 63 **the Sonne:** Cupid

p. 63 **Vagrant from the Mother:** deserting from Venus

p. 63 **refuse:** rejection

p. 63 **powre:** pour

p. 63 **Who:** those who

p. 63 **froward:** perverse

p. 63 **whether of the choice:** which of the two

p. 63 **former:** first

p. 64 **bate:** dispute

p. 64 **barre:** law-court

p. 64 **to other:** to the other

p. 65 **whether:** which

p. 65 **pide weeds:** varicoloured garments

p. 66 **of annoy:** over distress

p. 67 **on to passe:** to go further

p. 67 **roome:** place

p. 67 **such wise:** in this way

p. 69 **caitife:** captive

p. 69 **seaze:** seize

p. 70 **blaying:** bleating

p. 70 **unjust decaying:** unmerited decline

p. 70 **vext:** troubled

p. 70 **Captainnesse:** commanding officer

p. 70 **cates:** delicacies

p. 71 **long-staid:** long delayed

p. 71 **history:** story

p. 71 **laud**: praise
p. 71 **Without**: unless
p. 71 **endite**: express
p. 71 **hed**: head
p. 72 **seeing jets**: black eyes
p. 72 **wood-globes . . . skies**: celestial globes
p. 72 **Indian ware**: precious material
p. 72 **cutted**: laconic
p. 73 **seaze**: seize
p. 73 **licorous**: wanton
p. 74 **vexed**: distressed
p. 74 **Caitif's**: wretch's
p. 74 **quite**: acquit
p. 74 **harbengers**: fore-runners
p. 74 **caitife**: wretch
p. 74 **causefull**: justified
p. 74 **thy life**: (Grief's existence)
p. 75 **maine rage**: mad fury
p. 75 **kind**: nature
p. 75 **liverie**: uniform
p. 75 **one degree**: the same rank
p. 75 **moisture**: dew
p. 75 **mazefull**: terrifying
p. 75 **gastly**: fearful
p. 75 **stur**: stir
p. 75 **fur**: by far
p. 75 *Phœbus'*: the Sun's
p. 75 **weedes**: garment
p. 75 **doth dight**: dress herself
p. 75 **peere**: companion
p. 76 **shortly rained**: reined in
p. 76 **winke**: close
p. 76 **marke-wanting**: lacking a target
p. 76 **mazde**: confused
p. 76 **charme**: song
p. 76 **wight**: man
p. 77 *Zephires*: south-west breezes
p. 77 **annoy**: distress
p. 77 **conclusions tries**: engages in rivalry
p. 77 **heaven stuffe**: heavenly material
p. 77 **faire encrease**: lovely blushes

p. 77 kindly: natural
p. 77 weeds: garments
p. 77 vade: fade
p. 77 selfe engraind: herself dyed
p. 77 hackney on: jog onward
p. 77 furre: far
p. 77 sturre: stir
p. 78 *Tems*: river Thames
p. 78 planets: (her eyes)
p. 78 rigrows: harsh, severe
p. 78 empty glasse: empty windows, because Stella is not looking out from behind them
p. 78 From out my ribs: by tiring out my heart
p. 78 playneth: complains
p. 78 vulgar: common
p. 79 minds to nourish: indulge such memories
p. 79 get anger: become angry
p. 80 race: progress
p. 80 Nectar mist: missed your heavenly refreshment
p. 80 Bare me in hand: beguiled me
p. 80 thou: Hope
p. 80 charme: music
p. 80 mould: earth
p. 80 right: true
p. 81 Lieftenancy: delegated command
p. 81 fornace: furnace
p. 81 *Phoebus'* gold: sunlight
p. 81 use: enjoyment

The Defence of Poesie

p. 83 commendation: credit
p. 83 practise: skill
p. 83 *Pedanteria*: (Italian) pedantic trifle.
p. 84 silly: simple
p. 85 policie: statecraft
p. 86 *Indians*: West Indians
p. 86 *Areytos*: Spanish, *aréito*, from a West Indian word for a kind of dance accompanied by singing
p. 86 Authors: originators
p. 86 Sciences: branches of knowledge

p. 86 *Vates:* (Latin) prophet.

p. 86 conjoined: related

p. 86 *Vaticinium:* (Latin) a prophecy

p. 86 *Vaticinari:* (Latin) to prophesy

p. 86 *Sortes Virgilianae:* (Latin) lots drawn from Virgil's works

p. 86 *Carmina:* (Latin) verses/incantations

p. 87 interpreted: translated

p. 87 *Prosopopeias:* (Greek) προσωποποιίαι different kinds of personification

p. 87 *Poiein:* (Greek) ποιεῖν to make

p. 88 thereon hath his name: takes his name from this.

p. 88 thereon give artificial rules: suit their invented rules to this

p. 88 supernaturall: above physical nature

p. 88 knowe: discover

p. 89 imaginative: fantastic

p. 89 substantially: factually

p. 89 that maker: Xenophon

p. 89 erected wit: aspiring intelligence

p. 89 infected: corrupted

p. 89 with some probabilitie of reason gave: had strong arguments for giving

p. 89 opening: view

p. 89 principall: supreme

p. 89 *Mimesis:* (Greek) μίμησις imitation

p. 90 naturall: concerned with the natural order

p. 90 properly: in fact

p. 90 most properly: most fully

p. 90 rayned with: restrained by

p. 91 numbrous: using scansion

p. 91 versified: wrote in verse (as opposed to prose)

p. 91 *effigiem iusti imperii:* (Latin) the image of a just empire.

p. 91 sugred invention: sweet discovery

p. 91 peyzing: weighing

p. 91 Anatomies: analyses

p. 92 scope: capacity

p. 92 serving: supporting

p. 92 *Arkitecktonike:* (Greek) ἀρχιτεκτονική the master-science; Aristotle, *Ethics* I i 4

p. 92 shewe: demonstrate

p. 93 interogative: question

p. 93 specialities: particulars

p. 93 onely: alone

p. 94 poynt: conclusion

p. 94 *Formidine poenae*: (Latin) by fear of punishment

p. 94 *Virtutis amore*: (Latin) by love of virtue

p. 94 naughtines: wickedness

p. 94 hard of utterance: obscurely expressed

p. 94 mistie to bee conceived: opaque to the understanding

p. 95 peerelesse: unequalled

p. 95 but a wordish description: a merely verbal account

p. 95 conceits: understanding

p. 95 judicial: accurate

p. 95 *Genus* and Difference: species and sub-species

p. 96 historicall acts: actual events

p. 97 *Philosophoteron*: (Greek) φιλόσοφοτερον loving wisdom more

p. 97 *Spoudaioteron*: (Greek) σπουδαιοτερον more earnest

p. 97 *Katholou*: (Greek) καθόλου in general

p. 97 *Kathekaston*: (Greek) καθέκαστον specific

p. 97 *wayes*: weighs

p. 97 imposed: chosen

p. 97 ful ill-favoured: very ugly

p. 98 as for to move: as far as exciting the passions is concerned

p. 98 verifying: proof

p. 98 like: similar

p. 98 honest dissimulation: admirable deceit

p. 99 faction: deed

p. 99 little animate: hardly encourage

p. 99 then: at the moment

p. 99 *Literas nescivit*: (Latin) he was illiterate

p. 99 by: with reference to

p. 100 *Occidendos esse*: (Latin) that they must fall

p. 100 of: over

p. 100 *Philophilosophos*: (Greek) φιλοφιλόσοφος but possibly Sidney's own coinage: lover of the love of wisdom

p. 100 moving: stirring the passions

p. 100 not *Gnosis* but *Praxis*: (Greek) γνῶσις ... πρᾶξις not knowing but doing. Aristotle, *Ethics* i.

p. 101 *Hoc ... est*: this is labour indeed. Virgil, *Aeneid* VI 129

p. 102 *indulgere genio*: (Latin) give in to appetite

p. 102 as: that

p. 102 apparent shew: obvious signs

p. 102 (for that time): for that early period

p. 102 **insinuations**: hints

p. 102 **Maximes**: precepts

p. 102 **familiar**: friendly

p. 102 **each others'**: all the others'

p. 102 **notorious**: famous

p. 103 **ungratefullie**: wrongfully

p. 103 **defectious**: imperfect

p. 103 *Species*: (Latin) types

p. 104 **who**: the elegiac poet

p. 104 **abuse**: corruption

p. 105 **oblique . . . right**: (angles)

p. 105 **odde . . . even**: (numbers)

p. 105 **badge**: characteristic

p. 105 *Pistrinum*: (Latin) a mill where slaves did penal labour

p. 105 **So as**: so that

p. 106 **Liricke**: lyric poet

p. 106 **wel accorded**: well tuned

p. 106 **Crouder**: fiddler

p. 106 *Lacedemonians*: Spartans

p. 106 **field**: field of battle

p. 106 **lusty men**: men in their prime

p. 106 **as**: so

p. 106 *Olympus*: the Olympic Games

p. 106 **fearefull felicities**: joys so great as to arouse fear of the Gods' displeasure

p. 107 **holyday**: festive

p. 107 **tablet**: note-book

p. 107 **Worthies**: heroes

p. 107 **religious ceremonies**: household Gods

p. 107 **government**: behaviour

p. 108 **conceite**: concept

p. 108 **severed dissections**: aspects examined separately

p. 108 **of**: above

p. 108 **a playing wit**: perverse cleverness

p. 109 *Oratio . . . Ratio*: (Latin) Speech . . . Reason

p. 109 **without, perchaunce**: unless, perhaps

p. 109 **great affinitie**: close relationship

p. 109 **accuseth**: calls attention to

p. 109 **the follower**: what follows

p. 110 **to**: against

p. 110 **abuse**: corruption

p. 110 **to eare:** to sow (Chaucer: *Knight's Tale* 1. 28)

p. 110 *petere principium:* (Latin) look for a starting point

p. 111 **aver:** state as a fact

p. 111 **affirme:** assert

p. 111 **cloudy:** unclear

p. 111 **circles:** magic circles

p. 111 **conjure you:** cast a spell on you

p. 111 **his entry:** the opening of his work

p. 111 **good invention:** worthy theme

p. 111 **without:** except

p. 111 **affirmatively:** literally

p. 112 **conceite:** assumption

p. 112 **lively:** life-like

p. 112 **abuseth:** corrupts

p. 112 **Elegiack:** elegiac poet

p. 112 **hard:** difficult

p. 112 **wit:** mind

p. 112 *Eikastike:* (Greek) ʼεικαστική able to represent

p. 113 *Phantastike:* (Greek) φανταστική able to suggest an appearance (Plato's distinction, *Sophister*, 235–6).

p. 113 **better hidden matters:** matters better hidden

p. 113 **conceiveth his title:** bases its value

p. 113 **rampier:** rampart

p. 113 **in price:** valued

p. 113 **chaine-shot:** shot linked by chains to destroy masts, rigging etc.

p. 114 **ordinary doctrine:** common teaching

p. 114 **Camps:** military encampments

p. 114 **quiddity:** nature

p. 114 *Ens:* (Latin) being

p. 114 *Prima materia:* (Latin) first matter

p. 114 **Corslet:** body armour

p. 115 **the former:** the earlier (Cato the Censor)

p. 115 **carried:** taken

p. 115 **unmustered:** not enrolled

p. 116 **abused:** corrupted

p. 116 **followed:** used

p. 117 **very:** true

p. 117 **them:** the poets

p. 117 **gards:** ornaments

p. 119 **strew the house:** (with fresh herbs, in welcome)

p. 119 **inclinable:** inclined

p. 120 *Genius*: (Latin) guardian spirit

p. 120 *Orator fit, Poeta nascitur*: (Latin) an orator is made, a poet is born one.

p. 120 *Quodlibet*: (Latin) whatever you please

p. 120 wants: lacks

p. 120 meetely: aptly

p. 121 reason: sense

p. 121 very: true

p. 121 circumstaunces: plot

p. 121 inartificially: inartistically

p. 121 conceived: understood

p. 121 Upon . . . that: immediately

p. 121 traverces: trials

p. 121 sence: common sense

p. 122 most tragicall conveniencie: as best suits tragedy

p. 122 *Calicut*: in South West India, now called Kozhikode

p. 122 *Nuntius*: messenger

p. 122 *Ab ovo*: from the egg: Horace, *Ars Poetica* 1. 147

p. 122 slight: trick

p. 122 delivery: birth

p. 122 conceive: understand

p. 122 carrieth: demands

p. 123 daintily: delicately

p. 123 admiration: wonder

p. 123 Comedians: writers of comedy

p. 123 conveniencie to our selves: fitting our own natures

p. 123 byas: bias

p. 123 as for . . . of them: out of respect for them

p. 124 Clowne: rustic

p. 124 busy: impertinent

p. 124 names: characters

p. 124 honesty: chastity

p. 124 of which: about whom

p. 124 but we . . . have: without always having

p. 124 occasions: discoveries

p. 125 bewrayed: recognised

p. 125 *Energia*: (Greek) ἐνέργεια energy, vitality

p. 125 figures and flowers: elaborate rhetoric

p. 125 artificially: by art

p. 125 choller: anger

p. 125 hale . . . sometime: quote them sometimes

p. 125 **store:** many
p. 125 *Similiter Cadenses*: (Latin) the closing of successive phrases in the same rhythmic pattern
p. 125 **sounde:** agree with
p. 125 **gravitie:** solemnity
p. 125 **daintinesse:** grace
p. 125 **Sophister:** a speaker using fallacious tricks of argument
p. 126 **opinion:** reputation
p. 126 **seeming finenesse:** apparent skill
p. 126 **ende:** purpose
p. 126 **rifled up:** seized on
p. 126 **set by:** set store by
p. 126 **knacks:** tricks
p. 126 **generally:** frequently
p. 126 **curiously:** skillfully
p. 126 **professors:** claimants
p. 126 **pounded:** penned up
p. 126 **which is not:** which is not to presume
p. 127 **bend:** turn
p. 127 **mingled:** mixed
p. 127 **wanteth:** lacks
p. 127 **end:** purpose
p. 127 **quantitie:** length of syllables
p. 127 **number:** number of syllables
p. 127 **Whether:** which
p. 127 **divers:** various
p. 127 **in fine:** to conclude
p. 127 **Vulgar:** modern, vernacular
p. 127 **Dutch:** German
p. 127 *Antepenultima*: (Latin) third from last
p. 128 **ryme:** rhythm
p. 128 **quantity:** length of syllable
p. 128 **ryme:** rhyme
p. 128 **Poet-apes:** would-be poets
p. 128 **fables:** fictions
p. 128 *Quid non?*: (Latin) what not?
p. 129 **mome:** buffoon

Two Pastoralls

p. 131 **Mates:** close friends
p. 131 **gratefull:** delightful

p. 131 **prest:** induced
p. 131 **jointly:** closely
p. 131 **E.D. F.G. P.S.:** Edward Dyer; Fulke Greville; Philip Sidney.
p. 132 **grange:** farm enclosure
p. 132 **but:** except
p. 132 *Phœbus':* Apollo: the sun
p. 133 **pyde:** varicoloured
p. 133 **wonted:** accustomed
p. 133 **Shepheards' God:** Pan
p. 133 **retayning:** bound in service
p. 133 **malecontent:** discontented
p. 133 **tell:** relate
p. 133 **electing:** choosing
p. 133 **this effecting:** to this effect
p. 133 **Voyde of me:** lacking me
p. 133 **lovely:** affectionate
p. 133 **Never . . . loving:** never competing except in the strength of our love for each other
p. 133 **base:** humble
p. 133 **Seely:** simple
p. 133 **are not witting:** do not know
p. 133 **disclose:** reveal
p. 133 **skill:** artifice
p. 134 **pufft in minde:** swollen with conceit
p. 134 *Junoe's . . . pride:* peacocks
p. 134 **treaty:** entreaty
p. 134 **relying:** devoted
p. 134 *Sir Ed. D. and M.F.G.:* see p. 131 n.
p. 134 **reflected:** appeased
p. 134 **meane estate:** lowly station in life

The Psalms of David

p. 135 **prating:** pointless tattle
p. 135 **life:** continued existence
p. 135 **but . . . holdeth:** except what depends on Thee
p. 135 **what:** what is
p. 135 **of:** from
p. 135 **It:** that it
p. 135 **should . . . attended?:** should merit any attention from God
p. 135 **upon:** to rule over

p. 135 **That even . . . raigned:** so that indeed they are under his power

p. 135 **Thou . . . hast:** Thou has placed both sheep and oxen wholly under his dominion

p. 136 **Dissever:** cut off

p. 136 **careful sprite:** troubled spirit

p. 136 **with:** against

p. 136 **troublous:** aggressive

p. 136 **Ditty:** theme

p. 137 **mates:** companions

p. 137 **If:** whether

p. 137 **power:** protection

p. 137 **recomfort:** resource

p. 137 **comfort:** strength

p. 137 **green . . . his:** either 'in his green pasture', or 'in green pasture as one of his flock'

p. 138 **me besetst:** art near me

p. 138 **comfort:** strengthen

p. 138 **sure:** certain

p. 138 **upon . . . raigneth:** rules over

p. 138 **hurtless:** innocent

p. 138 **vanity:** folly

p. 138 **Vainly . . . up:** doth not fill his mind with empty pride

p. 138 **search of:** the search for

p. 138 **leave:** abandon

p. 139 **chafed:** heated

p. 139 **brayeth:** gasps

p. 139 **ill-feeding:** poorly nourishing

p. 139 **in troops:** with groups of companions

p. 139 **appaleth:** is faint

p. 139 **deep:** water-course

p. 140 **wasting wonders:** marvels of destruction

p. 140 **last:** endure

p. 140 **naughty:** wicked

p. 140 **present:** immediate

p. 140 **in fine:** to conclude

p. 140 **cruel sprites:** malicious minds

p. 140 **dressed:** disguised

p. 141 **tho:** therefore

p. 141 **Gratefull meaning:** pleasing intent

p. 141 **dole:** misery

p. 141 **What . . . discomfort?:** what causes thee distress?

NOTES

The Lady of May

p. 3 title: The Earl of Leicester owned Wanstead from 1577. The Queen visited him there eight times, but only twice in May: in 1578 and again in 1579. The comparatively simple versification of the songs in particular suggests that *The Lady of May* was probably written for the first of these occasions (see Ringler, p. 362). It is the earliest self-contained dramatic pastoral compliment in English, not forming part of any more elaborate local entertainments such as those of Kenilworth in 1575. The device whereby a distinguished guest comes upon the action by apparent accident was well established, however. The surface impression of the piece is misleading: the fun and charm play transparently over serious political hopes and expectations. The Queen's Judgement in favour of Espilus undercut these, quite deliberately. See nn. p. 14 below.

p. 4 *Maister* Rhombus: 'spinning-top' (Greek), or 'turbot' (Latin). The pun may be meant to include futile mental activity with flat stupidity. The ignorant but pedantic and self-important village schoolmaster is a stock comic character at this time and later. Shakespeare's Holophernes in *Love's Labour's Lost* is the most famous example.

p. 4 Lalus: 'chattering'. Sidney gives the name to a young shepherd in the First Eclogues of the *Old Arcadia*.

p. 5 *this learned oration*: Master Rhombus' style is a wicked burlesque of the current fashion for 'inkhorne terms': words dragged anyhow into English to satisfy pedantry and grandiloquence. E.K., in his introductory *Epistle* to Spenser's *Shephearde's Calendar*, 1579, attacks this tendency directly: '. . . peces and rags of other languages, borrowing here of the french, there of the Italian, euery where of the Latine, not weighing how il, those tongues accorde with themselves, but much worse with ours: So now they haue made our English tongue, a gallimaufray or hodge-podge of al other speches'.

p. 5 *Potentissima Domina*: Most powerful Lady.

p. 5 *Parcare ... superbos*: for, parcere subiectis et debellare superbos: 'to spare the conquered and subdue the proud', Virgil, *Aeneid* VI 853. Master Rhombus' Latin is magnificently unreliable.

p. 5 *solummodo*: unaccompanied.

p. 5 *Pecorinus Asinus*: a farmyard ass.

p. 5 *Dixi verbus ... est*: for, dixi verbum sapienti sat est: I have said, a word to the wise is sufficient. Proverbial, from, dictum sapienti sat est: one sentence to the wise is enough, Plautus, *Persa* 729.

p. 5 *Haec olim memonasse juvebit*: for, (forsan et) haec olim meminisse iuvabit: (perhaps) one day it will bring joy to recall these things. Virgil, *Aeneid* I 203.

p. 5 *ad propositos revertebo*: for, ad propositum revertam: I will return to my premiss.

p. 5 *Pulchra puella profecto*: undoubtedly lovely girl.

p. 5 **Dame Maia's month**: the brightest sister among the Pleiades is Maia, mother of the god Mercury. The month of May in which their constellation rises takes its name from her.

p. 6 *O Tempori, O Moribus*: for, O tempora, O mores: What times are these! what manners! Cicero, *Against Cataline* I 1.

p. 6 **a certain Gentleman**: the Earl of Leicester, the Queen's host.

p. 6 *Therion*: wild beast (Greek).

p. 6 *Espilus*: felt-presser (Greek).

p. 8 *Dorcas*: gazelle (Greek).

p. 8 *Rixus*: from *rixa*, a quarrel or dispute. So, quarrelsome.

p. 9 *Midas*: King of Phrygia. Rixus refers to the story of his giving the prize to Pan rather than Apollo in a musical contest. As a comment on his poor judgement, Apollo changed his ears to those of an ass.

p. 10 *Heu ... populorum!*: probably for ... *insipientia, inscientia* ... Ah me, well, alas for the stupidity and ignorance of common people!

p. 10 *Corpusculum*: diminutive of 'corpus', 'body', so 'puny form'. A joking reference to the actor's physical appearance may be intended.

p. 10 *prius ... gratia*: for, *prius dividenda oratio antequam definienda, exemplae gratia*: a speech must first be subdivided, then (its headings) defined, for example ...

p. 11 an *Enthememe a loco contingentibus*: an enthememe derived from things close to each other. An enthememe in rhetoric is a 'deduction from contraries', so 'the Poet' may stand for 'Homer', or 'the City' for the City of London specifically.

p. 11 *a conjugatis*: as with those linked together (in marriage).

p. 11 *Et ecce homo blancatum quasi lilium*: this is an elaborate muddle. Rhombus is trying to say 'a man white (pure) as a lily'. The correct word would be *candidus*; *blancatus* does occur in medieval Latin, from French *blanc*, white: it seems to be used exclusively of woollen and linen stuffs, hence 'blanket'.

p. 12 **one ... most excellent chace**: a reference to the failed hopes of the Queen's many suitors, and probably those of Leicester in particular.

p. 12 *Bene, bene, nunc de propositione prepositus*: for *praeposita*. Rhombus' translation is more accurate than his Latin.

p. 13 **wanton *Pan* ...**: Ovid (Fasti II, 303–58) tells the story of how Faunus (Pan) attempted to seduce Hercules's mistress, the Amazon Queen Omphale, and got into Hercules' bed by mistake. Sidney uses the story again, *Old Arcadia*, iv. 213, substituting another of Hercules' mistresses, Iole, for Omphale.

p. 13 **such a one**: the Queen.

p. 13 **My foule mishap ...**: the song was written to accommodate the Queen's judgement in favour of either suitor, but the analogy with Pan would have better suited Espilus had the more belligerent Therion been preferred. I am inclined to agree with Ringler's suggestion that Leicester's hope of England's active military involvement in the Protestant cause in the Netherlands is the underlying point at issue. Elizabeth's choice of the peaceful Espilus is likely to have been intended to underline her rejection of any such open confrontation with Spain. See Ringler, p. 362.

p. 13 **my litle companie**: the actors may have been members of the professional company patronised by Leicester.

Certaine Sonets

p. 15 **title**: 'Sonet' or 'sonnet' was at this time a term used for short poems generally, as well as for the formal sonnet: John Donne's *Songs and Sonnets* are a later example of this usage. Sidney probably composed the poems in this collection between 1577–81, while he was also working on the *Old Arcadia*. It includes a number of translations and metrical experiments, not represented here. I have otherwise made a selection intended to show range as well as accomplishment, retaining Ringler's numbering for ease of reference.

p. 15 stopped eares: a reference to the story of Odysseus, who ordered his sailors to block their ears with wax in order to escape the lure of the Sirens' song.

p. 16 To the tune of Non credo ... amante: 'I do not believe there has ever been a more unhappy lover'; the tune Sidney had in mind has not yet been identified. The verses appear again in the *New Arcadia* III xv, and William Corkine set them in 1612.

p. 16 The earth ... keepeth: the earth, not the sun, is here the centre of the universe.

p. 17 For Thereus' force ... O Philomela faire: Philomela was raped by brother-in-law Tereus, who cut out her tongue to prevent her accusing him. She wove a tapestry telling the story, and her sister avenged her. The Gods turned all three into birds; by long poetic tradition Philomela is the nightingale. Some feminist critics see this poem as based on masculine aggression and egocentric insensitivity. Comparison with other of Sidney's writings however rather suggest a sharply ironical distaste for mawkish self-indulgence. See for example *AS: Second song* and n.

p. 17 Devyse: a 'Devyse' or device here is an *impresa*: a picture glossed by a motto so as to display an opinion or state of mind. They were often carried or worn in tournaments, and formed part of the visual language of love. In Shakespeare's *Pericles*, Thaisa's suitors enter the lists to win her hand each with a 'device' of this kind on his shield.

p. 17 Seeled: 'Seeling' is still sometimes part of a falcon's training: the eyelids are sewn shut until it becomes accustomed to being handled. The operation (which is painless, a bird's eyelids having no more feeling than the human fingernail) was also performed on doves, which would then soar to provide hunting practice for high-flying hawks. Sidney uses the seeled dove again in *New Arcadia* I 15: with the same meaning of helpless love.

p. 17 Non mi vuol e non mi trahe d'Impaccio: 'He does not want me and does not release me from my pain.' The motto is adapted from a line in Petrarch's Sonnet 134, where Love is the tormentor.

p. 17 if she no bondage tried: if she did not try to escape.

p. 18 Edward Dyer: Sir Edward Dyer was a close friend of Sidney, see below, the first of *Two Pastoralls* and n. Very few poems can now be confidently attributed to Dyer. This sonnet and Sidney's answer (16a) exemplify a playful form of collaboration and/or rivalry common at this time.

p. 18 Prometheus: a Titan who brought fire down from the Gods to men. The story of the Satyr was well known, and appears in some sixteenth-century editions of Aesop's *Fables*.

p. 18 ... for dread: Sidney may have had in mind one of Alciati's *Emblemata*, which first appeared in the Paris edition of 1534. The engraving shows a satyr blowing a horn, and with the motto *In subitum Terrorem* (About Sudden Terror) expresses the nature of irrational panic. Sidney has turned the meaning round, so that his satyr terrifies himself.

p. 21 Let Dirge ... rightly read: in the Latin rite *Dirige*, Direct (O Lord my way in thy sight) is the first word in the antiphon at Matins in the Office of the Dead. The anglicised form comes to mean any song of mourning. Trentals were a series of thirty Masses, said for the relief of souls in Purgatory. For Sidney, as a convinced Protestant, both terms would carry ironic overtones.

p. 21 Thou web ... wrought: whose end is never reached. Sidney may be making an ironic reference to Penelope's weaving, which was intentionally never finished: a trick to put off her suitors while she waited for her husband Ulysses to return.

p. 22 Splendidis ... nugis: I bid a long farewell to glittering vanities. This expresses the devout mood of the preceding sonnet rather than any kind of fixed resolve on Sidney's part. In fact he did not turn his attention as a writer towards religion and philosophy until about six years later.

Astrophil and Stella

p. 23 Astrophil and Stella: it is clear from the manuscripts and from early references that Sidney did not give his sequence a title. 'Stella' recurs throughout, but 'Astrophil' only three times: twice in the eighth and once in the ninth *Songs*. See below, pp. 66, 67, 69 and nn. 'Astrophil' is the spelling which occurs in all known references before the first edition of 1591, which gives the title as *Astrophel and Stella*. This spelling is retained in the edition of 1598, and in most subsequent editions. 'Astrophel' is also the spelling used by many contemporary writers when referring to Sidney, including Spenser. It may result from a manuscript mis-reading, but together with the play on star/Stella it could refer to the bitterness of the lover's experience: 'Astrophel' is the name of a plant, probably derived from Latinised Greek *Astrophyllum*: 'star-leaf', and Spenser calls it 'bitter *Astrofell*' (*Daphnaida* 347). 'Astrophil' combines the Greek words for 'star' and 'love': so 'star-lover', as well as playing on Sidney's own name, Philip, as he does in *AS* 83 and with his *persona*'s name, Philisides, in the *Old Arcadia*. Ringler (p. 458) has shown conclusively that 'Astrophil' is the preferred reading, though references to 'Astrophel' from 1591 onwards may be picking up and over-emphasising a deliberate pun. Sidney clearly intended that Astrophil should be recognisably related to himself, and Stella to Penelope Rich, but how and to what degree may well have been calculated with a number of different possible readings in mind; this question is discussed in the Introduction, pp. xlii–xliii, and see nn. to *AS* 13, 24, 30, 35, 37.

p. 23 **looke . . . write:** Stella's image is fixed in his heart and is his true subject. Sidney plays on this idea throughout the sequence, for example in *AS* 32, 88, 105.

p. 23 **dribbed shot:** in archery, a weak or random shot.

p. 23 **mine:** a tunnel dug under fortifications during a siege.

p. 23 **like slave-borne *Muscovite* . . . Tyrannie:** sixteenth-century English travellers in Russia comment frequently that the natives seemed to prefer slavery to freedom.

p. 24 **problemes old:** *Problems* are questions posed for discussion, originally as an academic exercise: Petrarch and others used them as a poetic device. *AS* 58 is an example.

p. 24 **Of herbes . . . hold:** crowded and eclectic imagery of this kind is a feature of the style popularised by Lyly's *Euphues*, 1568. Sidney also comments on it in the *Defence*, see p. 126 and n.

p. 24 **old *Catoe's* brest:** Cato the Censor, noted for his rigour and austerity.

p. 24 **for thy hard bit:** this is the first use in the sequence of what develops into a key image, variously deployed and inverted. See nn. *passim*. Here its application is the same as in Petrarch's *Triumph of Death* II 88–120, where in a vision the dead Laura tells her lover that her apparent cruelty to him was the discipline of virtue:

. . . Vertue for ayde did then with loue aduise:

> If spurr'd by, thou took'st some running toye,
> So soft a bitt (quoth I) will not suffice . . .
>
> > > > (trans. Mary Sidney)

p. 25 Whereof . . . breed: human beauty, physically composed of the four elements of fire, air, water and earth, is only a shadow of beauty itself, which transcends form. This idea, very widely referred to in the Renaissance period, originates in Plato: *Symposium*, 210, 214.

p. 25 our countrey: Heaven, the true home towards which we travel all our lives.

p. 25 Of hopes . . . freesing fires: deliberately hackneyed oxymera. Throughout this sonnet Sidney is playing on the over-use of certain techniques in the love-poetry of his own time and earlier.

p. 25 Some one . . . golden raine: a common group of mythological references. *Jove*, or Jupiter, took the forms of a bull, a swan and a shower of gold to woo Europa, Leda and Danae respectively (Ovid, *Metamorphoses* VI 103–13).

p. 25 Another . . . retires: Spenser's *Shephearde's Calendar*, 1579, had popularised the use of pastoral *personae*.

p. 25 like painter wise: Sidney was interested in techniques of painting, and this passage may relate to his observation of portrait-painting in Italy.

p. 25 That whereas . . . flow?: Penelope Rich's black eyes and golden hair were celebrated by Constable in the second of his two *Sonets* addressed to her, where he also uses a heraldic conceit very similar to that developed by Sidney in *AS* 13: *The Poems of Henry Constable*, ed. Joan Grundy, Liverpool University Press, 1960 p. 151. The paradox black/beautiful was common even then. Shakespeare, for example, uses it in Sonnet 127.

p. 26 his native place: Cyprus, by whose shores Cupid's mother Venus was born, was taken by the Turks in 1573. Cupid as a runaway child appears first in a poem by Moschus, second century BC, and is so found throughout the Renaissance, but this neat contemporary context for his flight is Sidney's own idea.

p. 26 Turkish hardned hart: the Turks had a proverbial reputation for cruelty.

p. 26 He burnt . . . fly away: this image is again a recurrent one, but the explanation, that Cupid lost his wings while seeking shelter from the northern climate, is again Sidney's own. This light-hearted myth-making looks forward to the painful imagery of imprisonment and mutilation in the final sonnet, see *AS* 108 and nn.

p. 26 **Queene ... *Stella's* face**: this is an elaborate example of the very common 'Blazon of Beauty', in which the poet itemises the Lady's charms by rich simile or elaborate metaphor. The image of the body as a palace or temple, the dwelling-place of the soul, is also well-established. It occurs for example in the fifteenth-century morality play, *The Castle of Perseverance*, and Spenser develops it in the episode of the House of Alma, *Faerie Queene* II ix.

p. 26 **Of touch ... touch**: in *AS* 91 Sidney calls Stella's eyes 'seeing jets'. Jet, like amber, will attract fragments of paper, or straws, if it is rubbed to produce static electricity.

p. 26 **Or reach ... tree**: this is obscure. Stella herself may be the tree, the fruit of which is her love: see below *AS* 82 and n.

p. 27 **lookst ... eyes**: sees himself reflected in tiny form in her eyes.

p. 27 **thy day-nets**: 'For as the Larktaker in his day Net hath a glasse whereon while the birds sit and gaze, they are taken in the Net ...' Pettie's *Petite Pallace*, 1579, quoted by Ringler, p. 465. Stella's eyes are the mirror, and her hair the net.

p. 28 **Eagle sables ... young *Ganimed***: Jove, or Jupiter, has on his shield a black eagle; his sacred bird, whose form he took to carry off Ganymede, a beautiful Phrygian youth, to be cup-bearer to the Gods. Ovid, *Metamorphoses* x 155–61, gives Jupiter's motive as homosexual passion.

p. 28 **Each had ... did reare**: Mars was Venus' lover, and he carries her glove as a favour in his helmet. Only Jupiter could wield thunderbolts, the instruments of his divine anger. Sidney's heraldry reveals both gods as false lovers: Jupiter's love for Ganymede is homosexual, and Mars' for Venus adulterous.

p. 28 **Where roses ... field**: the colours are those of Stella's complexion, but the Devereux arms had three torteaux gules (three red discs, suggesting roses) in a silver field.

p. 28 **scantly Gentlemen**: hardly entitled to a coat of arms.

p. 28 **my friend**: see also *AS* 21 and 69. The friend in question may actually be Fulke Greville, a number of whose own poems in *Caelica* can be read as replying to or commenting on various of Sidney's sonnets (for example *Caelica* 12: *AS* 8). Greville's attitude to such a predicament as Astrophil's might well have been bracing rather than sympathetic.

p. 28 Then did ... the fire: Prometheus gave men fire that he had stolen from the Gods: as a punishment he was bound to a rock in the Caucasus, and a vulture was sent each day to tear out his liver, while each night he recovered from his wounds.

p. 28 Rubarb words: rhubarb was used as a bitter, purgative drug. See *AS* 21 and n.

p. 28 Which ... *Parnassus* flowes: Mount Parnassus, in Greece, one of whose summits was sacred to the Muses. Like *AS*3 and 6 this sonnet is criticising the fashionable abuse of poetic conventions.

p. 28 rimes ... rattling rowes: a parody of the alliterative technique popular at this time. Spenser does something very similar a little earlier in *October* 75 and *Teares of the Muses* 213.

p. 29 poore ... woes: Petrarch lived 1304–74.

p. 29 You seeke ... Fame: Sidney's attitude to Fame as earned by the poet and bestowed by him, is oddly ambivalent. See below, *AS* 28, First Song *AS* 64 and *AS* 90 and nn.

p. 29 But while ... plaid: the fable of the lion-cub brought up by a shepherd that grew up and devoured his flocks; applied by Aeschylus to the ruin Helen brought to Troy (*Agamemnon* 717–36).

p. 29 their first loving state: Venus, though married to Vulcan, took Mars as her lover.

p. 30 And not ... unfit: with potential for great achievement.

p. 30 my friends: this is the only time in *AS* that Astrophil addresses 'friends' in the plural, probably as a rhetorical expansion of the central conceit of Cupid's ambush.

p. 31 my friend: by contrast, the reference to 'caustiks', corrosive and therefore painful medicines, is likely to be specific. See *AS* 14 n.

p. 31 faire twinnes' gold'n place: in mid-June, under the sign of Gemini.

p. 32 the Prince ... tries: 'Prince' can apply to a ruler of either sex, but at this time Sidney's own duties at Elizabeth's court were frustratingly undemanding. See Chronology.

p. 32 *Tantal's* smart: Tantalus was a king of Lydia, who for his crimes was punished after death by eternal hunger and thirst: he stands in a pool of water that recedes as he tries to drink, beneath a fruit-laden tree he can never quite reach.

p. 32 with foule abuse ... blot: Penelope Devereux's marriage was not happy, though no details are known. Certainly she left her husband in 1588 and lived openly for many years with Sir Charles Blount, later Lord Mountjoy and later still Earl of Devonshire.

p. 32 in only follie rich: the whole sonnet plays maliciously on Penelope's married name, Rich. See also *AS* 35, 37 and n.

p. 32 By *Phœbus'* doome: the 'wisest scholler', Plato, related that Apollo's Oracle at Delphi judged Socrates to be the wisest of men (*Defence*, see p. 117 and n.).

p. 33 Though ... Astrologie: Sidney took astrology seriously enough to have his horoscope cast (Oxford, Bodleian, MS. Ashmore 356, 5).

p. 33 those Bodies ... low: the earth is at the centre of Sidney's universe; the stars above shed their influence on it like rain.

p. 34 You that ... to make: this line is often cited as indicating Sidney's aversion to allegory. However, his objection here seems rather to the current enthusiasm for finding allegorical meaning in texts where none was intended.

p. 34 brasen fame: fame's trumpets may be made of brass, or fame itself be of little worth, like the metal. Both meanings devalue fame itself.

p. 34 quintessence: the fifth, imperishable element, thought to be the substance of the physical heavens above the moon, and to be latent even in earthly matter. Its extraction as the elixir of immortality was one of the chief aims of alchemy.

p. 34 Turkish new-moone: the crescent moon was the standard of the Turks, who threatened invasion of Europe at this time and later. See *AS* 8. The questions on international affairs put to Astrophil by 'busie wits' would all together have been relevant only in the summer of 1582, as Ringler points out (p. 470), and it is likely that this sonnet was written at about that time.

p. 34 How *Poles'* ... hoast: Stephen Bathory was elected and crowned King of Poland in 1576. In 1580 he invaded Russia (Muscovy). A treaty was negotiated in January 1582, but news travelled slowly, and in any case Sidney may not have thought it would lead to lasting peace.

p. 34 ill-made fire: Bathory used red-hot cannon balls in his siege of Pskov.

p. 34 three parts: the Catholic, Huguenot and Politique factions who were struggling for power in France.

p. 34 the _Dutch_ in their full diets: 'diet' was a term only used in Germany; 'the Dutch' here (Deutsch) are the Germans, and their diet that of Augsburg, 1582.

p. 35 good townes: the Spanish Duke of Parma took a number of towns in the Low Countries during 1581–2, including Tournai and Oudenarde.

p. 35 pleasing _Orange_ tree: the Protestant William of Orange ruled and defended Holland and Zealand from 1576 until his assassination in 1584.

p. 35 that same golden bit ... halfe tame: Sidney's father, Sir Henry, had been Lord Deputy in Ireland for three terms, the last, during which he pacified Ulster, ending in 1578; in 1582 he was considering a fourth. The 'golden bit' is the cess, a tax on landowners revived by Sir Henry to fund the English military presence in Ireland.

p. 35 for still I thinke of you: Astrophil's love for Stella distracts him from his public concerns. The compliment is back-handed.

p. 35 Is constant love deemed there ...: irony is intended rather than pathos. The lunar sphere is above earthly change and fallibility.

p. 35 Do they call ... ungratefulnesse?: 'do they there call ungrateful-ness virtue?'

p. 35 _Morpheus_ ... sleepe: Morpheus (Shaper), a son of Somnus (Sleep), brings into 'death-like' sleep dreams that have 'life-like' human shape (Ovid, _Metamorphoses_ XI ii 635).

p. 35 as humours fly or creepe: the balance or imbalance of the four humours in the physical constitution of the individual will make him excited or depressed, and his dreams will be conditioned accordingly. This applies only to dreams arising from natural causes: for example ill-health, or, as here some overwhelming preoccupation such as love. Visionary or oracular dreams of warning or revelation are sent to the dreamer by grace, or in direct answer to a prayer.

p. 35 my sire: Sleep; while Astrophil is asleep and unaware, Morpheus can steal Stella's image from his heart.

p. 36 No lovely _Paris_ ... his: the Trojan prince Paris stole Helen from her husband King Menelaus, causing the Trojan War. Astrophil has no such grievance, and no one to blame but himself.

p. 36 But to my selfe ... the blow: this line has been taken to indicate that Sidney actively furthered Penelope Devereux's marriage to Lord Rich, and then came bitterly to regret it. How precisely Astrophil's

view of his situation coincides with Sidney's here and elsewhere is very
questionable, however.

p. 36 Nestor's counsell: Nestor was the Greek leader most respected
for his wisdom during the siege of Troy.

p. 37 Doth even grow rich ... name: a play on Penelope Devereux's
married name. See AS 24, 37 and nn.

p. 37 but stone ... priviledge: stones and trees, which are insensate,
are still not safe from the enchantment of your voice.

p. 37 Towardes ... dwell: Aurora is the Goddess of the Dawn, so,
'eastward'. The Nymph is Stella/Penelope Rich. Her husband's family
seat was in Essex, in the east of England.

p. 37 ... but that Rich she is: the sestet is made up of an elaborate
play on Penelope Devereux's married name.

p. 38 not onely shines but sings: Stella's image sings as her namesake,
a star, makes the music of the spheres. Compare AS 32.

p. 38 what in closde ... away: paradoxically, the vision is peceptible
only when his normal senses are drowned in sleep.

p. 38 I will ... do so: Sidney is recalling Chaucer's *Book of the
Duchess*, 250–61, where the narrator promises Morpheus a richly
furnished bed if he will send him sleep.

p. 38 A rosie garland: this signifies silence and secrecy, as in *sub rosa*.

p. 38 thou shalt ... see: see AS 32.

p. 39 that sweet enemie *Fraunce*: Sidney regularly took part in tournaments, in particular in two which were held in January and May
1581, when Penelope Devereux had newly come to court. These took
place before her marriage. There were French visitors and participants
at these, and at other such occasions earlier. Ringler, pp. 473–4, gives
details, and argues that it is impossible to specify what particular
occasion Sidney may be recalling here. It seems to me likely that the
tournament was real, but that Stella's part in Astrophil's triumph is a
fictive re-working, and that this is so also of the tragi-comic inversion
of AS 53.

p. 39 My bloud ... in this: Sidney's father and grandfather, as well as
his uncles the Earls of Leicester and Warwick had all taken part in
tournaments, achieving high reputations for their skill.

p. 39 And if ... sacred lights: 'and if the stars (Stella's eyes) whose
heavenly power overcomes merely human faculties, decree my death
...'

p. 40 Those daintie dores ... blisse: Stella's ears, through which his complaints enter her mind and heart.

p. 41 Then thinke ... tale of me: if Stella thinks of Astrophil's grief as a tragic fiction, she may be more touched than by the reality. Sidney gives this idea serious consideration in the *Defence*: see below p. 105. Here it carries irony, probably of more than one kind.

p. 42 And now ... so right: see *AS* 4 n. The image of Love riding her lover occurs several times in Petrarch, for example 71, 161, 173. It is used to express not only love's power, but also the nature of love as an educative discipline. Spenser, for example, uses it of Marinell's realisation of his love for Florimell, by which at long last he comes to maturity and self-knowledge: — *but not really here: the dominant sense is submission.*

> Thus while his stony heart with tender ruth
> Was toucht, and mighty courage mollifide,
> Dame *Venus* sonne that tameth stubborne youth
> With iron bit, and maketh him abide,
> Till like a victor on his back he ride,
> Into his mouth his maystering bridle threw,
> That made him stoupe, till he did him bestride:
> Then gan he make him tread his steps anew,
> And learne to loue, by learning louers paines to rew.
>
> *FQ* IV xii 13.

Astrophil's 'delight' in this training is, however, short-lived. See below, *AS* 98 and n.

p. 43 But find ... *Atlas* tyr'd: the Titan Atlas carries the heavens on his shoulders; Hercules was said to have relieved him of the burden for a time.

p. 43 unsuted speech: the styles appropriate for grave matters and public affairs jar with the delicate rhetoric of love. See *AS* 30 n.

p. 44 Muses ... ayde: Sidney seldom invokes the Muses; he may intend the reader to note that Astrophil has not taken to heart his Muse's instruction as recorded in *AS* 1.

p. 45 Far far too long ... without booke: to long to learn by heart.

p. 45 your large precepts misse: forget your weighty instructions.

p. 45 In thy cold ... delight: the phlegmatic humour is cold and moist, contrary to the 'fire' of his longing.

p. 45 but them ... sing: it is possible that Lady Rich, among others, did in fact sing poems written by Sidney to various tunes; see above, pp. 16–17 for examples. Some of the *Songs* occurring later in *AS* may be in question, though no settings so early are known. As with the 'tournament' sonnets, *AS* 41, 53, it is likely that this episode has at least been tailored to Astrophil's situation.

p. 46 ... his golden chaine ... doth bind: Alciati's emblem *Eloquentia Fortitudine praestantior* (Eloquence is stronger than strength), shows Hercules leading a crowd of people by a chain which leads from his mouth. The image occurs in Lucian's *Heracles* (Hercules).

p. 46 Deare ... then me?: comparisons between the situations of the lover and his lady's pets are common. See also *AS* 83 and n.

p. 46 my songs ... doth prove: see above, *AS* 57 and n.

p. 47 Angel's sophistrie: the angelic Stella's arguments, reduced to a scholastic paradox. Ringler (p. 478) suggests that there may also be a play on the title given to the great Saint Thomas Aquinas – Doctor Angelicus.

p. 47 And therefore ... to flie: Astrophil's does not escape from 'vaine love', and his witty inversion of the greater for the less marks the downward turn of the sequence as a whole.

p. 48 now *Io Pean* sing: Ringler points out (p. 478) that the illustrative quotation for the celebratory cry *Io Paean!* in Cooper's *Thesaurus*, 1565, is Ovid's *Ars Amatoria*, II 1–2, where he rejoices in his success as a seducer: the 'petita praeda', the long-sought prey, has fallen into his snares. Astrophil is indulging in wishful thinking.

p. 48 For Grammer says ... affirme: this is true of Latin, but not of sixteenth-century English. Besides, the repetition of 'no' is emphatic only. Astrophil's misunderstanding is deliberately perverse.

p. 48 *First Song*: *AS* 1–63 are an unbroken progression of sonnets; now, as Astrophil's negative passions and self-concern begin to be admitted and indulged, the downward, closing movement of the sequence is interrupted and quickened by the *Songs*, whose forms reflect shifts in mood and register.

p. 49 Only with you ... wonders: probably an inversion: 'Only with you miracles are not wonders', but deliberately ambiguous.

p. 49 I do not envie ... to frame: Astrophil's abnegation of scholarship, military achievement and public ambition marks his acceptance of the distraction commented on in *AS* 30 as a norm.

p. 50 Since in thine armes ... arrow head: the Sidney arms have 'a phaon azure', a silver arrow-head. See *AS* 13 for a parallel heraldic reference to Penelope Devereux. Astrophil's witty claim to kinship with Cupid has ominous overtones. See below, *AS* 73, 108 and nn. in particular.

p. 50 Fortune . . . slow: my fortunes remain the same; in particular Stella has not admitted to loving me.

p. 50 But failst . . . hie?: have you not perhaps mistranslated that heavenly language (of Stella's eyes)?

p. 51 *Amphion's* lyre: Amphion was a musician, who learned his skill from the God Mercury himself. He was said to have built the city of Thebes, moving the stones into place by the power of his music.

p. 51 my friend . . . wo: see above, *AS* 14, 21 and nn.

p. 51 Nectar . . . I *Jove's* cup do keepe: Ganymede was cupbearer to Jove, or Jupiter (see above, *AS* 13 and n.); nectar was the drink of the Gods. There is an astrological play on words here: Jupiter is a most fortunate planet, and Astrophil is intoxicated with delight. There may also be a glancing referencing to Sidney's office at Court, of Cupbearer to the Queen.

p. 51 Sonets . . . annoy: sonnets are not forced to serve the turn only of grief.

p. 52 night-birds: the owl in particular is often used as an emblem for various of the vices.

p. 52 *Venus* . . . to flie: Venus, Goddess of love and beauty, and Diana, the virgin huntress, the Moon and patroness of chastity are proverbially at odds. See below *Fifth song* n.

p. 52 Vertue's gold . . . dart: Cupid has two arrows, one of gold, which causes love, one of lead, which causes love to be rejected (Ovid, *Metamorphoses* I 468–72). Sidney has shifted the meaning of the golden arrow.

p. 53 . . . for no more taking: Sidney's sympathy for Astrophil's behaviour here, as with the attitude expressed in the *Song*, pp. 16–17, would have been slight. In *New Arcadia*, III 1 the disguised Musidorus attempts to kiss Pamela; her response is furious disdain, provoking the most abject of apologies. In *Old Arcadia* I when Pamela is pursued by a bear, she faints, and Dorus takes advantage of the situation to kiss her: her reaction as she regains consciousness is anger. In *New Arcadia* IV Pamela sleeps, guarded by Musidorus, and he is tempted to rape her: only a sudden attack by rebel brigands prevents this. The bear and the brigands are not only narrative conveniences; they express the base impulses which Dorus/Musidorus must fight and conquer in himself. Astrophil, like the singer, is too self-absorbed for such moral analysis.

p. 54 **Sweet ... not humble I:** Astrophil's identification of himself with Cupid is an uneasy attempt to laugh off his fault. See above, *AS* 65 and n.

p. 54 **Those scarlet judges ... paine:** Stella's lips, through which she speaks her anger, are scarlet, like the court robes worn by judges.

p. 54 *Aganippe* **well:** a fountain on Mount Helicon, near the Grove of the Muses.

p. 54 **... in shade of *Tempe* sit:** a valley in Thessaly, praised by the poets for its beauty.

p. 54 **Poets' furie ... meane by it:** Astrophil disclaims knowledge or experience of the 'divine fury' which Sidney speaks of at the end of the *Defence*.

p. 54 **impe feathers oft ... :** this refers to the practice in falconry of 'imping out' the feathers of a hawk's wing. Broken or damaged wing-feathers have new feathers grafted on to them, using a double pointed iron needle to make the join. As this rusts slightly the join becomes permanent.

p. 54 **To lose ... his Love:** The reference is to Edward IV's marriage with Elizabeth Woodville, which took place while the Earl of Warwick (the Kingmaker) was negotiating a French match for him. Warwick was deeply insulted, and turned against Edward, driving him into exile. He only regained the throne some years later after defeating and killing Warwick in battle. Edward was a proverbial type of carnality and uxoriousness: at least two readings of this sonnet are possible. It can be taken as expressing Astrophil's bitter and self-reflexive irony, or the continuing degradation of his sense of values by the distraction described in *AS* 30 and 53.

p. 55 **like *Aurora*:** Aurora is the Goddess of the Dawn, and see *AS* 37 and n.

p. 55 **more then *Atlas* might:** that is, more than the weight of the heavens. See *AS* 51 and n.

p. 56 **that such ... wants hornes:** horns are the mark of a cuckold. The figure of Jealousy is here fused with that of Stella's husband.

p. 56 **coupling Doves ... right:** Venus' chariot is drawn by doves, which are sacred to her.

p. 57 O kisse ... ties: the idea that a kiss links the souls of the two lovers occurs frequently. For example, Marlowe's Faustus says when he has kissed the succuba in Helen's shape: 'Her lips suck forth my soul; see where it flies.'

p. 57 His who ... glasse: Narcissus, who fell in love with his own reflection and pined away.

p. 57 Or hers ... did see: Venus, who appeared naked at the Judgement of Paris.

p. 57 the Cherrie tree: Stella's lips are the cherries which she guards from thievish kisses.

p. 57 th' *Esperian* tast: the golden apples which Juno gave to Jupiter on their wedding day were kept in the island Garden of the Hesperides, daughters of the Evening Star.

p. 57 Good brother *Philip*: sparrows were popular ladies' pets, and 'Philip', 'Phip', or 'Pip' as typical a name for one as 'Polly' is for a parrot today. Sidney takes advantage of this to pun on his own name. Sparrows were also sacred to Venus, and associated with lechery. This sonnet is intended to recall Skelton's much longer poem *Philip Sparrow*, especially ll. 115–42.

p. 58 If *Orpheus'* ... make them move: Orpheus' music had the power to halt rivers, tame wild beasts and move trees.

p. 58 If stones ... did yeeld: see *AS* 68 n.

p. 58 To make a Lyzard ... endlesse night: These references are to accounts of animal fidelity in Pliny's *Natural History* viii 61 and x 19. A dragon rescued from brigands a man who had cared for it when young, and an eagle befriended by a young girl flew to its own death on her funeral pyre.

p. 58 Highway ... *Pernassus* be: the road that leads toward Stella is my road to inspiration.

p. 59 apt sprites to enlarge: prone to set free mental energies.

p. 59 *Fourth Song*: This and the *Eighth* and *Eleventh Songs* are the only occasions in the sequence when Stella's own voice is heard, though it is overheard through Astrophil's responses throughout. Paradoxically, it is in these songs that Astrophil's dramatic fantasising is most evident.

p. 61 like spotlesse Ermine: the ermine was a symbol of chastity, because of the belief that it would allow itself to be killed rather than escape by a way that soiled its white coat with any filth. Petrarch gives the heraldic ermine, collared with a crown, as Chastity's emblem:

> Borne in greene field, a snowy Ermiline,
> Colored with topacee, sett in fine gold,
> Was this faire companies unfoyled signe.
> (*Triumph of Death*, I 20–23. Trans Mary Sidney)

The portrait of Queen Elizabeth I known as the 'Ermine Portrait', now in the collection of the Marquess of Salisbury, uses the same motif.

p. 61 Fift Song: Ringler (p. 484) argues convincingly that this *Song* is adapted from an earlier version originally intended for inclusion with the *Eclogues* which conclude the Fourth Act of the *Old Arcadia*, where Philisides expresses his vengeful reaction when Mira has rejected him. In its present context it aptly demonstrates Astrophil's oscillations of mood.

p. 62 hidnest gifts infused: poured in your most secret gifts.

p. 63 For wearing *Venus*' badge ... didst flee: your beauty shows you dedicated to Venus, Goddess of Love, but you have deserted her for Diana and her virgin company. See above, *AS* 72 and n.

p. 64 The Common Sence: the faculty by which impressions received by the physical senses are interpreted and made available to the imagination and rational understanding in turn.

p. 65 *Eighth Song*: Fulke Greville's *Caelica* 76 may have been written in response to this.

p. 66 Did for mutuall comfort meete: see above *Fourth Song* and n.

p. 66 Her faire necke a foule yoke bare: alluding to the bonds of her marriage.

p. 66 With armes crost: a posture signifying grief.

p. 68 Go my flocke: Ringler argues that the Pastoral idiom is out of keeping here (Introduction, p. xlvi). Like the *Fifth Song*, see above and n., the *Ninth Song* may have been adapted from an earlier version, or even simply carried over into *AS*, where the brief switch into a pastoral persona tends to heighten the reader's sense of Astrophil's emotional disorientation.

p. 70 Because in brave array ... a present pay?: because this (other) lady tries to attract me, dressing finely, and offering immediate gratification ...

p. 71 *Stella* ... a Poet's name: see above, *AS* 15 and n. Here Astrophil disclaims any desire of fame for himself, as did many other poets, including Petrarch, to whose frequent play on 'Laura' and 'laurel' (the poet's crown, sacred to Apollo) he here alludes. Petrarch did however give Laura fame, and his *Triumph of Fame* succeeds his *Triumph of Death*. Astrophil's re-working of the central theme of *AS* 1, 3, 6 and 15, his sole dependence on Stella for his inspiration, has become introverted, an end in itself.

p. 72 *Tenth Song*: this was set as early as 1589, by William Byrd, *Songs of sundrie natures*.

p. 74 **even** *Stella* **vexed is**: there is no hint of what Astrophil may have done to hurt Stella, though the rather self-centred spite of the *Fifth Song*, for example, written when his 'wit' was 'confus'd with too much care', might have done so.

p. 75 **my mate-in-arms**: translation of the French 'compagnon d'armes'.

p. 75 *Dian* **... each mortall wight**: Diana, the moon goddess, leads her nymphs, the stars to hunt in the heavens, from whence their beams strike those on earth.

p. 75 **a Lady**: perhaps the same who appears in *AS* 88.

p. 76 **Ah Bed ... traind**: this invocation is traditional, but Sidney's handling of it is unusually dark.

p. 76 **Spurd ... hard hand**: see above, *AS* 49 and n. The contrast between Astrophil's earlier 'delight' and his present nightmare is painful.

p. 76 *Aurora* **... daunce**: Aurora, Goddess of the Dawn, before whom Night and Sleep flee as she precedes Phoebus Apollo in his chariot of the Sun.

p. 76 **Lillies ... Roses**: (of her complexion).

p. 76 **O honied sighs ... to flow**: as Stella sighs her creamy breasts rise above her fashionably low-cut bodice.

p. 77 *Gallein's adoptive sonnes:* old-fashioned followers of the famous Roman physician, Galen, whose theories were being displaced by new developments in medicine, especially in Italy.

p. 78 *Æols' youthes*: the breezes, sons of Æolus, God of the Winds.

p. 78 **But if I ... (though but of empty glasse)**: I only have to pass by the happy window that is Stella's, wearing armour ornamented with stars, in whatever state of mind or body, and even though Stella's window is empty you will interpret every detail as an allegory of what

; in my heart. (In the engravings made by Thomas Lant for Sidney's funeral procession his armour is shown embellished with stars.)

p. 79 the faithful Turtle dove: turtle doves were emblematic of constancy in love.

p. 79 Lest that *Argus* eyes perceive you: Argus had a hundred eyes, and was set by Juno to watch over Io, Jupiter's current mistress, whom she had turned into a cow. Proverbial for a guardian of feminine virtue.

p. 80 And from lowts to run away: the love scene dissolves at the end into pathetic farce.

p. 81 To this great cause ... and art: Astrophil asks to be seconded from Stella's service to that of the state, for which he is fitted by experience (use) and art (training). Sidney may have had in mind specifically his father's proposal that Philip join him in Ireland, though this came to nothing. See above AS 30 and n. The shift from private involvement to public concern is very sudden, and cruelly subverted in the final sonnet that follows.

p. 81 When sorrow ... only annoy: Astrophil's symbiosis with Cupid is complete. The whole sonnet plays on the opening and conclusion of Petrarch's *Triumph of Chastity*, where Amor, with his face of fire in which the lover burns (*ch'al volto à le faville ond' io tutt' ardo*) and his fiery darts is outfaced by Laura's purity (ll. 34–69). He is made captive and his wings are clipped (ll. 132–5), and after he has been led in Laura's Triumph he is left with her victorious spoils in the temple of noble Chastity in Rome (ll. 181–5). Astrophil expresses his own situation of impotent frustration from Cupid's point of view.

The Defence of Poesie

p. 83 title: It is likely that Sidney himself never gave his essay a formal title. It was written at the same time as or shortly after *Astrophil and Stella*, and it then circulated in manuscript. Two editions appeared in 1595, by William Ponsonby, as *The Defence of Poesie*, and by Henry Olney, as *An Apologie for Poetrie*. References both before and after 1595 suggest that both titles were in use. It was included in the 1598 edition of Sidney's works with Ponsonby's title, and based on his text. This is a little fuller than that of Olney, and its quotations are more exact. Olney's however is generally more carefully printed; in particular it has crisper paragraphing and punctuation. The text given here is generally based on that of 1598; its layout on that of Olney's edition.

It also follows Olney in giving English transliterations of Greek words in the text: the Greek, with translations, will be found in the Glossary. The spelling of some proper names has been normalised, for ease of reference.

p. 83 *Edward Wotton*: later Baron Wotton, 1548–1626, was employed on the Continent by Walsingham. Sidney met him in Vienna in the summer of 1573, on his first visit there.

p. 83 *Pugliano*: see Introduction, p. xxxii.

p. 84 the Hedghog . . . host: a proverbial type of ingratitude.

p. 84 the Vipers' . . . their Parents?: vipers are viviparous. It was believed that the young tore their way out of their mother's body, killing her.

p. 84 *Musæus, Homer* and *Hesiod*: Greek poets, of the very early period. Musæus was said to be the son or disciple either of Orpheus or Linus: see below n. None of his works survive: the poem *Hero and Leander*, on which Marlowe's poem is based, is by a much later poet of the same name. The Homeric *Iliad* and *Odyssey* are the foundation of European epic, through Virgil to Sidney's own time and later. Hesiod's poem *Works and Days* is a philosophic treatise on agriculture, a genre developed by Virgil in his *Georgics*. His *Theogony* is the earliest known descriptive account of the Greek Gods, their mythology and worship.

p. 84 *Orpheus, Linus*: see below p. 90 n. Linus is said by some ancient authorities to have been the first poet in Greece, and to have had Orpheus himself as a pupil. Nothing survives that can be reliably attributed to him.

p. 84 *Amphion . . . Thebes*: see *Astrophil and Stella* 68 n; *Third Song* n.

p. 84 *Orpheus . . . people*: see *Astrophil and Stella, Third Song* n. Some mythographers interpreted the magical power of Orpheus' music as symbolising the influence of civilisation on barbarism.

p. 84 *Livius Andronicus* and *Ennius*: Livius Andronicus lived most of his life in Rome from *c.* 220 BC, and was one of the first Latin dramatists. Ennius, his near contemporary, was the most famous among the early Latin poets.

p. 85 *Thales, Empedocles* and *Parmenides*: Pre-Socratic Greek philosophers. Many of Sidney's examples and supporting arguments are derived from Continental critics of his own time. Detailed references and discussion can be found in Gregory Smith's notes to his edition of Olney's text: *Elizabethan Critical Essays*, Vol. I, pp. 383–403. See Suggestions for Further Reading.

p. 85 *Pythagoras* and *Phocylides*: Pythagoras was said by Cicero to have invented the term *philosopher*. He died in about 497 BC. His school was interested in the power and symbolism of number and music, and believed in reincarnation. Phocylides was a Greek poet and philosopher who lived a little earlier.

p. 85 *Tirteus*: properly Tyrtaeus, a Greek poet, flourishing in about 680 BC, famous for his battle songs.

p. 85 *Solon*: a great Athenian law-giver. He died in 558 BC.

p. 85 by *Plato*: Plato's enormously influential descriptions of Atlantis occur in *Timaeus* 24–9, 296, and in *Critias* 108–10.

p. 85 *Gyges'* Ring: a magic ring that made the wearer invisible. Plato makes a number of references to it, and to the fantastic adventures of its owner, notably in *Phaedrus* 230B.

p. 85 nine *Muses*: The nine Books of Herodotus's famous *History*, completed in 445 BC were named after the Nine Muses.

p. 86 the auncient *Brittons*: interest in Wales as the retreat of the Celtic, 'British', people after the Saxon invasions was high in Sidney's time. The Tudors were Welsh, and Henry VII had supported his very weak claim to the throne by claiming descent from ancient British Kings, of whom the greatest had been Arthur.

p. 86 *Arma amens ... rationis in armis*: Distraught I seize my weapons, having no plan of battle (Virgil, *Aeneid* II 314).

p. 86 performed it: the Emperor Albinus died in 198 AD. This story is taken from the popular *Sex Scriptores Historiae Augustae* (*Six Writers on the History of Augustus*), and Sidney might have read any one of a number of editions published in France.

p. 86 this word *Charmes ... cometh*: Sidney's derivation is correct. *Carmen*, a song, has the other, and probably earlier, meaning of 'incantation': rhythmic verses or a chant having sacred or magical power.

p. 87 a *Maker*: this term for a poet is found most often in fifteenth-century Scottish poetry. A famous example is William Dunbar's *Lament for the Makeris*.

p. 88 divers sorts of quantities: measurement and number.

p. 88 *Heroes ... Furies*: most of the Greek Heroes were of divine parentage on one side: Aeneas' mother, for example, was Venus. By Demigods Sidney may mean those, who like Hercules, received divine honours after death. The one-eyed giants, the Cyclops, and the fire-breathing goat-lion-dragon Chimera, are monsters overcome by heroes: Ulysses and Bellerophon. The snaky-haired Furies are supernatural agents of vengeance. They torment the sinful dead, and pursue those still alive, like Orestes who killed his mother, who are guilty of kin-slaying.

p. 88 *Theagines*: the hero of a Greek prose romance, *Theagines and Chariclea* or *Aethiopica* by Heliodorus, written in the third century. It was highly valued by Renaissance critics, and was translated into English *c.* 1569 by Thomas Underdowne.

p. 88 *Pylades*: the faithful friend of Orestes. See above, n. p. 88.

p. 88 *Orlando*: the hero of Ariosto's epic poem *Orlando Furioso*, 1532.

p. 88 *Xenophon's Cyrus:* Xenophon, an Athenian historian and philosopher, lived in the fourth century BC. He served under Cyrus the Great, King of Persia. Sidney is following Plato and Cicero who both state that his *Cyropaedia* is not a literal account of Cyrus' reign, but a moral extrapolation from it of what a ruler should be.

p. 89 *Idea* ... *it selfe*: the original conception, to which the actual work will approximate.

p. 89 **that second nature**: man, being made in God's image, has the power to create, but only God can create from nothing: the creations of man are derived from God's Creation.

p. 89 **accursed fall of *Adam***: since the Fall mankind is incapable of good without divine help. This doctrine was strongly emphasised in Protestant teaching. See Genesis 3.

p. 89 **theyr *Hymnes***: Exodus 15: 1–19; Deuteronomy 32: 1–43; Judges 5.

p. 89 *Emanuell Tremelius* and *Franciscus Junius* ... **Scripture**: the title page of the second volume of the Latin Bible produced by these two Protestant scholars refers to its contents as the 'poetical Books'.

p. 90 *Orpheus* ... *Hymnes*: the *Hymns* attributed to Orpheus may express the philosophy of his followers, but are not actually by him. Amphion's works are known by reputation only: see above, *Astrophil and Stella*, *Third song* n. There are 'Homeric' *Hymns* extant.

p. 90 **Saint *James* his counsell ... merry**: *Epistle of St James* 5: 13.

p. 90 consolation ... goodnesse: reading and singing of the *Psalms* was a central part of Protestant devotion. Here Sidney may also have been thinking ahead to his own translation, left unfinished on his death and completed by his sister, Lady Pembroke. See below pp. 135–41 and nn.

p. 90 Tirteus ... Cato: see above, p. 85 nn.; the *Disticha de Moribus* (couplets about good behaviour), attributed to Dionysius Cato, were used as a text-book in Elizabethan schools.

p. 90 Lucretius: an Epicurean poet, author of *De Natura Rerum* (Of the Nature of Things), a philosophical epic. He died *c.* 54 BC.

p. 90 Virgil's Georgicks: written after the *Eclogues* and before the *Aeneid*: four long poems dealing with aspects of farming. *Georgic IV* includes the best-known version of the Orpheus story. See above, p. 84 n.

p. 90 Manilius and Pontanus: Caius Manilius, in the first century AD and Jovianus Pontanus in the fifteenth: authors of Latin scientific epics on astronomy.

p. 90 Lucan: a Latin poet who conspired against the Emperor Nero and was ordered to commit suicide. His only surviving work is the *Pharsalia*, a very highly wrought account of the Civil Wars between Julius Caesar and Pompey.

p. 90 Lucretia ... fault: Lucretia was raped by Prince Tarquin while he was a guest in her house. The next day she called her husband and family together, told them what had happened, and stabbed herself. The Tarquins were driven from Rome and the Republic established. Shakespeare tells the story in his narrative poem *The Rape of Lucrece*.

p. 91 Cyrus ... Poem: see above, pp. 88–9.

p. 91 Heliodorus ... Chariclea: see above p. 88 n.

p. 92 Demigods: 'A sound Magitian is a Demi-god': Marlowe, *Doctor Faustus* (B text). Faustus misuses 'supernatural' philosophy.

p. 92 supernaturall Philosophers ... divine essence: possibly Sidney here has in mind some of the ideas put forward by Giordano Bruno. See *Introduction*, pp. xlix–l.

p. 93 Definitions ... Distinctions: formal divisions of an argument.

p. 93 little world: the microcosm; man is made in the contracted, and the physical universe in the expanded, image of God.

p. 93 [Historia vero] Testis ... vetustatis: [History is indeed] the witness of the times, the light of truth, the life of memory, the mistress of life, the messenger of antiquity. Cicero, *De Oratore* ii 9.36.

p. 93 *Marathon . . . Agincourt*: the Athenians overcame the Persians at Marathon, in spite of being very greatly outnumbered: 490 BC. Julius Caesar defeated Pompey at the battle of Pharsalia: 48 BC. Poitiers and Agincourt are battles where the Black Prince and Henry V respectively were victorious over the French: 1356 and 1415.

p. 93 *directed . . . history*: have been guided by the thought of their future reputations.

p. 94 *Brutus . . . Aragon*: Marcus Junius Brutus, who led the conspirators who assassinated Julius Caesar, 44 BC: Alphonsus V of Aragon and I of Sicily, 1416–58.

p. 94 *chiefe of Vertues*: because in a fallen and imperfect world no other virtue can thrive in its absence. *Ius* (Latin): Law.

p. 95 *Tullie*: a common way of referring to Marcus Tullius Cicero.

p. 95 *Troye's flames*: Virgil, *Aeneid* II 701–3.

p. 95 *Ulysses . . . Ithaca*: Ulysses stayed for seven years with the nymph Calypso in her island paradise, but longed to return to his homeland, Ithaca. Homer, *Odyssey* VII.

p. 95 *Ajax . . . Greeks*: the *Ajax* of Sophocles deals with the hero's madness and death.

p. 95 *Agamemnon* and *Menelaus*: brothers, kings of Mycenae and Sparta. Menelaus was the husband of Helen of Troy. Agamemnon was the leader of the Greek forces in the Trojan War.

p. 96 *Ulysses*: Ulysses (Greek, Odysseus) fought with the Greeks at Troy. He was famous for his wisdom and cunning.

p. 96 *Diomedes*: one of the Greek heroes in the Trojan War. Sidney may here be thinking of his restraint when he returned home to find his wife had been unfaithful; he left her and his homeland to found a city elsewhere.

p. 96 *Achilles*: the greatest of the Greek heroes. His killing of the Trojan Prince Hector in single combat is the climax of Homer's *Iliad*.

p. 96 *Nisus* and *Euryalus*: Trojans in Aeneas' following. They died in battle, each trying to defend the other. Virgil, *Aeneid* IX ll. 176ff.

p. 96 *Oedipus*: son of Laius and Jocasta, King and Queen of Thebes. Despite all attempts to evade the prophecy that he should kill his father and marry his mother, he did both, in all ignorance, becoming King of Thebes. When eventually he discovered what he had done he blinded himself and went into exile. Sophocles: *Oedipus the King*.

p. 96 *Agamemnon*: see above p. 95 n. On his return to Mycenae his wife Clytemnestra spread purple cloths before the palace for him to walk on. He accepted this semi-divine honour as his due. Once inside the palace, he was murdered by Clytemnestra and her lover, Aegisthus.

p. 96 *Atreus*: Atreus' wife was seduced by his brother, Thyestes, and had children by him. In revenge Atreus invited his brother to a banquet, and served him with the children's flesh.

p. 96 the two *Theban* brothers: Polynices and Eteocles, sons of Oedipus, see above p. 96 n. They killed each other in single combat in the war over who should be King of Thebes.

p. 96 sowre-sweetnes ... *Medea*: Jason, Captain of the Argonauts, won the Golden Fleece from Colchis with the help of the Colchian enchantress Medea. When he deserted her for Glauce, she sent the new bride a poisoned mantle which burned her to death, and killed her own children by Jason before fleeing to Athens. Euripides, *Medea*.

p. 96 the *Terentian Gnato*: the name of Gnatho, a character in Terentius' comedy *Eunuchus*, became proverbial for a parasite.

p. 96 *Chaucer's Pandar*: Pandar brings the lovers together in Chaucer's *Troilus and Criseyde*. Pandar is synonymous with bawd in Elizabethan English.

p. 96 *Sir Thomas More's Eutopia*: the usual title of More's account of an imaginary island and its government, 1516, is *Utopia*, but both may have been in use.

p. 96 *Mediocribus ... Columnae*: Not Gods, nor men, nor booksellers' stalls will acknowledge indifferent poets. Horace, *Ars Poetica* ll. 372–3.

p. 96 *Dives* and *Lazarus*: Luke 16. 19–31.

p. 96 the lost Child ... Father: the parable of the Prodigal Son, Luke 15. 11–32.

p. 97 *Vespasian*: Emperor of Rome; died in 79 AD.

p. 97 *Justine*: Justinus, a late Roman historian.

p. 97 *Dares Phrygius*: his *History of the Ruin of Troy* was composed certainly as late as the sixth century AD, but was thought in Sidney's time and earlier to be authentic and much more ancient. It gives a far from flattering account of Aeneas.

p. 97 *Horace* sweareth: *Odes* V. 5, where Horace ridicules Canidia's pretensions to sorcery.

p. 98 *Tantalus*: a King of Lydia: he attempted to deceive the Gods by serving them at a banquet with the flesh of his own son, Pelops. His punishment in Hades is to stand in a pool of water from which he can never stoop to drink, under a tree hung with fruit he can never reach.

p. 98 *Scipio*: There were many famous members of this family, but Sidney is probably referring to Scipio Africanus, so-called because he defeated the Carthaginian leader, Hannibal, in 202 BC.

p. 98 *Quintus Curtius*: a late Roman historian, author of a *Life* of Alexander the Great.

p. 98 *Tarquinius* **and his sonne**: the Roman Historian Livy tells how Sextius, the youngest son of Tarquinius Superbus, the last King of Rome (see above, p. 90 n.) deceived the citizens of Gabii into thinking he had quarrelled with his father and been cruelly beaten by him. They trusted him, and he then helped Tarquin to take the city.

p. 99 **heaven . . . hell**: in the *Divina Commedia*.

p. 99 *Miltiades* **. . . fetters**: after defeating the Persians at Marathon (see above, p. 93) Miltiades was accused by the Athenians of treason, and died of his wounds in prison.

p. 99 **The just Phocion . . . like Traytors**: Phocion was an Athenian statesman, famous for his incorruptible virtue. He was falsely accused of treason and condemned to death *c.* 318 BC, when he was over eighty years old. Socrates was condemned in about 400 BC, on trumped up charges of corrupting the young men of Athens and blaspheming against the Gods. His disciple Plato gives a deeply moving account of his judicial death by hemlock poisoning in *The Death of Socrates*.

p. 99 **the cruell** *Severus* **. . . The excellent** *Severus*: the Roman Emperor Lucius Septimus Severus, was known for his vengefulness and harsh government. He died in 211 AD, aged 66. The Roman Emperor Marcus Aurelius Severus was a young man of strict morals, and the firm discipline he imposed on his soldiers during his campaigns was so resented that they murdered him in 235 AD, at the age of 28.

p. 99 *Sylla* **and** *Marius*: Marius was a general who gained the Consular power in Rome, which he governed with great harshness. Sylla successfully challenged him for supreme power; his rule was if anything more bloodthirsty and corrupt. The Civil Wars between Caesar and Pompey followed soon after Sylla's abdication and death.

p. 99 **vertuous** *Cato*: Cato Uticensis supported Pompey against Caesar. After Pompey's defeat at Pharsalia he committed suicide.

p. 99 Rebel Caesar ... honor?: Shortly before the final phase of the Civil Wars, Julius Caesar became technically a rebel against the Roman State when he crossed the Rubicon with his army on to territory immediately under the Senate's jurisdiction.

p. 100 Cipselus ... Dionysius: infamous tyrants of antiquity.

p. 101 Aloes ... Rubarb: bitter herbs used medicinally as purgatives.

p. 101 Amadis de Gaule: a late medieval Spanish romance. Sidney may have known it from the French version by des Essarts, 1540.

p. 101 Aeneas ... his back: On their flight from Troy Aeneas carried his aged father Anchises, who held their household Gods. Virgil, *Aeneid* II. ll. 707–720.

p. 102 Fugientum ... est?: And shall this land see me a fugitive? But then, is it so wretched a thing, to die? Virgil, *Aeneid* XII 645–6.

p. 102 Cherries: a syrup of cherries was used as a medicine for coughs and sore throats.

p. 102 Menenius Agrippa: a Roman general at the time of the Sabine Wars.

p. 102 the whole people of Rome: the Plebians, the common people, who up to this time had no voice in the government. Agrippa was responsible for their having representatives, the Tribunes.

p. 102 Geometrie ... conceived: Sidney may have in mind some of the highly mathematical passages in Plato.

p. 103 This applied ... ensued: Shakespeare uses this episode in the opening scene of *Coriolanus*.

p. 103 by telling ... bosome: Nathan's parable refers to David's adultery with Bathsheba, and his murder by proxy of her husband, Uriah. II Samuel 11–12.

p. 103 (... the second and instrumental cause): David having first heard the story then rightly applied it to himself and was moved to repentance.

p. 103 Psalme of mercie: probably Psalm 102: 'Hear me O Lord'.

p. 103 Sanazzar: Sanazzaro's Italian pastoral romance *Arcadia*, by which Sidney's own *Arcadia* was influenced.

p. 103 Boethius: His *De Consolatione Philosophiae: Of the Consolation of Philosophy*, was written in about 524 AD while he was in prison awaiting execution. It has been translated into English by among others King Alfred, Chaucer and Queen Elizabeth I.

p. 103 the poore pype: the pipe of reeds or oat-straw, expresses the 'lowly' pastoral as the lyre does the 'higher' registers of poetry.

pp. 103–4 *Melibeus'* mouth . . . highest: Virgil, *Eclogue* I.

p. 104 *Haec . . . nobis*: I remember these things, and that Thyrsis is overcome (in singing) and strives in vain. From that time Corydon, Corydon is our choice. Virgil, *Eclogue* VII ll. 69–70

p. 104 *Heraclitus*: a pre-Socratic Greek philosopher. It was said that he wept continually for the wretchedness of the world.

p. 104 Iambick: Sidney is thinking of the early use of iambic (long-short syllabic) verse by the vituperative Greek poets Archilochus and Hipponax.

p. 104 *Omne . . . ludit*: the subtle man pinpoints all his friends vices, and makes him laugh, while sporting among his vitals: Persius, *Satire* I ll. 116–17, slightly adapted.

p. 104 *Est . . . aequus*: even in (remote) Ulubrae (you will be content) if you keep a serene mind. Horace, *Epistle* I ll. 30.

p. 105 foile: At this period the cutting of diamonds was crude, and it was usual in setting the stones to back them with dark metal foil to enhance their lustre.

p. 105 *Demeas*: a character in Terence's play *Adelphi*.

p. 105 *Davus*: 'the slave'. Characters so-called appear in the *Andria* of Terence and the *Phormio* of Plautus.

p. 105 *Gnato*: see above p. 96 n.

p. 105 *Thraso*: a braggart soldier in Terence's *Eunuchus*.

p. 105 *Qui . . . redit*: A cruel man who governs his dominions by harsh authority fears those who fear him, and brings fear back to its origin. Seneca, *Oedipus* l. 705.

p. 105 *Alexander Pheraeus*: a Tyrant of Pherae in Thessaly. He was murdered by his wife.

p. 106 naturall Problemes: see *Astrophil and Stella* 3 n.

p. 106 Percy and Douglas: a reference to a version of the ballad *Chevy Chase*, or perhaps to that of *The Battle of Otterbourne*.

p. 106 rude stile: such ballads were still current in the oral tradition: part of the repertoire of popular entertainers.

p. 106 that uncivill age: the medieval period was generally regarded in Sidney's time as having been unrefined in manners, artistically crude and intellectually obscurantist.

p. 106 *Pindar*: perhaps the greatest of the Greek lyric poets, born in 522 BC.

p. 106 *Hungary*: Sidney visited Hungary briefly in the course of his European travels, 1573. See Introduction, p. xxxii.

p. 106 **rather of sport than vertue**: the only complete works of Pindar to have survived are his *Odes*, composed for the celebration of victories at the Olympic and other Greek Games.

p. 106 *Phillip of Macedon*: father of Alexander the Great.

p. 106 *Tydeus*: a famous hero. He took an important part in the Wars of Thebes. See above p. 96 n.

p. 106 *Rinaldo*: one of the knights in Ariosto's epic *Orlando Furioso*, 1532. He plays a more major part in Tasso's epic *Gerusalemme Liberata*, 1593. There were unauthorised editions in 1576 and 1581, either of which Sidney might have seen.

p. 107 **love of her beauty**: Cicero, referring to Plato: *De Finibus* ii. 16 and *De Officiis* i. 5.

p. 107 **to leave *Dido***: Dido, Queen of Carthage gave hospitality and welcome to Aeneas with his followers, and they became lovers. Jupiter sent the God mercury to command Aeneas to leave Carthage and sail to Italy, where he was to found the Roman state. He obeyed reluctantly, and Dido killed herself.

p. 107 *Melius . . . Crantore*: better than (the philosophers) Chrysippus and Crantor. Horace, *Epistle* I 2.4.

p. 108 *Misomousoi*: (Greek) Μισόμουσοι, haters of the Muses. Possibly Sidney's own coinage.

p. 108 **the Spleene**: thought to be the seat of angry passions.

p. 108 *Ovid's* verse: *Ars Amatoria* II l. 662. Ovid's text reads: *Et lateat vitium proximitate boni*: and vice may lie hidden close to virtue. Sidney has reversed the point deliberately.

p. 108 *Ut . . . mali*: as virtue lies hidden next to evil.

p. 108 *Agrippa . . .* Science: Henricus Cornelius Agrippa of Nettesheim, 1486–1535. A scholar and student of the occult, with a popular reputation as a magician. Sidney refers here to his *de Vanitate et Incertitudine Scientiarum*: of the Foolishness and Uncertainty of (all branches) of Learning, 1530.

p. 109 *Erasmus . . .* follie: in *The Praise of Folly*, 1509.

p. 109 **without versing**: in prose: at this time 'poetry' is used of any kind of imaginative or fictional writing.

p. 109 *Scaliger* **judgeth:** Julius Caesar Scaliger 1475–1558, one of the greatest scholars of the period and editor of many critical editions, in his *Poetice* (i. 2) contends that the term 'poetry' should be used only of writings in verse.

p. 110 Art of memory ... knowne: see Introduction p. xxx and n.

p. 110 *Percontatorem ... est:* I always avoid an inquisitive man; he talks too much. Horace, *Epistle* i. l. 18.

p. 110 *Dum sibi ... sumus:* so long as everyone pleases himself we are a trusting crowd. Ovid, *Remedii Amoris* l. 686.

p. 110 verses: mnemonic verses to help young students to memorise rules of grammar and other disciplines were a teaching aid in schools throughout the medieval and Renaissance periods. Some of them indeed survived until about forty years ago.

p. 110 Nowe then ...: in this passage Sidney is specifically addressing Gosson's arguments in his *Schoole of Abuse*, 1579, which had been rashly dedicated to Sidney himself. See Introduction, pp. xliv–xlv, and nn.

p. 110 *Syren's* **sweetnes ... Serpent's tayle:** the Greek Sirens whose sweet singing lured sailors to their destruction had the heads and bodies of lovely women, and the wings and claws of ravening birds. Later they become conflated with mermaids; half fish. Sidney may here be combining the sweetness of their perilous singing with the common iconography of the Serpent in pictures of the Fall, showing a serpent with a human head and torso. An example is Michelangelo's *Fall of Man* in the Sistine Chapel, Rome.

p. 110 *Robin Hood:* the Ballads of Robin Hood were very popular at this time.

p. 110 his Common-wealth: in the *Republic* (II 364 ff.) where very strong censorship of all kinds of fiction is proposed.

p. 111 *Charon:* the ferryman who carries the dead over the rivers Styx and Acheron to Hades.

p. 112 *John of the Stile ...* **case:** fictitious names used in legal debate, equivalent to 'John Doe' and 'John Roe', still used in American law.

p. 113 *Abraham ... Goliath:* Genesis 22 1–14: the Apocryphal book of Judith: I Samuel 17.

p. 113 scarcely *Sphinx* **can tell:** the Sphinx of Thebes, who asked riddles and devoured those who could not answer them. Oedipus solved her question, and she killed herself. In gratitude Jocasta, the widowed Queen of Thebes, married him. See above, p. 96 n.

p. 113 the _Albion_ Nation: Albion is the name given by a number of Latin writers to the island of Great Britain itself, using Britannia to refer to the whole British Isles.

p. 114 Iubeo stultum esse libenter: willingly I allow the foolish man to be so. Adapted from Horace, _Satire_ i l. 63.

p. 114 _Orlando Furioso_: Ariosto's epic poem, 1532.

p. 114 Onlie . . . serve: the single example of Alexander may suffice.

p. 114 though . . . not: even if Plutarch had not.

p. 114 the _Phoenix_: Sidney is here comparing Alexander to the Phoenix as being unique in its splendour, without reference to its self-immolation and resurrection.

p. 114 tooke . . . with him: Alexander the Great is said to have always carried Homer's works with him.

p. 114 _Callisthenes_ . . . stubburness: a philosopher who accompanied Alexander the Great on his expeditions to the East, having been recommended to him by Aristotle. He became involved in a conspiracy, and was executed.

p. 115 Cato . . . _Ennius_: Cato the Censor, great-grandfather of Cato Uticensis (see p. 99 n.). He was famous for his severity, and for his distrust of Greek culture. The poet Ennius (see p. 84 n.) accompanied the commander Marcus Fulvius on campaign during the Carthaginian wars.

p. 115 _Pluto_ . . . _Latine_: Pluto is the god of the Underworld, King of the dead.

p. 115 _Scipio Nasica_ . . . _Sepulcher_: Scipio Nasica fought with distinction in Spain, and was famous for his virtue. His cousins Scipio Africanus and Scipio Asiaticus were so-called because of their military successes in Africa and Asia. Ennius was a close friend of Africanus in particular. His bust was placed in the tomb of the Scipio family after his death, but he was probably not buried there.

p. 115 Which . . . them: which the delight the poets gave prevented them from doing.

p. 116 _Simonides_ . . . a just King: Simonides was a Greek poet of the sixth century BC, famous for the sweetness of his verse. Only some fine fragments are now extant. Hiero of Syracuse was his patron for a time.

His influence and that of Pindar (see above p. 106 n.) is said to have moderated the savagery of Hiero's early rule.

p. 116 *Plato* ... slave: In the *Dio* Plato tells how he first visited Dionysius of Sicily, and was sold into slavery at Aegina, then at war with Athens. He later visited Dionysius' son, the younger Dionysius and had for a time great influence over him. Dionysius came to resent and distrust him, and imprisoned him. On his release he returned to Greece. Sidney here seems to be conflating the elder Dionysius with his son.

p. 116 *Plutarch*: a historian and moral philosopher of the first century AD. His most famous work is the parallel *Lives* of famous Greeks and Romans.

p. 116 filthines, as they doe: the Greeks and Romans had no prejudice against homosexual love.

p. 116 communitie of women: in the *Republic* (V 448 ff.) Plato says the State should itself be a family: that women should share duties and responsibilities as far as possible equally with men; that they should be held in common, and their children be brought up away from their parents and unknown to them, to avoid the evils of family ambition, litigation and feud.

p. 116 Saint *Paule* ... a Prophet: St Paul's references to the Greek poets are said to be: Titus l. 12: 'One of themselves, even a prophet ...': Epimenides of Crete, from a lost work *On Oracles*: Acts 17, 28: 'as certain also of your own poets have said ...': Aratus of Cicilia, *Phaenomena* and Cleanthes, *Hymn to Zeus*; I Corinthians 15, 33: 'evil communications corrupt good manners', Menander, *Thais*.

p. 116 *Isis* ... ceased: in the *Isis and Osiris* and *Of the Decay of Oracles*.

p. 117 *Qua* ... *exigendos*: which authority certain rough and barbarous men may have desired to misuse, with the aim of expelling poets from the state. Scaliger, *Poetice* i 2.

p. 117 in ... *Ion* ... to Poetrie: *Ion* 533 ff. See below p. 129 n.

p. 117 *Laelius*: a Roman consul and patron of letters.

p. 117 the Greeke *Socrates* ... wise man: Plato, *Phaedo*, 61.

p. 118 *Musa* ... *laeso*: Muse, call to my mind the cause, by what offended deity ... Virgil, *Aen.* l.8.

p. 118 *David* ... *Germanicus*: David, King of Israel and Psalmist. Hadrian, Roman Emperor, second century AD, author of some charming verses. He also built Hadrian's Wall. Sophocles' tragedies include

Oedipus the King (see above p. 96). He was also a distinguished military commander and statesman. Germanicus Caesar, nephew of the Emperor Tiberius, was an outstanding general. He also wrote comedies and other poetic works.

p. 118 a *Robert* ... **of Scotland:** Robert II of Anjou and Sicily, 1275–43, the friend of Petrarch and Boccaccio: Francis I of France, 1515–47, an enthusiast of Italian art and literature, whose patronage ensured its influence in France: James I of Scotland, 1394–1437, follower of Chaucer and author of *The Kingis Quair*, a semi-autobiographical love-allegory.

p. 118 *Bembus* **and** *Bibiena*: Cardinal Piero Bembo 1470–1560, and Cardinal Bernardo Bibiena, 1470–1547: famous humanist scholars and patrons of the arts.

p. 118 *Beza* **and** *Melancthon*: Theodore Beza, 1519–1605, was a close associate of Calvin, best known for his work on the Protestant Latin edition of the New Testament. He published some *Juvenilia* of his own, 1548. Melancthon, 1497–1560, was a Protestant theologian, and also a humanist Greek scholar and writer on educational theory.

p. 118 *Fracastorius* **and** *Scaliger*: Hieronymus Fracastorius, 1483–1533, author of some Latin poetry and an essay on poetry. Scaliger: see above p. 100 and n.

p. 118 *Pontanus* **and** *Muretus*: Pontanus: see above p. 90 n. Marcus Antonius Muretus, 1526–85, wrote Latin poetry.

p. 118 *George Buchanan*: 1506–81: poet and historian.

p. 118 that *Hospitall* **of** *Fraunce*: Michel de l'Hôpital, 1505–73, Chancellor of France.

p. 119 trumpet ... loudest: Mars is the God of War, so 'in time of war'.

p. 119 over-faint quietnes: Like his uncle the Earl of Leicester, Sidney at this time favoured a more militant foreign policy than did the Queen. See Introduction, *passim*, and *The Lady of May* p. 13 n.

p. 119 the *Mountibancks* **at** *Venice*: a mountibank is a quack or charlatan, but Sidney may here be using the term figuratively. In a letter to his brother Robert, written probably in 1578, he says: 'And for the men you shall have there [i.e., in Venice] although some in deede be excellentlie lerned, yett are they all given to soe counterfeit lerning, as a man shall learne of them more false groundes of thinges than in anie place ells that I doe knowe . . .' III p. 127.

p. 119 *Vulcan*: Vulcan, the God of fire and the metal-smith of the Gods, was the husband of Venus. When he discovered that Mars was her lover he set a net of unbreakable metal mesh around their bed. Having trapped them, he called the Gods to come and laugh at them, but Venus was so beautiful that they all wished themselves in Mars' place. This tale is one singled out for condemnation in Plato's *Republic* (III 390) as presenting the Divine in false terms of human folly and corruption. See above: p. 116.

p. 119 *Epaminondas* ... **highly respected:** he was a great Theban general, famous also for his personal virtues, who even when he had been degraded to a private soldier after one defeat successfully turned another into victory, and was reinstated with due honours.

p. 119 *Helicon*: a mountain near Corinth, sacred to the Muses.

p. 119 *Queis* ... *Titan*: for whom the Titan Prometheus made entrails of finer clay, Juvenal, *Satire* XIV l. 35. Prometheus was said to have made the first man and woman out of clay, which he brought to life with fire stolen from heaven.

p. 119 *Pallas*: Pallas Athene, or Minerva, Goddess of Wisdom.

p. 119 *Daedalus*: a master-craftsman who when he had to flee from Crete made artificial wings for himself and his son, Icarus. He reached Italy safely, but Icarus flew too near the sun, and the wax that held his wings melted; he fell into the sea and was drowned. Sidney is using the reference metaphorically.

p. 120 *Quicquid* ... *erit*: anything I may try to say becomes verse. Adapted from Ovid, *Tristia* iv 10. 26.

p. 120 **cleare age** ... **after him:** see above pp. 96, 106 and nn.

p. 120 *Mirrour of Magistrates*: the first edition of *A Mirror for Magistrates*, a collection of nineteen narrative poems by different hands relating exemplary lives of kings and other great men, appeared in 1559. There were several later, expanded, editions.

p. 120 **the Earle of** *Surrie's Liricks*: Henry Howard, Earl of Surrey, 1517–47; the publisher Richard Tottel included forty of his shorter poems in his famous anthology *Tottel's Miscellany*, 1557, and printed his translation of *Aeneid* II and III in the same year.

p. 120 **The** *Sheapheards Kalender* ... **Eglogues:** Spenser's *Shephearde's Calendar* was printed in 1579, and was dedicated to Sidney.

p. 120 **old rustick language:** Spenser was experimenting with Chaucerian and dialect words and forms, attempting to broaden literary English from its native resources.

p. 121 not without ... against: the wit of the early Tudor comedies tends to be crude, and at times obscene.

p. 121 Gorboduck: *Gorboduc* is one of the earliest English tragedies by Norton and Sackville. It was performed in the Inner Temple Hall in 1567. Its subject, like that of Shakespeare's *King Lear*, is taken from the (legendary) Chronicles of Britain. It is written in blank verse, and the action is described, not performed on the stage, as in Classical drama.

p. 121 Seneca his stile: Seneca's tragedies were favourite models for early English tragic dramatists.

p. 121 Aristotle's precept: in the *Poetics* Aristotle sets out the Unities of time, place and action, though rather as a guideline than as the hard and fast rules that later critics took them to be.

p. 121 the ordinary Players in Italie: the professional actors of the improvised drama of the *Commedia dell' Arte*.

p. 121 Eunuchus in Terence: this is a slip on Sidney's part. It was the time-scheme of *Heautontimorumenos* that was much discussed at this time and later.

p. 122 Plautus: one of the greatest writers of Roman comedy. He lived in the second century BC.

p. 122 Pacolet's horse: in *Valentine and Orson*, an English version of an early French romance translated by Henry Watson, *c*. 1550, the dwarf Pacolet has a little magic horse made of wood which carries him instantly wherever he wishes.

p. 122 Hecuba: the Queen of Troy, wife of Priam and mother of Hector as well as Polydorus. After the fall of Troy she was taken with other captive women in the Greek ships, which stopped at Thrace to sacrifice her daughter, Polyxena, at the tomb of Achilles. By the sea she found Polydorus' body. Sidney outlines the plot of Euripides' *Hecuba*.

p. 122 Apuleius: a writer of the second century AD. His best-known work is *The Golden Ass*, which includes the first literary version of the Cupid and Psyche legend.

p. 123 Horn-pypes and Funeralls: merriment and tragedy.

p. 123 Omphale's commandement: Omphale was a Queen of Lydia, with whom Hercules fell deeply in love. To please her he exchanged clothes with her: she wore his lion's skin, and he dressed as a woman and spun. See also pp. 13–14, *Therion's* Song, and n.

p. 124 **Nil habet ... facit**: wretched poverty has nothing in itself more disagreeable than that it makes men ridiculous. Juvenal, *Satire* iii ll. 152–3.

p. 124 **a busy ... Traveller**: these are all common character-types. 'busy loving Courtiers' are described by *Dorcas* in *The Lady of May*, p. 11, and Maister *Rhombus* is 'a selfe-wise-seeming schoolemaister'. Shakespeare's *Pistol*, Henry IV II and Henry V, is 'a hartlesse threatening *Thraso*' (see above p. 105 n.), and in his travels his *Pericles* is cruelly changed by every kind of undeserved misfortune. The Elizabethans, not without reason, regarded travel abroad as rash unless necessary, and dangerous in itself.

p. 124 *Buchanan*: see above p. 118 n.

p. 125 **coursing of a letter**: excessive alliteration, fashionable at this time.

p. 125 **method of a Dictionary**: choosing words as they appear under any one letter of the alphabet. See *Astrophil and Stella* 15 and n.

p. 125 *Tullie*: referring to Marcus Tullius Cicero.

p. 125 *Nizolian* **paper-bookes**: collections of notes, excerpts and annotations on various authors, on the model of the *Thesaurus Ciceronianus* of Marius Nizolius, 1498?–1596.

p. 125 *Indians*: Sidney is probably referring here to natives of the West Indies.

p. 125 *Tullie ... Catiline*: Catiline's Conspiracy took place in Rome during the Civil Wars of Pompey and Caesar. Cicero discovered his plans, and denounced him in the Senate. He was forced to flee the city: his associates were executed and he himself with his few remaining followers later died in battle.

p. 125 *Vivit. vivit? imo in Senatum venit &c*: He lives. He lives? yes indeed; he comes into the Senate itself ... Adapted from Cicero *In Catilinam* I i.

p. 126 **similitudes ... conceits**: Sidney is referring to the fashionably elaborate and decorated Euphuistic style.

p. 126 *Antonius* and *Crassus*: Antonius Gnipho had a school of rhetoric in Rome, which Cicero attended for a time. Lucius Licinius Crassus was a famous orator and successful statesman, praised by Cicero on both counts.

p. 127 best of both: that is the best of both the Germanic and Latin elements of the English language.

p. 127 cumbersome ... Tenses: characteristic of Greek and Latin, both heavily inflected languages.

p. 127 the Tower of *Babylon's* curse: the tower that was built to reach heaven. At this time there was only one language, but God, angry at the pride of men, changed this so that they could not understand each other, Genesis 2: 1–9. Babel here means 'confusion', and is sometimes conflated with Babel (Babylon), the chief city of King Nimrod, Genesis 10: 10.

p. 127 greatest beauties ... language: Sidney himself makes frequent use of this possibility, e.g. 'long with love acquainted eyes' and 'her eye's-speech'; *Astrophil and Stella* 31, 67.

p. 127 Elisions: between vowels, e.g. 'dell' Arte' for 'della Arte'.

p. 128 Dactiles: in Latin and Greek scansion, a dactyl has a long syllable followed by two short. The Italian *Sdrucciola* discussed below has the same pattern, by accent rather than quantity.

p. 128 Female: feminine rhyme: the term seems not to have been current in Elizabethan English.

p. 128 *Motion, Potion*: at this time given three syllables. See n. 'Dactiles' above.

p. 128 the first ... civilitie: Cardinal Bembo (see above p. 118 n.) was one of many scholars who believed poetry to have been the earliest of the arts, and the first means by which civilisation was established.

p. 128 *Clauserus* ... Cornutus: Sidney refers to Conrad Clausner's Preface to his Latin translation of Annaeus Cornutus' Greek work written in the first century AD: *On the nature of the Gods*, a Stoic interpretation of Classical myths.

p. 129 many mysteries ... abused: the idea that allegory in particular can be used to express meanings intended to be understood only by some readers, while leaving the work as a whole generally accessible on a simpler level is widely held at this time.

p. 129 *Landin* ... fury: Cristofero Landini, 1424–1504?, a humanist scholar. The concept of the poets' 'divine fury' derives from Plato, *Ion* 534: '... the lyric poets are not in their right mind when they are composing their beautiful strains: but when falling under the power of music and metre they are inspired and possessed; like Bacchic maidens who draw milk and honey from the rivers when they are under the

influence of Dionysius, but not when they are in their right mind.'
(Jowett's translation.)

p. 129 of kinne ... Preface: many dedicatory poems will carry your
name.

p. 129 *Libertino patre natus*: born of a father who was a slave and is
a freedman.

p. 129 *Herculea proles*: a descendant of Hercules. Adapted from
Horace, *Satire* i. 6. 6.

p. 129 *Si quid mea carmina possunt*: if my verses have any power.
Virgil, *Aeneid* IX l. 446.

p. 129 dull-making ... *Nilus*: the great waterfalls of the Nile; the
Cataracts proverbially stunned and deafened anyone standing close by.

p. 129 Planet-like Musick: Sidney is referring to the music of the
spheres; the harmony produced by the movement of the stars and the
planets, which is inaudible on earth except, faintly, by the purest and
most exalted of men.

p. 129 *Momus*: the God of jokes, cast out of Heaven for ridiculing the
greater Gods.

p. 129 Asse's eares of *Midas*: Midas, King of Phrygia gave judgement
for Pan against Apollo in a musical contest. By way of comment on his
taste, Apollo changed his ears to those of an ass.

p. 129 as *Bubonax* was: Sidney has somehow conflated two names
here. Hipponax, a satiric poet who lived in Ephesus *c.* 500 BC so
cruelly ridiculed a sculptor, Bupalus, that he hanged himself.

p. 129 to be rimed to death ... in Ireland: the supposed ability of Irish
poets to destroy their enemies by the vituperative power of their verses
was proverbial at this time. In *As You Like It* Rosalind plays on this
idea and the Pythagorian doctrine of reincarnation: 'I was never so
berhym'd since Pythagoras' time that I was an Irish rat, which I can
hardly remember.' *As You Like It* III ii 163–5.

Two Pastoralls

p. 131 title: The *Two Pastoralls* were first printed as the first two
poems in Fancis Davison's anthology *A Poetical Rhapsody*, 1602. They
appear to have been carefully printed from a reliable manuscript, now
lost. The editor was the son of a friend and associate of Sidney: William
Davison, courtier and diplomat, whom Sidney succeeded as Governor

of Flushing in 1585. The book is dedicated to the young William Herbert, Earl of Pembroke, eldest son of Sidney's sister, one of whose poems is included. On metrical grounds Ringler takes these poems to have been written after 1581.

p. 131 **Sir Edward Dier ... Maister Fulke Grevill:** Edward Dyer and Fulke Greville are likely to be the 'friends' and 'friend' addressed in *Astrophil and Stella* 20. 21: see nn. Dyer was not knighted until 1596; his title as given here has been supplied by the editor, like the marginal initials, pp. 131, 134.

p. 131 *Pan* **our good God:** the God of shepherds and the countryside.

p. 131 *Joyne ... three:* the idea that unity of mind transcends individuality is a common expression of love or friendship from Classical times. Shakespeare uses it in *The Phoenix and the Turtle:*

> So they lov'd as love in twain
> Had the essence but in one;
> Two distincts, division none:
> Number there in love was slain.

p. 131 **Ye Hymnes ... giving:** Apollo is the God of poetry and leader of the Muses.

p. 131 **our reedes:** the reed-pipes of pastoral music properly belong to Pan. A nymph, Syrinx, whom he pursued, was turned into a reed to escape from him. He cut the reed, and made the first pan-pipes. Sidney is playing here on the famous rivalry between the two Gods. The poetry of himself and his friends, and the mental harmony between them are sufficient reason for Apollo to overcome his contempt for rustic music. See above p. 129 and n.

p. 131 **Sweete** *Orpheus'* **... moved:** see *Astrophil and Stella*, Third song and n.

p. 131 **Trinitie ... Unitie:** Sidney is playing on the idea of their triple friendship as a microcosm of the Christian Trinity of Father, Son and Holy Ghost.

p. 131 **The number best beloved:** three; the number associated with love, since the third brings two from opposition into balance, as well as being the number of the Trinity.

p. 132 **the Turtle-Dove ... liveth:** the turtle-dove is proverbial for married love and constancy.

p. 132 **metamorphoz'd wonder:** a mysterious transformation. See above p. 131.

p. 131 *Disprayse of a Courtly life*: the disillusioned courtier who retires to the country and a private life is a stock figure in literature of this time and later.

p. 133 **a man I met**: the later reference to 'my two loves', and the editor's marginal gloss identifying them, suggests that Sidney has subdivided his *personae* in this poem: 'I' is the narrator who learns from overhearing the complaint of 'a man', who projects a particular state of mind, perhaps correlative to that of Astrophil towards the close of *Astrophil and Stella*.

p. 133 **to whom ... is knowne**: the 'arte of Love' refers to the conventions and attitudes of love as a courtly game with no real feelings involved, and is a play on the title of Ovid's *Ars Amatoria*: *The Art of Loving*.

p. 134 **Oten Reedes**: see above p. 131.

p. 134 **Striving ... song**: there is only one specifically identifiable example of this poetic 'rivalry': the variations on the common theme by Sidney and Dyer: *Certaine Sonets* 16a and 16: see above p. 18 and n. A number of the earlier poems in Fulke Greville's *Caelica* pick up and play with themes from *Astrophil and Stella*, and he says they were 'Written in his Youth, and familiar Exercise with Sir Philip Sidney.'

p. 134 **blacke Swannes**: proverbial for something impossible or non-existent.

p. 134 *Pan*: invoking the God of the countryside, to which he has retired, and of rural poets, whom he wishes to rejoin.

The Psalms of David

p. 135 **title**: Seven of Sidney's Psalms are given here: the choice has been made to show something of their variety. They were begun probably in 1585, and *Psalm XLIII* was the last to be finished before Sidney's death. Between 1586 and 1599, when she presented the work, with a Dedication, to the Queen, his sister Mary, Countess of Pembroke, completed the work, revising her brother's versions as she did so. The *Psalms* circulated widely in manuscript, but there are no early editions. The two most important modern editions are those of Ringler, *The Poems of Sir Philip Sidney*, 1962, pp. 270-337, and J. C. A. Rathmell, *The Psalms of Sir Philip Sidney and Mary Countess of Pembroke* 1963; Suggestions for Further Reading. The aims of the editors are almost exactly opposed. Ringler sets out to go behind his sister's revisions to Sidney's own text; the complexity of his manuscript sources is discussed in *Poems*, pp. 500–505. Rathmell sees the work as a whole: a joint production of which the Countess's revisions and her own versions are an integral part. The text here is based on that of Ringler, with some modifications of capitalisation and punctuation. For ease of comparison, verse numbers are given as in the Prayerbook, in the left-hand margin.

Sidney had no Hebrew, and he made no use of the Latin Vulgate text. He would have known the Prayerbook Psalter, retained from Miles Coverdale's version in the Great Bible of 1539, almost by heart. He would also have known the English metrical version, *The Whole Book of Psalms* by Thomas Sternhold, John Hopkins and others, which was appended, with musical settings, to the Coverdale Psalter in the Book of Common Prayer. He is likely to have sympathised with its aims, while deploring its crudity. It is improbable however, that he intended his own version to replace it for public worship. Translation and/or versification of the Psalms was a common devotional exercise at this time and earlier: a (just) pre-Reformation example is the *Penitential Psalms* of Sir Thomas Wyatt, 1549. It is likely that Sidney saw his metaphrase in this light, and specifically as a dedication to God of his mature poetic virtuosity. This he deploys throughout to enhance differences of register and theme: each of the forty-three Psalms he completed has a different verse-form. He made use of a number of the recent poetic versions available in Latin, French and English, as well as the careful translation given in the Protestant Geneva Bible, 1560. He is likely also to have consulted the most recent scholarly commentaries on the Psalms, in particular that of Beza, of which the London edition in Latin and English, 1580, was dedicated to Sidney's uncle and aunt, the Earl and Countess of Huntingdon.

p. 135 Psalm VIII: the verse form is taken from Clement Marot's French version of Psalm IX, in Sidney's most important stylistic source: *Les CL Psaumes de David, mis en rime Françoise*: metrical versions by Marot and Beza with musical settings by Claude Goudimel.

p. 135 this earthly mate: Man was created on earth, and of earth, in the image of God, to have dominion over it under Him: Genesis 1: 27–31; 2: 1–7. Sidney is playing on the words 'earthly', and 'mate': friend, co-worker.

p. 135 The Bird ... embraceth: Sidney has given the meaning of this verse precise definition. Coverdale reads: 'The foules of the ayre, and the fyshes of the sea: and whatsoever walketh through the pathes of the seas.'

p. 136 Psalm XIII: the stanza form was probably suggested by the opening in Coverdale: 'How long wylt thou forget me (O Lorde) for ever: how long wylt thou hyde thy face from mee.'

p. 136 Psalm XIV: Ringler compares the stanza form to that of Marot's Psalms 114, 115. Sidney, like Marot in his version, omits two verses (5–7 in Coverdale), following the more accurate Geneva text.

p. 137 Clayey race: mankind: a double allusion to Adam having been created from earth (see above p. 135 n.), and to the spiritual dullness of his descendants.

p. 137 These Canibals: OED gives 1553 as the first occurrence of this word in English. It is derived from Carib or Caribes, a savage tribe of the West Indies, reputed to eat human flesh.

p. 138 With oyle ... his hall: Sidney's version of verses 5–6 necessitates an extra half-stanza, eliminated in his sister's revision:

> Thou oil'st my head thou fill'st my cupp:
> > Nay more thou endlesse good,
> > Shalt give me food.
> To thee, I say, ascended up,
> > Where thou, the Lord of all,
> > Dost hold thy hall.
>
> (Rathmell, *Psalms*, p. 49)

p. 138 makes battails fight: brings victory in battle. The rhyme-scheme has led to over-compression here.

p. 139 Psalm XLII: Sidney has based his stanza form and its divisions of the argument on Beza's French version. See above p. 135.

p. 140 Psalm XLIII: this is the last Psalm to be completed by Sidney himself.

SUGGESTIONS FOR FURTHER READING

Modern editions of Sidney's Works:

POETRY

The Poems of Sir Philip Sidney, edited by William A. Ringler Jr. Oxford University Press, 1962.
   Fully annotated, with Introduction, Textual Apparatus, Notes and Commentary. Includes the poems from *The Lady of May* and the *Old Arcadia*.

The Psalms of Sir Philip Sidney and the Countess of Pembroke, edited with an Introduction by J. C. A. Rathmell. This is the text of Sidney's *Psalms of David* as completed and revised by his sister.

Sir Philip Sidney, Oxford Standard Authors, edited with Introduction and Notes by Katherine Duncan-Jones, Oxford University Press, 1971. Includes selected poems from the *Old Arcadia* and also extracts from the *New Arcadia*, and a selection of Letters.

Silver Poets of the Sixteenth Century, revised and expanded edition, edited by Douglas Brookes-Davies, Everyman, London, 1994. Includes poems from the *Old Arcadia* and from *Certain Sonnets* as well as *Astrophil and Stella*. It also gives representative selections from the poems of Sir Thomas Wyatt, Henry Howard, Earl of Surrey, Sir Walter Raleigh, Mary, Countess of Pembroke, Michael Drayton and Sir John Davies.

PROSE

The Prose Works of Sir Philip Sidney, in four volumes, edited by Albert Feuillerat, Cambridge University Press, 1912; revised edition 1962. Includes *The Lady of May* (Vol. II) and gives Ponsonby's text of the *Defence*, 1595 (Vol. III). There have been a number of manuscripts discovered since Feuillerat's first edition, and his text is at times unreliable in other ways. The revision of 1962 was intended to keep an improved inclusive text available until others could be produced taking full advantage of recent discoveries and of modern scholarship. It is now being replaced by volumes appearing in the Oxford edition of Sidney's *Works*, which at present include:

The Defence of Poesie, edited with an Introduction and Notes by Jan Van Dorsten, Oxford University Press, 1971.

The Countess of Pembroke's Arcadia, the *Old Arcadia*, edited with Introduction, Textual Introduction and Commentary by Jean Robertson, Oxford University Press, 1973.

The Countess of Pembroke's Arcadia the *New Arcadia*, edited with Introduction, Textual Introduction and Commentary by Victor Skretkovicz, Oxford University Press, 1987.

Miscellaneous Prose of Sir Philip Sidney, edited by Katherine Duncan-Jones and Jan Van Dorsten, Oxford University Press, 1973. Includes the *Discourse on Irish Affairs*, 1577, and the *Letter* to Queen Elizabeth, opposing her proposed marriage with the Duc d'Alençon, 1579.

Other editions include:

An Apologie for Poetry; or The Defence of Poesy, edited by Geoffrey Shepherd, Manchester University Press, 1973.

An Apology for Poetry (Olney's edition, 1595): in *Elizabethan Critical Essays*, 2 vols. Oxford University Press, 1904, Vol. I pp. 148–207. ed. G. Smith. Also includes: a Bibliographical List of pamphlets defending and attacking the Stage, 1577–87, Vol. I pp. 61–3; Sir John Harington, *A Preface, or rather a brief Apologie of Poetrie*, 1591, Vol. II pp. 194–222, and Thomas Nashe's *Preface* to Newman's pirated edition of *Astrophil and Stella*, 1591, Vol. II pp. 223–8. The survey of developments in critical thought over this period given in the Introduction is still useful, and the Notes are full and detailed.

The Countess of Pembroke's Arcadia, edited with an Introduction and notes by Maurice Evans: Penguin, 1977. The *New Arcadia*, with the conclusion taken from the *Old Arcadia*. The most easily accessible text.

The Correspondence of Sir Philip Sidney and Hubert Languet: the Latin text edited with an accompanying translation, by Steuart A. Pears, William Pickering, London, 1845.

English writers of Sidney's period cited in the Introduction and Notes

Gascoigne, George (1525?–1577)
The Glasse of Government and other Works, edited by John W. Cunliffe, Cambridge University Press, 1910. Includes *The Princely Pleasures at Kenilworth Castle*, 1576, pp. 91–131.

Greville, Fulke, Lord Brooke, (1554–1628)
The Prose Works of Fulke Greville, Lord Brooke, edited by John Gouws, Oxford University Press, 1986.

Poems and Dramas of Fulke Greville, First Lord Brooke, 2 vols., edited with Introductions and Notes by Geoffrey Bullough, Oliver and Boyd, Edinburgh, 1938.

Fulke Greville, Lord Brooke, The Remains, being Poems of Monarchy and Religion, edited by G. A. Wilkes, Oxford University Press, 1965.

Raleigh, Sir Walter (1552?–1618)
The Poems of Sir Walter Raleigh, edited by Agnes M. C. Latham, Routledge and Kegan Paul, London, 1951.

Spenser, Edmund (1552–1599)
Poetical Works, edited by J. C. Smith and Ernest de Selincourt, Oxford University Press, 1912.

Wilson, Jean (ed.)
Entertainments for Elizabeth I, D. S. Brewer, Boydell and Brewer, Woodbridge UK, 1980. Includes *The Four Foster Children of Desire*, 1581, pp. 61–85.

Critical Works on Sidney and his writings:

Up until the last fifty years or so Sidney's reputation, in particular as crystallised in the work of Fulke Greville, tended to colour any assessment of Sidney's life and work with a kind of romantic reverence. This is specially true of *Astrophil and Stella*, which after the decline of *Arcadia*'s enormous early popularity was Sidney's best-known work. The discovery of new material, and of extant manuscripts of the *Old Arcadia* in particular, has led to modern critical editions of Sidney's work, which in turn have sparked off energetic and varied responses in every area of modern critical engagement. The works cited below represent a fair and helpful range, but a very small proportion, of what is currently available. Works dealing solely or primarily with *Arcadia* have not been listed, nor have articles in periodicals. The first three items however present a wide and inclusive basis for further reading, and the *Sidney Newsletter and Journal*, edited by Gerald J. Rubio, University of Guelph, Ontario, provides on-going access to new material through summaries of recent papers as well as articles and reviews.

Duncan-Jones, Katherine, *Sir Philip Sidney, Courtier-Poet*, Hamish Hamilton, London, 1991.

Hager, Dennis, *Dazzling Images: the Masks of Sir Philip Sidney*, University of Delaware Press, 1991.

Hannay, Margaret P., *Philip's Phoenix: Mary Sidney, Countess of Pembroke*, Oxford University Press, 1990. The best of several recent studies of Mary Sidney's work and its relationship to that of her brother.

Kay, Dennis (ed.), *Sir Philip Sidney, An Anthology of Modern Criticism*, Oxford University Press, 1990. Includes Thomas P. Roche's important essay *Astrophil and Stella: a Radical Reading* (slightly condensed). Generally a widely representative collection, with a useful retrospective Introduction on Sidney's critical heritage.

Kinney, A. (ed.), *Sidney in Retrospect*, 'Recent Studies in Sidney 1940–69, 1970–77, 1978–86', Amherst, Mass., 1988.

Rees, Joan, *Sir Philip Sidney* and *Arcadia*, Associated University Press, London, 1991. Her discussion of the development of Sidney's growing interest in the potential of women from *Astrophil and Stella* onward is especially valuable.

Robinson, Forrest G., *The Shape of Things Known: Sidney's Apology in its Philosophical Tradition*, Harvard University Press, 1972.

Rudentstine, Neil L., *Sidney's Poetic Development*, Harvard University Press, 1967.

Spiller, Michael, *The Development of the Sonnet: An Introduction*, Routledge, London, 1992. Sets *Astrophil and Stella* (Chapter 7) in its full context of tradition, sources and their expansion. Stimulating and perceptive.

Washington, Mary A., *Sir Philip Sidney, An Annotated Bibliography of Modern Criticism*, University of Missouri Studies LVI, Columbia, 1982.

Critical works of general relevance including those cited in the Introduction and Notes:

Berry, Philippa, *Of Chastity and Power: Elizabethan Literature and the Unmarried Queen*, Routledge, London, 1989.

Chanduri, Sakunta, *Renaissance Pastoral and its English Developments*, Oxford University Press, 1989.

Cooper, Helen, *Pastoral: Medieval into Renaissance*, D. S. Brewer Ltd, Ipswich, 1977.

Fowler, Alastair, *Triumphal Forms: Structural Patterns in Elizabethan Poetry*, Cambridge University Press, 1970.

French, Peter J., *John Dee: the World of an Elizabethan Magus*, Routledge and Kegan Paul, London, 1972.

Greenblatt, S. J. *Renaissance Self-Fashioning*, University of Chicago Press, 1980.

Greenblatt, S. J., (ed.) *Representing the English Renaissance*, University of California Press, 1988.

King, John N., *Tudor Royal Iconography: Literature and Art in an Age of Religious Crisis*, Princeton University Press, 1989.

Norbrook, David, *Poetry and Politics in the English Renaissance*, Routledge and Kegan Paul, London, 1984.

Pagen, Anthony, *European Encounters with the New World: from Renaissance to Romanticism*, Yale University Press, 1993.

Yates, Frances A., *Giordano Bruno and the Hermetic Tradition*, Routledge and Kegan Paul, London, 1964.

Yates, Frances A., *The Occult Philosophy in the Elizabethan Age*, Routledge and Kegan Paul, London, 1979.

Yates, Frances A., *The Art of Memory*, Routledge and Kegan Paul, London, 1966.

Young, Alan, *Tudor and Jacobean Tournaments*, Sheridan House, New York, 1987.